Print editions of "The Dark Side of Europe" are available in English, Serbian and Greek. The book is available for publishing (print and digital) in other languages. For further information contact the author, *Basil(at)Coronakis(dot)com*

Brussels 2018

THE DARK SIDE OF
EUROPE

Basil A. Coronakis

The Dark Side of Europe

5   **RISE AND FALL OF AN EMPIRE**

12   AND YET, IT MOVES

URBI ET ORBI

1/1 14,666 The Divinity of Numbers

If anything of what I say in this book was not true, by now I would be deep in jail, probably in Saint Gilles since the publication of my first book under the title "The Deep State of Europe", in Brussels, April 2016.

I know Brussels upside-down as for the last 26 years I work for New Europe, the oldest and most powerful mainstream media group of Brussels, reporting on European affairs. It should be considered that none of our media, ever, received not even a single Euro or any favor from the European Commission or the European Parliament.

In these 26 years, we witnessed many newspapers and magazines and any kind of media you can imagine passing by Brussels and after collecting subsidies, subscriptions even programs and projects generously granted by the charitable institution, one morning vanished, like the dreams which are vanishing in the morning.

However, nobody was ever held accountable and business in Berlaymont, continued as usual. Think that once the Commission set-up in midsummer a tender aiming at granting to a friendly media concern a few million Euro, by coincidence I got them with the hands in the jar with the candies, I addressed complaint to the media Commissioner for the "photographic tender". The tender was cancelled and was not repeated, just cancelled. The beneficiary who was depicted in the tender's specs after a month closed business and nothing happened afterwards. No inquiry as to who and why, no referral to the case to OLAF or at least to the Internal Audit Service, absolutely nothing. Simply to remember Jules Dassin (Never on Sunday) after the "murder" everybody went happily to the beach. It was mid-summer, after all, and it was beach time.

Although New Europe is a clear pro-EU independent newspaper never had good relations with the Commission System as it always wanted the European Commission transparent and accountable. As far as I am concerned I have sensed the aporrhaid with all my senses. Yet what I only did was to uncover scandals resulting in losses for the Community budget.

Twenty-six years of constructive and benevolent criticism gave the opportunity to the Commission to produce a dossier for me, this book and my newspaper of 14,666 documents recorded in the ARES system of the Commission which does not include emails, press clippings and notes.

That was confirmed to me, in writing, by the Commission which refused, however, to grant me access to any of the 14,666 documents directly concerning me, althoughit is compelled by Regulations 1049/2001 (Access to Documents) and 45/2001 (Access to Personal Data). Think that explained to me in writing that among others the Commission has in its possession 152 documents in which my last name comes first and my first name comes second. Only security services, prosecution authorities and secret services in their correspondence put the last name of the subject first.

However, I will take the matter to the Court as such a situation is unacceptable. I will not do it for violation of (EC) Regulations 1049/2001 and 45/2001 for refusal to give access to documents or personal data because no matter what the Court will say, the Commission will disregard the Court Decision and it will not be the first time.

I will take the Commission to the Court for non-contractual liability for damages caused by its servants in the performance of their duties resulting 26 years of malevolent exclusion, proven in the 14,666 documents it refuses to release. Article 340 (ex 288 TEC) of the Treaty of the Functioning of the European Union (TFEU). I can do it in the next five years.

The issue, however, which reflects our legal civilization, is not why the Commission violates the law by non-delivering 14,666 document with my personal data. The issue is why the European Commission keeps 14,666 documents for a citizen with clean record and what is the legal background which authorizes the Commission services to keep undisclosable records for citizens.

As to the Commission letter, which admits the existence in its official records (ARES) of 14,666 documents which concern me I will not publish it, but you can get a copy straight from the European Commission with the Access to Documents procedure as it is foreseen by Regulation 1049/2001, explained in detail in this book. However, it is very simple. Write an email to the European Commission Sg-Acc-Doc@ec.europa.eu with the following text:

On the ground of Regulation (EC) 1049/2001 on Access to Commission Documents, please provide me with the letter sent by the Commission to B. A. Coronakis, Anenue de Tervuren 96, Brussels 1040, on 20/10/2017, under Ares (2017)5128047.

Sign the letter with your full name and address details, and enjoy.

1/2 Urbi et Orbi

In my first book (April 2016), I have categorically anticipated the Brexit and I explained why. It was the decision of most of the Brits, to leave the European Union taken on June 23, 2016. However, when and how the United Kingdom will be out it is not easy to say, as Europe is the last colony of the British empire. Theoretically, the United Kingdom is set exit the European Union on11 pm UTC, 29 March 2019. Theoretically.

This book is a revelation. It is addressed to the city (of Brussels) and the world (Europe and beyond) and it will raise contempt without limits, but also praise without limits.

This paperback will demystify the legend of the European Commission. You might find it irrelevant or provocative, insulting or malicious, but whatever the case you will read the truth from beginning to end. Truth liberates.

In the last two decades, the European Commission has paid billions over billions of your money to manage your perceptions. All what you know and all what you do not know about Europe is what the Commission wants you to know. "1984", not more, not less. This is the art known as propaganda, Just one example. Ask from any Commission Info Point to get you a free copy of the booklet "Europe in 12 lessons," translated in all 22 languages It is the basic text book to learn about the European Union.

In that "textbook" while you will get a lot, of useless information, crucial and important knowledge to the citizen's, is missing. Specifically, there is not a single word to the right citizens have for free access to documents of EU Institutions. It is the most important right European have vis-a-vis the European Union. Have a look in the chapter "Access to Documents" in this book, then download or ask for a free copy of "Europe in 12 lessons" and try to find such information there. You will not.

This book will reveal the secrets and the Machiavellian mind-set of the Brussels 'nomenclature' that rules the daily life of half a billion Europeans and many more, without any moral or political legitimacy. It will bring the Commission "gods" and "semi-gods" back down to Earth from their thrones on Mount Olympus.

It will uncover their weaknesses and their deviousness and will make the "gods" feel like ordinary people, naked and ridiculed, in the eyes of their subjects.

Our purpose is not to destroy Europe. Others before, methodically and efficiently, have done it, seemingly with success. Instead, we want to motivate citizens and provide them with the arguments and information needed to win Europe back.

REQUIEMS FOR A DREAM

2/1 Anatomy of a Massacre

When people refer to Brussels as "Sin City," they are not referring to drugs, prostitution or the traditional mafia. They are referring to the sins against the European Project. The sins they might have heard about at a café or witnessed in their daily jobs. Countless such sins have come and gone, and these eleven scandals I am sharing with you are just the tip of the iceberg.

These just happened to fall upon citizens who have a conscience and who felt compelled to lift the weight off their shoulders by sharing their documented stories against the very mainstream grain of Brussels. In some cases, they were employees of the Commission, in other cases they were journalists. As far as I'm concerned, they were all true Europeans who sought to make us more united.

In all eleven episodes, if had occurred in any Member State, the protagonists would have been referred to justice and some would certainly be still, deep in jail.

In the European Commission, however, systemic functionaries are untouchable and can violate administrative and penal laws at their discretion. They are never being referred to justice and are never interrogated by the otherwise decorative Internal Audit Service. On the contrary, they all maintain their positions and are promoted on "merit."

In the European Commission, those who are running the show of transgressing the law, are not very many. On the contrary, the great majority of officials are honest people who are forced to violate the rules under the threat of being side-lined. This explains the incredibly large number of therapy medicines used in Brussels.

In December 4, 2015, one hard working honest lawyer, under the pressure of his superiors to approve an illegal procedure reportedly involving certain satellite contracts, committed suicide. He jumped out of the window from the second floor of the Breydel building after he locked himself in his office while his superior and his secretary were standing behind the door. As the issue was serious and hot dossiers were left open on his desk, the Commission, claiming diplomatic immunity, did not allow the Belgian police to enter the building and examine what the suicide had left behind. However, the Commissioner who visited the place of the suicide immediately after, ordered to remove the flowers that his friends had put in the place of the suicide and took away all documents from the desk of the suicide.

The Spokesperson service, in an off-the-record briefing, advised the media not to report on the suicide. Exception was New Europe which reported the story of the suicide of (French) Gauthier Pierens, one of the best lawyers of the Commission. Pierens, was expecting for his promotion for two decades. Instead of, when he refused to approve the concession contract for a highway project in a big Member state he was demoted and transferred in the Space Unit of DG Grow. There, he refused to approve the contract for launching the satellites of Galileo (the European GPS) by the Russian conglomerate Soyuz. Eventually, under unbelievable pressure by his superiors, he prefeared to commit suicide instead of signing.

ONE How Court Decision Become Opinions

It is fun. When the Commission against its own regulations appointed the Head of the Athens Representation office, three officials who participated in the procedure for getting the post applied to the Court of Justice of the EU against the appointment. The Court annulled the appointment but the Commission kept the irregularly appointed in his post. However, in order to pacify other Heads of Representations who were appointed in a similar illegitimate manner, the Deputy Director General of the Department of Communication, issued a tranquilizing circular, to all Representations. The circular, which was published by New Europe, said, the Commission will study the Opinion of the Court and will take the necessary actions to maintain all appointees in their positions. The Commission showed its contempt to the Court by labelling its binding decision as an "opinion."

TWO The Monstrous Roaming *Affair*

With dubious legitimacy, the European Commission managed to prevent mobile operators from paying billions in penalties. At the same time, the Commission's competition authorities not only lied, but deprived European Union citizens from the binding evidence that would have allowed them to seek damages after years of illegal roaming overcharges. The benefit to the industry has grown to over €100bn. Yes, billions!

THREE Europe by Satellite

It is the TV channel of the European Commission. In violation of any rule and all logic, the European Commission managed to move the broadcast from the most popular satellite Hotbird 7A to a lesser known Swedish satellite used for (among other things) encoded adult entertainment channels. As for the old frequency of the EbS, it was taken over by Kirmizicam, a free- to-air, hard-porn network. Beyond the world's obsession with pornography (which is not Europe's fault), viewers in many European Union member states needed to upgrade to a larger satellite dish to gain access…

FOUR The Confession

European Commission President Jose Manuel Barroso saw one Commissioner ousted during his presidency. Maltese Commissioner for Health and Consumers Affairs, John Dalli, was implicated in a scandal which the EU's antifraud body, OLAF, had thoroughly investigated.

While there was little doubt in Barroso's mind from the resulting report that Dalli should not be a member of his commission, Dalli was not given the opportunity to rebut the alleged circumstantial evidence.

Even though the Treaty of Lisbon allowed Barroso to fire Dalli, the President asked him to resign. Under extreme pressure and unprecedented protocol, Dalli asked for time to consult with his wife and legal team, which was denied. Although Dalli immediately agreed (verbally) that he would, in due course, resign, he never signed a resignation letter. I know this because I did not allow him to do so. I know this because I took this paper from him. In the days to come, the President and the European Commission continued to allege that Dalli resigned. A cleaning lady at the European Commission needs to sign at least six different papers before her resignation is accepted. Moving on from Barroso's administrative failure, the content of the final Tobacco Products Directive, which Dalli was allegedly trying to sell, was watered down in favour of the tobacco industry. Dalli's original version, paradoxically, was much tougher on tobacco…

FIVE The Sinking of Samina Express, 81 Dead

The European Commission purposely did not launch infringement proceedings against Greece for not transposing an EU directive for crisis management and crowd management for crews of passenger ships. Many of the 81 people who died in the sinking of the liner Samina Express in the Aegean Sea, might have survived had Greece followed EU law or if it had been obliged by the European Commission as it was its duty, to train its crews to handle crises and crowds as provided for by the directive.

SIX Eximo, Small but Beautiful

As a scandal, it is perhaps worthless; a little more than €20m was at stake. It is however, representative of how the European Commission can cover up dossiers that are harmful.

SEVEN The Thing and the Flight of €134m

An organisation claiming to be international received from the Commission over €130m without being an international organisation eligible for such contributions. High-ranking employees of the Commission were seemingly involved in this case, which was uncovered by OLAF (the anti-fraud body of the EU), while New Europe committed its investigative journalism team to making sure the EU institutions never made the same mistake again.

EIGHT Licence to Pollute until 2050

International ship owners, thanks to their connections with the European Commission, managed to exclude the shipping industry from paying Carbon dioxide tax. All other transporters (airlines, trucks and cars), however, have to pay this tax. Shipping, however, was exempt until the year 2050 and the EU budget is losing over €20bn as a result.

NINE The Cancelled Tender

In mid-summer 2013, to develop an "Izvestia" type media outlet for the European Union (Izvestia was the newspaper of the Soviet Union government), the Commission issued a tender worth over €5m. The call was photographic to ensure that one particular company would win it. I informed Commissioner Viviane Reding of this. Unaware of the mid- summer machinations of her services, she immediately cancelled the tender. But as much as that.

TEN The Athens Airport Robbery

This is a robbery bigger than that of the Great Train Robbery in England, 1963. Much bigger. The project was co-financed by the European Commission, while the European Investment Bank granted a loan of €1bn for the project. The total cost of the project came to €2.25bn. The real cost, I believe, was less than €300m. Beyond this, and among many transgressions, which can fill at least one whole book, the robbery in this case included some 'light' falsification by the European Commission. You see, an ordinary limited liability company co-owned by the German Hochtief and the Greek state, and managed by Hochtief, was stripped of its post-nominals (which were included in the application) and was upgraded to a State Authority.

ELEVEN The Audit of the European Science Foundation

A routine audit of a project seeking the recovery of just over €5m is cancelled with no explanation. The only logical reason seems to be that the Commission Director who initially signed the extension contracts with the beneficiary who happened to become Director-General and was removed after the publication of the scandal by New Europe. The Commission's lawyers ands the Legal Service, said that such extensions of the contracts were not quite in conformity with EU law. In this story, you will see the documents that exemplify the ethos of the European Commission.

Eleven incredible cases each one worthy to be the subject of a PhD thesis in European studies at university!

2/2 Beyond Fantasy

You cannot win the System. It is strong, merciless, determined and has no hesitations.

In this book, you will learn about the Commission System. You cannot win it, it is strong, merciless, determined and has no hesitations.

However, as a citizen of Europe you must understand it find out how it acts a why and survive. To understand it, you must to forget all rules and ethics you and must think in medieval terms keep always in mind the myth of the Gyges ring (Plato The Republic, book II). People are doing what they do either by pleasure or fear. In the Commission there is not fear because there is no punishment. There are only orders.

Few months before the Brexit referendum in the UK, I learned that the European Commission paid tens of millions of Euro to certain British media concerns for... subscriptions. Strange, since in the years before subscription payments to same media were at the level of just a few hundred thousand Euro. It seems the real reason behind this generous move was to get their support in the Brexit referendum, against the Brexit. Indeed, the System wanted the UK to stay in the EU, at any cost.

We tried to check the information, asking the Commission through the "Access to Documents" procedure for the contracts they signed with the various media organisations over the past three years. They did not refuse. However, the Department of Communication of the European Commission informed us in writing that they would need 200 working days to provide in partial lots the information requested. That's nine months without counting official holidays.

In other words, it was five months after the Brexit referendum! Regulation 1049/2001 provides for a maximum delay of a total of four weeks (one month). The truth is that there is no rule that can stop the System from violating the law if any lunatic thinks that it is done for the "intérêt du service." In this case, however, there is no lunatic blocking the procedure, but the System that wants to keep Great Britain in the barn, at any cost, despite the Brexit.

What is the moral of the story? That rules and regulations are good and strictly applied to ordinary citizens and small Member States, only. With a little bit of imagination and basic historical knowledge, one can easily notice interesting resemblances. The eleven scandals you got the summaries in the previous chapters, are chosen among the hundreds of cases that came across my attention over the past two decades. They cover a wide spectrum of areas and involve practically the entire Commission System. All these scandals were reported in detail by New Europe, the leading independent newspaper in the "Sin City." The European Commission did nothing except to write nonsense letters desperately trying to justify the unjustifiable, without denying or apologizing. It is not so rare that New Europe articles have been the reason for moving to other positions high-ranking officials for wrongdoing, yet no one has ever been referred to the Prosecutor. This, in real life terms, is called omertà. However, New Europe was never taken to court by any European institution despite accusing top Commission executives of Community law violations.

A few years ago, a Deputy Director General of the Commission invited me for coffee to tell me: "I recognise that you recommended me with the government of my country to get the position I have today. Yet, if you continue writing negative things about us in your newspaper, you will not get any money from the Commission". I replied: "For 17 years my newspaper (this year 25) never received a single Euro from any EU Institution because it never asked for and will continue this way for the next 117 years".

By the way, the subject of the meeting was aimed at "buying" my silence in another scandal, the one under the title "How Court Decision Become Opinions" (p.10)

Corruption, a legitimately conferred type of anomaly, which can be found only in the European Commission is the real reason Europe is fading out. Corruption in the "Sin City" is systemic, horizontal and vertical, encompassing the wider System of European Union officials. Which reminds me of the closing paragraph of George Orwell's "Animal Farm."

Twelve voices were shouting in anger, and they were all alike. No question, now, what had happened to the faces of the pigs. The creatures outside looked from pig to man, and from man to pig, and from pig to man again; but already it was impossible to say which was which.

WELCOME TO HELL

3/1 The Hell is Chinese

Why I Wrote this Book? Because I had to. The Chinese claim that a man has three obligations in his life. To plant a tree, make a son and write a book.

This is my book.

I am a Greek, one of those going around the world. To be Greek is a full-time job. In my life, I worked for the Italian and the American governments. I also served as Ambassador to a regional organisation in Brussels, a kind of post-communist structure based in Sarajevo, the Regional Cooperation Council (RCC), ex Stability Pact, overseeing the Brussels RCC diplomatic office. I never understood why the Stability Pact was closed and was replaced by RCC. The only thing I know is that when the Stability Pact, which had distributed several billion in unchartered lands was closed, nobody had asked to perform an in-depth audit to that charitable organization before closing.

For the past four decades, I have been living in Europe where I enjoy the wonderful world of media. Newspapers and magazines, TV and the web are my life. They are fascinating, amazing and of high risk. In media, you can learn about the real world if you keep your feet on the ground and your eyes wide open. I have worked for many newspapers and TV networks, but the most challenging has been New Europe, a media group I founded in 1978. New Europe has a great advantage, but also an ever-greater disadvantage, which can be summarised in one word: independence.

That is why I will tell you the truth about the European Union and, in particular, the European Commission. The truth that few know and nobody among those in the know dares to speak.

I wrote this book because I still believe in the European Union despite knowing pretty well what it really is. Indeed, it is in deep decay and is fading out. If we believe in the European Union it is our duty to stop its decay and open it to its citizens, transparent, democratic, accountable credible and forward looking so to survive.

In this book, you will learn a lot about the European Commission, the presumed government of the European Union, the inner circle of which I have labelled the System that often behaves as a legitimate "corporate gang". In this context, it must be made crystal clear that compared to the great majority of the European Commission staff members who are honest and decent people, giving their hart and their soul for the cause of Europe, the members of the "corporate gang" are very few. Yet these few are sufficient, like few malicious cells in an organism to drive the project Europe in risky adventures.

You will also learn about the other European Institutions, which seemingly shape your future although their real impact in the governance of the European Union is small.

Europa has entered into a rapid transition from the traditional systemic establishment to the emerging anti-System forces. The EU leadership, thinks that the aphorism that anti-systemic are far-right, will be enough to stop the change. Wrong it is not. The rise of the anti-System in Europe is due to wrong political choices. Euro was a wrong choice. Austerity was a wrong choice and over-regulation was a wrong choice. Whoever is opposing to the Euro currency, to austerity and to over-regulation, is not far-right.

However, the European Commission is all that we have, and it is our last hope. Therefore, we must keep it and protect it, but make it better to fit in with our original dreams and fulfil our hopes and expectations.

The European Union is the most sophisticated administrative machine on Earth. This machine is, in the wider sense of the term, the most "corrupt" government in Europe. However, it is ours and we must make it better and make it work for us. To do this, we need to have knowledge about it. We must know what it is made of, how it works and, since you pay for it, how you can benefit from it.

Knowledge is power and can liberate. In this book, you will find what you need to understand the European Union, how to become a part of it and how to take control of your legitimate interests. It will tell you how to become free from a System, which keeps you prisoner and rules your everyday life without any political or moral legitimacy.

In writing this book, I interviewed many experts and insiders all over the Union.

I will conclude my introduction with a conversation I had with an American friend, a veteran of the Cold War, now retired and now lives in Berlin very close to the location of Checkpoint Charlie. You see people first die and then loose the vice.

I was speaking to my friend about this book and telling him that while speaking to Brussels people, I realized as already said, people do what they do either out of fear or for pleasure. In Brussels, I concluded, it looks like fear reigns.

My friend thought a while and he said: "I understand with this book you will turn Brussels into Chinese hell".

He explained: "The Chinese hell is not a religious, but a deeply political concept. Life in the Chinese hell is an exact replica of life in this world. Everybody is doing exactly what he or she was doing here, same job, same rank, same position, yet with one difference. In the Chinese hell, everybody knows everything about everybody else. Example, the patron knows that his employee is cheating on him and the employee knows that his patron is screwing his wife."

This book will tell you all about your patrons who know everything about you, but until now you know nothing about them.

Welcome to hell!

3/2 Historical Outline

1951, April 18. Six countries, France, Italy, The Netherlands, Belgium, Luxemburg and West Germany, sign the Treaty establishing the European Coal and Steel Community (ECSC). The Treaty entered into force on July 23, 1952 and according to the Commission communication services was aimed to use the raw materials of war, namely steel and coal, as instruments of reconciliation and peace. Nice beautiful words. Future historians will tell you that ECSC was exclusively established by French initiative to control and make sure that the German industry of Ruhr would not be building riffles and tanks (Panzers) again.

1957, March 25. Same six countries sign the Treaties establishing the European Economic Community (EEC) and the European Atomic Energy Community (Euratom), which came into force on January 1, 1958. The two Treaties secured peace in the continent as since then not a single bullet has crossed the French-German border, except for bullets of hunters. With Euratom the winners of the 2nd war secured full control of the use of atomic energy by Germany for the exclusive production of electricity.

The unification of Western Europe did great steps immediately after the war, as the Western "bloc" had to confront with the East "bloc." In this context as the two "blocs" had diametrically opposed interests and ideologies, and relations between the "blocs" developed into a framework of mutual mistrust. This secured peace since the end of WWII until our days, as every part knew well its limits. It was after the fall of the Berlin Wall in 1989 that the mistrust was intelligently turned into enthusiasm and the soup turned sour.

1960, January 4. Under the initiative of the United Kingdom, which was left out of the EU because of Gen. Charles De Gaul firm objections, the Stockholm convention establish the European Free Trade Association (EFTA) including several Western European countries that were not part of the EEC.

1965, April 8. The three Communities (EEC, ECSC and Euratom) merge (effective July 1, 1967) creating a single Council and a single Commission. Thus, the European Communities (EC-6) was born.

1968, July 1. Customs duties on industrial goods between Member States are abolished and a common external tariff is adopted.

1973, January 1. Denmark Ireland and the United Kingdom join the European Communities (EC-9) while by Referendum Norway stays out.

1981, January 1. Greece joins the European Communities (EC-10).

1985, June 14. The Schengen (small town in Luxemburg) Agreement is signed by five of the ten Member States of the then European Economic Community and border controls among these Member States are abolished.

The Schengen agreement was extended to all Member States by the 1999 Amsterdam Treaty, except the UK and Ireland which obtained an "opt-out".

1986, January 1. Spain and Portugal join the European Communities (EC-12).

1986, February 28. The Single European Act (SEA) is signed in The Hague and came into force on July 1, 1987. It was the first major revision of the Treaty of Rome to complete the internal market by December 31, 1992.

1989, November 9. Fall of the Berlin Wall.

1990 October 3. The unification of Germany. The European Commission apparatchiks claim that "the European union encouraged German unification." Historians of the future might have a different assessment as the unification came overnight by Chancellor Helmut Kohl who "purchased" it from certain Soviet leaders as the Soviet Union had entered the typical chaotic situation which proceeded the collapse. The Soviet Union, officially dismembered in 26 November 1991. Kohl, without any reaction from the European Commission which is supposedly the "Guardian of the Treaties" ruled that one West Germany Mark is equal to one East Germany Mark, thus placing to the EU Member States the cost of billions of Marks printed at will by Erich Honecker and the Soviets.

1992 February 7. The Treaty on the European Union (EU) is signed in Maastricht (The Netherlands), and came into force on November 1, 1993.

1995, January 1. Austria, Finland and Sweden join the EU (EU-15)

1999, January 1. Following the Maastricht Treaty, the Euro currency enters virtually into effect while the actual coins and notes circulate in January 1st 2002. The Euro currency was designed by bank clerks with no sense of the real economy, who instead of following the denominations scale of the US Dollar (follow the leader principle), reinvented the wheel by making coins for one and two Euros thus pushing inflation up while introduced €200 and €500 just to help financing of terrorist groups, drug dealers and money laundering. Of this "criminal act" against EU citizens, the otherwise eloquent European Commission, never spoke.

2000, March 24. The Lisbon European Council encompasses the wishful thinking of the Brussels mandarins of reducing unemployment, modernizing the economy and strengthening social cohesion. To a certain extend this resolution reminds vaguely the five-year plans of the Soviet Union.

2000, December 8. The Nice Treaty institutionally opens the EU doors for granting membership to former communist countries.

2004, May 1. Czechia, Estonia, Cyprus, Latvia, Lithuania, Hungary, Malta, Poland, Slovenia and Slovakia join the European Union (EU-25).

2004, October 29. In Rome, 25 Heads of State sign the European Constitution, which however, is rejected by referenda in France and The Netherlands, in May after.

2007, January 1. Bulgaria and Romania join the European Union (EU-27)

2007, December 13. In Lisbon, the EU member states sign a "light" version of the rejected European Constitution, in the form of two treaties: the Treaty on European Union or TEU, and the Treaty on the Functioning of the European Union (2007) or TFEU, which replaces the Treaty of Rome of 1957.

12 June 2008. The Irish voters reject by referendum these treaties by a margin of 53.4% to 46.6%.

2009, October 2. After grotesque interventions of the European Commission and the System force Ireland to vote again. This time, again by referendum the Treaty of Lisbon is approved. That was the first (failed) attempt of a Member State to withdraw from the Union.

2013, July 1. Croatia joins the European Union (EU-28).

2016, June 23. The United Kingdom decides by Referendum to leave the European Union, which politically now becomes EU-27. Although some of the British leaders claim there should be a second referendum to validate the first, next morning the Minister of Economy of Germany, declares that the UK is out of the EU and there is no way back on the decision of the British people. Few hours later the three EU leaders, the President of the European Commission, the Council and the European Parliament, repeat the statement of the German Minister. However, if, when and how the United Kingdom will leave for good from its last colony, it remains to be seen.

2017, March 29. The United Kingdom triggers article 40 of the Treaty and informs officially the Council that it decided to withdraw from the European Union. This means that in two years' time (by March 20, 2019), the UK will be out of Union.

3/3 The European Union Made Simple

The European Union is still an association (rather than a union) of 27 independent states (plus the United Kingdom in the way out) of Europe and, as such, has a unique mode of operation. So far, after seven decades since its establishment, the European Union has yet to become a federation. Consequently, it has no common policy in the key areas of defence, foreign affairs or direct taxation.

Four basic institutions rule the European Union: the European Commission, the European Parliament, the European Council and the Court of Justice of the European Union.

The European Council, the assembly of the Heads of State or governments, has the real political power in the Union. Such powers are mostly demarcated by the three major Member States (Germany, France and until recently the UK), which channel major European policies in cooperation of the Commission's inner circle.

Ideally, the Commission should be the executive arm of the Council, a kind of Secretariat to the assembly of the Heads of State. This occurs, to a certain extent, when the political and financial interests of the big Member States are involved. For the great majority of all other issues, however, the Commission has developed a great degree of autonomy. This is something many Member States are concerned about, but do not dare to question.

To a great extent the European Parliament remains a decorative organization.

The inter-relations among Commission, Parliament and Council, characterize the EU decision-making process.

The European Council sets the policy objectives in the conclusions to its meetings similarly to the Central Committee plenums of the Chinese Communist party. These conclusions are addressed to the Member States and the other European institutions.

In compliance with the broad guidelines of the European Council – which sometimes were drafted by the secretary general or the head of cabinet of the Commission president, the Commission proposes legislation. The European Council (usually at the level of Ministers) and the European Parliament have the final say in approving and eventually amending legislation.

If, for one reason or another, the proposals of the Commission, as prepared by the System, are not approved, they will be withdrawn. But they can be brought back later, with different wording. Rephrasing and resubmission of proposals will be made again and again for as long as it takes for the rules, as formulated by the System, to be adopted.

The essence of this complicated, costly and excessively useless exercise is that it formally provides the European Commission its much-needed legitimacy, as technical expert and initiator of legislation, even if it is only a posture.

The European Commission is outstanding in matters of "political communication," the politically correct term for propaganda. In this context, we learn that the European Union promotes humanitarian and progressive values to ensure that humankind benefits; it secures solidarity among Member States; and many other achievements. Indeed, naïve citizens (they are not few), believe that Plato's utopia is finally real and Brussels is its capital.

When the European Union was founded it meant to fulfil the visions of its founders and the hopes and expectations of the peoples of western Europe for prosperity, peace and freedom.

Seven decades after, through a series of artificial genetic mutations, the wonderful dream of half a billion Europeans turned into nightmare.

A complex administrative machine, self- reproduced and non-accountable, serving its own puny interests and the interest of few big Member States at the expense of all others, without any kind of legitimacy.

Finally, in this beautiful setup of our Utopia, Commission staff members claim in private off-the-records talks on condition of anonymity, that way more than 50% of the Commission staff, is permanently on therapy drugs.

Sad realities meaning that if we do not change radically the European Union, we will lose it.

3/4 The Three Mistakes, UK, the Big Enlargement and the Euro

Complex structures based on delicate check and balances displaying power stemming from perceptions, cannot afford strategic mistakes. The European Union, sa far, has made three while one is enough.

Although the situation was dormant for years and business was running smooth as usual, In the last couple of years a series of unforeseen situations occurred, and the European Union entered into rough waters.

The United Kingdom became EU Member State in 1993. That was the big mistake since the European Union was since then manipulated by the Brits and never became a real Union. It remained an association of merchants capable of fixing the VAT and regulating the internal market. Gradually the Union became the new and only colony of Great Britain and as a colony was never allowed to develop common foreign and defense policy that would allow the deepening of the Union. The lack of a common defense policy

Instead of deepening, the Union choose to enlarge, and that was the second mistake. It enlarged with 11 former communist countries which altered the socio-economic profile of the Union and operate freely in the internal market area taking advantage of the opportunities but without the restrictions and the costs of the old member States.

The third equally catastrophic mistake was the introduction of the Euro. This made possible the adoption of austerity policies all over the Eurozone and the creation of a growing class of neo-poor with simultaneous galloping depletion of the middle class. The effects are already visible in Europe with the rising of the anti-systemic political powers, which are neither far left or far right but just anti-austerity.

3/5 …and the System was Born

This book is about you and the System.

You should read it because you will discover how a System of a few extremely smart, highly capable and corrupt senior officials (administrators not politicians), regulate every single aspect of your life. You may already suspect something is wrong and have some vague ideas as to what. This book will give you the global picture, the "real thing."

The "monster" called the European Union is the "real thing." Now you will discover what it is and what to do about it. You need no arms, no bombs and no guns. All you need is knowledge, intelligence, patience, determination to understand how the System thinks.

The European Union is ruled by two institutions, the European Commission, which institutes the deep state of Europe and the conclave, though non-acting independently, of two EU Member States, Germany and France. Before the Brexit referendum was also the UK. Together, Commission and the two Member States constitute the so-called "Commission System or simply, the System. The rule of the System is absolute and merciless; it does not have any kind of democratic legitimacy and often violates its own rules.

One cannot defeat or bypass the System. For as long as the European Union exists, this is the first axiom. EU citizens are trapped in the System which makes them believe that seemingly they can do nothing about it, or nearly next to nothing.

This "quasi-nothing," this minuscule capacity for change although minor and apparently irrelevant, may potentially constitute the "strange attractor" that will bring the EU to the change we need.

And while we can dedicate another book on discussing why the minuscule is not majuscule, it is the knowledge that allows you to achieve even this small change. The System is purposely keeping citizens in the dark about it. You will soon understand why.

Under the various European Commission initiatives to "communicate Europe," billions of Euros have been spent over the years and only a small number of companies and individuals have benefitted. Ultimately, however, Europeans know nothing about the European Union. From the System's perspective, the various "communicate Europe" packages have been allegedly very successful. Indeed, the strategic goal of these actions has been to keep half a billion EU citizens ignorant and distant from the European policymaking operation.

Just think about it for a moment. How many of the half a billion Europeans, including politicians of all ranks and parties in Member States, know the difference between the European Council, the Council of Ministers and the Council of Europe? What about the difference between a Regulation and a Directive?

Knowledge is power. It is knowledge that makes the world better and it is knowledge that can bring about change without bloodshed. Only if you know how the System works, what are its strengths and weaknesses, what opportunities it offers and how you can benefit from them, only then can you get "ownership" of Europe.

Ultimately, only in this way you will get "value for money," the money every year you contribute to the European Union and is administrated by the System. Everything consumed in the EU has a sales tax, known as VAT (Value Added Tax). A percentage of this tax goes to the EU budget and allows for the functioning of the EU. Money collected from import duties by EU Customs Authorities also contribute to the EU budget. However, most of the EU budget - 73.8 % in 2013 - is fuelled by direct contributions from the member states' budgets, calculated as a percentage of their respective gross national income. When you pay your income taxes, a part of those is channelled to Brussels. It is your money, this is it.

By default, the System is closed to outsiders, like a shell. Yet deceptively, it is open, so as to claim credentials of accountability but it is well protected from intruders. However, where there is an opening, even one well hidden, there exists an opportunity. This is what we will talk about.

This book will explain to you what the System is and how it works. Then it will tell you how to get familiar with it. Finally, we will lay out some ideas as to how you can contribute to bringing about the change we need.

This book concerns half a billion European citizens under the shadow of the Brussels nomenclature. It concerns all Europeans from ordinary people, men and women of Main Street waiting for the bus, to Ministers and Members of Parliament in Member States and from professionals and experts to prostitutes, cops and cab drivers. Because they all are Citizens of the EU and since everyone is required to pay for it, everyone deserves to know and benefit from it.

The European Commission, is the "Executive Body" of the European Union, let's say, the government of the European Union. The Council of Ministers is the body in which the permanent representatives of the Member States steer and amend the laws that the European Commission and Parliament are making. The Council of Ministers provide these laws with a legitimacy vis-à-vis national legislatures – who will be bound by their provisions. Member States can vote in the Council and are deemed supporting whatever the Council of Ministers approves by qualified majority. In addition, each Member State, including the smallest, are given the ceremonial honour to chair successively the Council of Ministers for six months. Officially, there are three main players shaping EU legislation: The Council of Ministers, the Parliament and the Commission. But in real terms, there is one, the European Commission, which generally can play out MEPs against the opposition from Member States in the Council. Considering the number of Member States, it became increasingly difficult for Member States to gather a blocking minority in the Council of Ministers to block legislation. You have already read that in earlier pages but *repetitio est mater studiorum.*

However, while for the big issues such as transatlantic relations or world trade matters the Member States have the final saying over the European Commission, "minor" issues such as the distribution of funds and other "trivialities" affecting everyday life of citizens, are the exclusive prerogative of the non-accountable and not elected, European Commission.

What is the difference between a Directive and a Regulation? They are both binding European laws, which are published in the Official Journal of the European Union printed in Luxembourg. Regulations have immediate effect and once published are enforced immediately, in all Member States as if they were published in the national Official

Journal. Directives are not binding immediately. Directives bind the Member States that have a time period to transpose their provisions into their national law, meaning to impose the obligations concerned on you and me, in the form of national laws. In practice, most of the laws adopted by national parliaments transpose obligations decided by the System. The sovereignty of Member States is in many domains more a legal fiction than reality.

3/6 Why it Matters

It matters because you may be living the last days of democracy, your last days of freedom, and the last days of the European Union.

This is a very good reason to understand what is going on and then see what you can do about it, and how.

As a citizen of the European Union, your life depends entirely on the System. But what is the System?

The System is a kind of living organism, composed by certain staff members who form the inner circle of the European Commission. It includes the President of the European Commission, yet not in the capacity of absolute ruler, certain Members of his Cabinet, few Directors General and very few other high-ranking, deeply "systemic" functionaries.

This group is atypical, has no institutional capacity and is under the direct yet unofficial control of the two, politically most powerful, Member States: Germany (Chancellery) and France (Palais de

l'Élysée). Few people, however, in the hard-core of the power structure in these two Member States and are the overlords of the System.

There is a noticeable difference between the two "components of
the System." The "inner circle" of the European Commission has a
stable configuration since the main element of change is retirement.
The "few people" from the important Member States have a higher
turnover as they originate from entities subject to rotation, Cabinets
of Heads of State, MEPs and Members in Permanent Representations.

The first goal of the Commission element of the System is to
maintain its autonomy and self-reproduction. This works fine. The
System has developed special abilities, procedures and techniques
to keep the political personnel of the Commission busy and out of
the way. Commissioners worry for the "irrelevant" thus ignoring
the "important." Certainly, they are politically responsible for their
portfolios, but few exert real political power. Indeed, in many cases, especially in the first years of their term they are intelligently
manipulated by their Cabinets and certain Director Generals, which
is the "long hand" of the System. They are continuously kept busy
with extensive travel, "important" meetings with representatives of
special interest groups and organisations, with the remaining time
filled in with various public relations exercises where the Commissioner is usually the most important personality of the event. Indeed,
there are cases of Commissioners who their role is rather ornamental
because decisions are already made by the System.

In the total absence of effective political supervision from the
Member States, the System thrives and decides almost everything
that impacts your life.

The System is using many ways and means to claim political legitimacy. One major argument is the progress achieved in the election of the
President of the European Commission directly by the citizens of Europe.

With the new, German inspired, procedure named "Spitzenkan-
didaten" in real terms, nothing changed but it adds deceptive legit-

3/6 WHY IT MATTERS

imacy to the Commission. Before the introduction of the "Spitzen-kandidaten," the political groups were proposing their candidates after the European election. The winning party was proposing the candidate and usually was approved by the European Council. Now, the parties simply present their candidate before the election, put its name in the party's ballot in all parties of the group, and the first winner gets the job. Big deal!

This brings us to the second strategic target of the System. It is to enlarge the democratic deficit of Europe, by further reducing citizens' freedoms, to exert greater control. This is being gradually achieved using a two-track progression based on the very noble ambitions; to eliminate tax evasion and fighting terrorism.

Tax evasion is a crime against the society and must be efficiently prevented. However, with the excuse of combating endemic tax evasion, the System in cooperation with the network of "sub-Systems" in Member States (the national administrations, equally eager for power) passed laws, which turned citizens into hostages of the tax authorities. This is wrong because at the end of the day citizens become more hostile to authorities and tax evasion is not efficiently controlled.

Such an approach is in direct conflict with the principle of freedoms guaranteed by our political civilization, even the Charter of Fundamental Rights of the European Union. However, in Member States, politicians prefer to keep a safe distance of questioning the constitutionality of such laws because they are afraid to be targeted. Indeed, with the connections the interested authorities have with the media, national tabloids, "character assassination" of a politician who dares to confront administrative decisions concerning tax evasion controls is very easy. Just spreading the rumour that x Member of Parliament, for opposing a certain decree aiming to fight tax evasion, must have a reason of his or her own to do it. This is enough to destroy any politician.

In this context, "Systemic" elements in Brussels, but also in certain

Member States, are preparing the political grounds to introduce legislation that will allow tax authorities to search private homes without warning and without a Court Order or the presence of a Prosecutor. If any cash or non-declared valuable items are discovered, the occupant will have to prove their legitimacy.

If this happens, the basis of our legal civilization, which is Roman law, will be changed and our society will shift to the principles of Soviet law. Therefore, once this legislation will be introduced, if the authorities ever discover any cash in your house or a golden jewel, you will have to prove that it is legal. The authorities will have to prove nothing. This was the Soviet pattern and still exists in certain eastern countries today. If you cannot produce sufficient documentation (i.e. bank withdrawal statements), your cash and other valuables will be confiscated and you will be charged with money laundering.

No politician dares to oppose such systematically organised new legal provisions, which will make citizens hostages of the System. Politicians are scared of being "exposed" by the administration in a targeted "name and shame" approach. This ensures politicians remain scared to challenge the legality of such actions.

And, we are not talking about drugs or prostitutions money. For that there is enough legislation. The issue is usual small business activities, which anyway, are dying every day because of over-regulation.

In a similar way, the issue of "fighting terrorism" has climbed to the top political and social agenda and is a priority of our society to maintain our safety and our freedom. Terrorism of any kind and for any reason must be eradicated. However, it is necessary to discourage politicians to overlook human rights and "close an eye" to the legal exaggerations occurring in the build-up of legislation aimed at monitoring citizens' actions.

Under the excuse of "suspected" relations with terrorist affairs, the authorities can arrest and detain citizens without external contacts (lawyers, family) for as long as they deem necessary. In many Member States, telephones and correspondence are monitored without any previous juridical authorisation. No systemic politician is opposing this, only the far-left and the far-right parties complain. However, nobody is listening to them as they are considered extremists. This is a matter the European Union should look at globally, but it doesn't.

The point is that under the pretext of fighting terrorism and tax evasion, Europe is heading towards a dictatorship run by the EU's administrative machinery. The European Commission, which should be the guarantor of the rights of its citizens, is keeping a safe distance from all such issues.

This is wrong. If we want to maintain the European Union in one piece, the European Commission must be carefully guarding new legislation and must always have, as its main constraint, the protection of the democratic freedoms of our society.

Anti-corruption oversight, security and regulation are all essential elements in any democratic society and are the basis of our political civilization. However, if these are not designed with the consensus of the people, if they are not governed by the rule of my ancestors "metron ariston" (moderation) and are employed "in the name of God" without any kind of accountability, they will ultimately serve only as tools for the next dictator.

The Union of Socialist Soviet Republics lasted 70 years. Just think how many millennia Communism would have survived if its founders, Lenin and Stalin, had invented our legislation and had access to current supporting technology.

3/7 Europhobic, not Eurosceptic

In Europe, in Europe proper, it is difficult to imagine someone being a Eurosceptic – that is, to be against his own interests.

There are people who are against the integration of the EU. There are people who feel nationalist and want independence to tamper with their national laws without having the OK of the EU. There are people who are genuinely opposed to their countries being in the EU. But they are only few.

"United we stand" is the secret of success of peoples and nations and the people of Europe have many things in common and many common interests to defend. Those against EU integration are not more patriotic than the others, but are simply uninformed or even, misinformed. They ignore what the European Union is and what benefits they and their country can get. If they only knew...

If they only knew, most of them would be in favour of the EU and only a few stubborn with extreme political views would remain against. They are the Eurosceptic.

Today, the System has conveniently named those who mistrust the European Commission as Eurosceptic. They are not, because in their great majority are neither stubborn nor extremists. They simply ignore.

The System, which over the years "devoured" billions of Euros to communicate Europe, intelligently did the opposite. It spent money only to keep citizens in the dark with no knowledge of what the European institutions really are and how they work. And it did this for obvious reasons.

The European Union belongs to its citizens, not to the civil servants. A United Europe is a great achievement and it will be against our own interests to destroy such a hope.

The general perception of ordinary people, including many government officials from Member States working with the EU institutions, is that the European Commission is, in one way or another, corrupt. They cannot specify the kind of corruption, but they do feel that something is wrong. As they know nothing, or almost nothing, of what the European Commission does but they understand it has a determining negative role in their daily life, they do not trust it. Yet the European Commission is our government and it is all we have.

We must mobilise our national leaders and ourselves as ordinary citizens to make our Union better. We must force them to make it democratic, honest, fair, open and transparent. And we must give to our Union a clear political dimension. The European Union is not an association of merchants who fix VAT. What we should become is the United States of Europe. But United States means transparency and accountability...

The clear majority of Europeans repudiates and does not trust European Institutions, especially the European Commission. This is also seen between the lines of the various Eurobarometer surveys, which, however, are presented in such a statistically "creative" manner that the substance is lost in the details.

Citizens have only a vague idea of "United Europe" considering it a closed System of self-appointed and self- reproducing rulers. Citizens asking embarrassing questions are classified as "anti-Europeans" and labelled as "Eurosceptic."

So who are all these Eurosceptic we hear about all the time who are presented by the System as a kind of shameful cult? They do exist in the mind-set of the System which invents imaginary enemies "within its walls" only to draw moral legitimacy.

What does exist, however, and is widely spread, are Europhobic. They are the Europeans who do not trust the System. They are many and keep growing in numbers every day.

The simple fact that you are reading this book means that potentially, you are one of them.

Welcome to the club!

TRUTH LIBERATES

4/1 The European Parliament

The European Parliament is supposed to be the supreme political institution of the European Union. In reality, it comes next to the Commission and next to the Council.

In the present term (2014-2019) it has 751 Members (MEPs) who were directly elected by the citizens of all 28 Member States for the usual 5-year term. In the election of May 2019, Great Britain will not participate, and the 27 Member States will elect 705 Parliamentarians, in direct proportion to the population of each Member State.

Political parties sharing the same political principles and values form political groups. However, political groups cannot propose legislation, only political parties can. However, no individual political party has sufficient number of members to table legislation. Consequently, the European Parliament is the only elected Parliament on earth that cannot propose legislation. Indeed, only the (non-elected) European Commission can. Members of Parliament can only approve or reject proposed legislation and can introduce amendments.

So far, there are two main political groups that have decisive importance in EU Parliamentary affairs. They are the Christian Democrats, the right-of-centre European People's Party (EPP) and the left-of-the-centre Progressive Alliance of Socialists and Democrats (S&D). The other political groups have no real role and move between screaming and holding events in order to justify their existence. As to the real political power it is in the hands of only a dozen of Parliamentarians who can be found in the two big political families. The Brussels environment is easy-going, and compromise is the real objective. One element to consider is that after so many years of coexistence with no real political role, the two big political families have become very close. Although in their own national environments the two parties, popular and socialists, often come to extreme confrontations reminiscent of the Montagues and the Capulets, in Brussels, they behave like blood brothers.

In the European Parliament, all kinds of lobbyists have free and unlimited access. They can walk the corridors where MEPs have their private offices, knocking on any one they choose. This allows for their over-familiarisation with MEPs and their assistants. In this context, many MEPs and lobbyists develop close relations over the years, which in some cases allow for serious wheeling and dealing in matters crucial to certain industries such as energy, tobacco, cars, shipping, chemicals and others. In this way, the various interest groups or individual conglomerates can influence the decision-making process by introducing amendments.

Among the frequent "clients" of the European Parliament facilities, in Brussels and Strasbourg, are certain Ambassadors of various "banana" and politically marginal "republics." Counties with little, if any, democratic rule and respect for human rights, which have an embassy in Brussels are usually accredited to all, the European Commission, NATO and the Kingdom of Belgium. As they all get accreditation to the European Parliament, they usually invite for lunch someone (MEP or assistant) in the Members' Restaurant in a kind of public relations exercise. This lunch where nothing important will be discussed will give the opportunity to the Ambassador to compile a detailed report afterwards, which will be sent directly to the President of the "republic", back home. The President will be happy because he or she will learn that talks during this lunch of great importance (!) were mainly focused on His Excellency. At the same time, the Ambassador will prove once again that he works hard in Brussels and he is eternally devoted to His Excellency. As for the MEP or the assistant, he or she will forget the name of the host and his wonderful country, before even getting into the elevator.

Another peculiarity of the European Parliament is that, despite its official seat is in Strasbourg (France), it has a second seat in Brussels, while more than 4000 staff is hosted in Luxembourg. In Brussels, facilities are bigger and more modern, and the Parliament convenes there, three weeks per month for its committee meetings, its group meetings and a few plenary sessions. Once a month everything is moved over to Strasbourg for the main plenary sessions. This is simply ridiculous as it reminds one of a travelling circus.

The annual budget of the European Parliament is €1.8bn (2016). Every Strasbourg week (12 weeks per year), besides the Parliament Members and staff, more than 5,000 people move to Strasbourg and this number includes Commissioners, Commission executives, Ambassadors and diplomatic staff, journalists, lawyers, lobbyists and all kind of Brussels "personalities" dealing with the System. They travel by chartered planes, convoys of lorries carrying documentation, fleets of cars and a long, slow train journey for the assistants. The annual cost of the Strasbourg week for the EU budget is €107m, which includes €5m for moving the Members of the Commission which have their weekly meeting of Tuesday, in Strasbourg and the necessary officials of the Commission and the Council.

The Parliament's Strasbourg week, a well-paid week (by taxpayers), is a full week of PR and lobbying. No more, no less.

The only real reason for the existence of the Parliament in Strasbourg is the French opposition to abolish it. The matter concerns the national pride of France, while it is a monthly financial injection to the city of Strasbourg and its business, primarily hotels and restaurants. Since the treaty of Lisbon, the location of the seat no longer figures in the treaties. Therefore, any change of the status quo must be decided by a unanimous decision adopted by the European Council. In this case, France has a veto right and will never allow change. In this context, to support the city of Strasbourg, the late French President François Mitterrand moved the famous National School of Administration (ENA) from Paris to Strasbourg.

The European Parliament exists because it is a "tool of convenience" for the System and for the political parties in the Member States. They all are happy with the existence of the European Parliament, as it is. The System draws its missing legitimacy from it, and this is worth the expenditure and the trouble.

As for the Member States, it constitutes a luxury parking space or holding pen for annoying political personalities. Party leaders in Member States dispatch to the European Parliament internal political opponents, as well as personalities, such as former Prime Ministers or Presidents and former Commissioners, who have national appeal and speak the truth as they are out of frontline politics. By sending them to the golden cage of the European Parliament, politicians in the field reduce their own internal party attritions, and Europe picks up the bill.

All Members of the European Parliament (MEPs) have the right to table written questions to the various Institutions and, by law, they must get an answer. No law specifies, of course, what the reply must contain. As of this parliamentary legislature (2014-2019) the number of questions, which was unlimited previously, was reduced to 10 questions per MEP, per month.

It should be noted that in the past, according to rumours in the Brussels "corridors," questions by MEPs to the EU Institutions could be "bought" for a few thousand Euros each. This was reportedly an additional source of (black) income, primarily for certain Parliamentary assistants who were keeping the relations of the MEP and the business community at arm's length. "Paid" questions were not tabled for getting an answer, but just for tabling the question. Once the question was tabled, the interested party was taking the question, translating into the national language and through a media relations' agency, was reprinting the question in national media.

Now questions have been limited to only 10 and MEPs are using them primarily to impress voters. In most instances, they table questions to satisfy their electorate. Indeed, once a question concerning a national (for their country) issue is tabled, they forward the question to the national press. All this, is in the context of a public relations exercise, which promotes the image of the MEP in his own constituency and has some sort of psychotherapeutic effect. The purpose is to make voters believe that their representative in Brussels "raised a strong voice to the Commission."

The questions in the European Parliament are considered a door of citizens (through their MEPs) to the System. However, if the question is on a sensitive matter, the Commission and other Institutions will use all means to circumvent the essence. However, such questions for the Commission are quite useful because they add to the apparent legitimacy of its operations. Thus, both sides are happy, MEPs and the Commission. As for the citizens, they are also happy because they think that through their MEPs they are in control, though vague, of the Brussels Institutions. This control, however, is only a product of fantasy.

Members of Parliament have many fringe benefits, which partially offset the lack of real political power of the only elected body of the European Union. Among the fringe benefits, every Member of Parliament can invite to Brussels (usually in groups of 15 to 30 citizens) up to 110 visitors from their own country per year, to visit the Parliament and be briefed about the Parliament and the Union. The Parliament pays for all expenses including air transport.

4/2 The European Council

The European Council is the assembly of the Heads of all 28 Member States, after the Brexit seemingly 27, along with the (non-voting) President of the European Commission and its own president. It decides the general political direction of the European Union. The assembly of the Heads of State has no legislative powers, yet it has the supreme political power in the European Union.

At a second level comes the Council of Ministers (officially, the Council of the European Union). The Council of Ministers meet 10 different configurations of 28 national ministers (one per Member State). Agriculture and Fisheries; Competitiveness; Economic and Financial Affairs; Education, Youth, Culture and Sport; Employment, Social Policy; Health and Consumer Affairs; Environment; Foreign Affairs; General Affairs; Justice and Home Affairs and Transport, Telecommunications and Energy.

Under the Treaty on the Functioning of the European Union, the Council in most fields, legislates jointly with the European Parliament. Too good to be true.

In practice, EU laws are drafted by the European Commission upon recommendation of the ruling Member States to the System. As to the Council of Ministers and Parliament, they must approve. If for any reason the proposed legislation fails to be approved, then the Commission withdraws the proposal, waits for a while and brings the proposal back, under a different wrapping.

The Council of Ministers is based in Brussels and should not be confused with the Strasbourg-based Council of Europe, which is a separate European organisation with 47 Member States. It focuses on protecting human rights, democracy and the rule of law.

4/3 The European Commission

For the great majority of ordinary citizens, but also for many national politicians, the European Union is a distant, untrustworthy and largely unknown structure of governance. As for the benefits they get, they concern only a few key groups; farmers, selected academic entities, NGOs concentrated in certain "intelligent" Member States and selected contractors of public projects.

Benefits for the few come from the EU Budget. The budget is based on three main sources. Roughly three quarters come direct contributions from the member states' budgets, calculated as a percentage of their respective gross national income, then come import duties collected for the EU by Member States (which keep 20% for collection expenses) and contributions of the Member States as a percentage of their Value-Added Tax (VAT) revenues. VAT rates vary in Member States from 5% to 25% depending on the State and the product. Furthermore, Member States pay to the EU budget fines for violations of EU Law, as well as competition and other penalties paid by companies.

The EU budget is approved through a very democratic- looking procedure, using the European Parliament and the Council as a façade.

In real terms, the budget is decided and allocated by the European Commission with the blessings of the two reigning Member States.

All EU citizens, rich or poor, employed or not, contribute their own money to the Community budget. Thus, they should at least know what the European Commission (the budget money manager) is, how it is made legitimate and to whom it is accountable.

The European Commission is the government of the European Union, theoretically headed by the college of 27 Commissioners (including the President minus the British Commissioner). In real life, a small team of technocrats rules the Commission. They are the better-paid civil servants on Earth and are self-reproducing. The Commission, enjoys a privilege of the "discretionary power". It a concept similar to the notorious "raison d'état" introduced in early 17th century by Cardinal de Richelieu, allowing decisions based on national interest violating principles of justice. This discretion allows the small team of technocrats to violate any rule and law and thus, in a real sense, they are not accountable to anybody, while the law is not violated for national interests.

You may argue that the Commission is accountable to the European Parliament. Yes, legally speaking the Parliament has the privilege and the right to ask the Commission questions. It also has the right to vote a motion for the Commission to resign, which has happened once with the Jacques Santer Commission (1999). This is true, but all was political and decided before by the inner circle of the big Member States and the System. Indeed, no matter how many questions are raised by the Parliament, it is not ensured that there will be adequate and satisfactory replies for all.

That is why citizens must be actively interested in learning about the European Union and its institutions. Knowledge is power, and this is the only tool to bring the change we need.

The European Commission is the most important and most powerful Institution of Europe. It is extremely efficient and it can make things happen. The European Commission, behind closed doors and without any kind of legitimacy, allocates the EU budget at will, after keeping a robust share for its own needs and remuneration (salaries and expenses). In this process, theoretically the last word is with the Council and the European Parliament. However, the essence of the budget is decided by the System (inner circle of the Commission and the big Member States) and is approved with few, mostly irrelevant, changes.

The European Commission is today the most sophisticated and complex administrative machine in the world. It rules half-a-billion people, using some 110,000 pieces of legislation, which are binding for all EU citizens. This legislation, however, is enforced "a la carte," and under unprecedented "discretionary powers." In this context, the Commission can derogate from its own rules and can even ignore Decisions of the Court of Justice of the EU, which if unpleasant, in the internal jargon are conveniently renamed into "opinions."

Around 25,000 permanent civil servants working for the European Commission are paid an approximate average of €10,000 per month net-pocket (the range varies from €4,000 to €19,000). However, at the level of decision-making only grade AD employees (Administrators) are involved, counting for about 35% of the total.

It is of extreme importance to realise that all European Union legislation, binding on the every-day lives of five hundred million citizens, although formally approved by the Council and the Parliament, has been formulated upon initiative of the European Commission. As for the Member States, they substantially participate in the formulation of new laws, but effectively, only at the level of the System, that is the big Member States.

It is also important to understand, or rather to digest, that European legislation supersedes any national legislation in Member States. Indeed, a simple EU Regulation is enough to supersede, without any further argument, even the Constitution of any Member State.

Finally, in any occasion, the Commission is insistently asserting that it is the Council which has the last word in decision-making. Theoretically, this is true. In practice, however, the Council is limited in major political issues (i.e. TTIP, World Trade, Terrorism etc.) and all decisions concerning every-day life of Europeans are exclusively taken by the Commission.

4/4 How Court Decision Become Opinions

This story shows how the Commission transgresses the laws, its own laws, in recruiting its executives. Not long ago, in 2007, the Commission, had published the post of the Head of its Representation in Athens.

Decision makers at the time were, Margot Wallström (Swedish Social Democrat, subsequently Foreign and Deputy Prime Minister in her country) Commissioner responsible for Communication (propaganda), Claus Sørensen (Danish) as Director General and Panos Carvounis (Greek) Deputy Director General. The latter was connected in a "best man" relationship with the Deputy Head of the Athens Representation Ierotheos Papadopoulos (Greek) who had also applied for the post and eventually got it.

Several candidates had applied for the post; amongst them, three Heads of Unit and a member of the Cabinet of the then Greek Commissioner. It has to be added that all Commissioners, in some kind of established practice, manage to appoint as Heads of the Representation in their country officials of their choice. However, formally, the final decision is, according to the rules, to be taken by the Commissioner for Communication, in cooperation with the human resources Commissioner. The Commissioner of the country has in reality the strongest say, but in this case the Greek Commissioner, abstained from the process. Once a "decision making gap" is identified it will be filled by others. This is how things have started and the last choice of the candidates got the post.

It is not by coincidence that the Greek wife of Sørensen was a sympathizer of the then PASOK socialist ruling party same as Papadopoulos and Carvounis, whereas the other short listed candidates were not. The Commissioner of Communication at the time was also socialist.

After the first selection panel, chaired by Carvounis, a short list was established with the three Heads of Unit - with one of them on the top of the list (meritocratic decision in the context of staged game), the member of the cabinet of the Greek Commissioner and Ierotheos Papadopoulos. These five candidates were interviewed by a second panel chaired by Sørensen who has selected Papadopoulos as his first choice and as his second choice the Head of Unit who was the first choice of the first panel.

It should be noted that according to one of the candidates a politically incorrect question was asked by Sørensen to the candidates on what their position would be in the case of a conflict between Greece and Turkey. This just to show how the Commission System sees its role. One wonders if Sørensen would have asked such questions about Gibraltar to the British or Spanish candidates for the Heads posts in London or Madrid. Presumably, on this question Papadopoulos gave the right answer and got the job.

The panel said that the other short listed candidates were also eligible and it was for the political leadership of the Commission to take the final decision. At this point the Machiavellian approach was staged by Sørensen and Carvounis, together with the Danish member of the Wallström Cabinet Anne Bergenfelt (married to a Greek too and friend of Sørensen's wife). They manipulated the neutralization of the two strong candidates, by setting one against the other. As the Greek Commissioner gave from the beginning signs that he would not be involved, he was ignored and the Propaganda micro-system rigged the deck.

To make the long story short, Papadopoulos was appointed as a "compromise". This was once again a "lowest common denominator" decision, convenient to the key actors that had manipulated the procedures and appointed their preferred candidate. Sørensen had his "yes man" and moreover a "political family comrade" in the country of his wife and Carvounis had somebody of trust to "keep him the seat warm." Indeed, after a while Carvounis, Deputy Director General of the European Commission, was appointed as Head of the Representation in Athens, a post purposely classified by the Commission, as of minor importance to appoint Papadopoulos in the first place.

Indeed, when the post was first published the requirements were very low. The Commission classified it as of minor importance requiring no high grades and thus no high budgetary requirements. That in the same position, the same Commission officials, shortly after replaced the low grade/salary chosen with a Deputy Director General with no excuse, is a practice we can see in the kingdom of Kim Jong-un but not in any EU Member State. Except for Brussels where everything is possible except the impossible. That, as in this case, takes some time.

Until here you had the beginning and the mid of the story. Now, the end of it. The three Heads of Unit rejected by the "witch of the tribe" challenged the appointment of Papadopoulos before the Civil Service Tribunal of the EU. The Tribunal delivered three judgments against the Commission and Papadopoulos, in 2009. In all three Decisions, the nomination of Papadopoulos was annulled and the rejection of the candidacies of the three applicants was judged illegal.

However, the Commission decided to keep Papadopoulos as "Acting Head of Representation" violating the Court Decision, conveniently renamed into "opinion."

But there is more. At that time, to pacify other Heads of Representation who were appointed in similar procedures and by the Court's Decision as a Case Law they should have been all removed, the Deputy Director General of Communication (who shortly after replaced the illegally appointee in Athens!) issued a circular to all Representations informing them that "the Commission will consider the opinion of the Court (!!!)" and it secured that it will manage for the status quo not to be bothered. Among other, he says:

.... As some of you might be aware, the Civil Service Tribunal issued on 2 April 2009 a judgment according to which the nomination of Ierotheos (Papadopoulos) as head of Representation in Greece, is annulled. The annulment is solely based on reasons related to the procedure chosen for the appointment; the qualifications of Ierotheos for the post were neither questioned nor examined at all in this judgment. The Civil Service Tribunal is of the opinion that HoR (Head of Representation) cannot be appointed by secondment in the interest of the service under Article 37, 38 of the Staff Regulations as it is currently the case under the Commission decision C (2004) 2662. HQ (Head Quarter) is currently examining together with DG ADMIN (Directorate General of Administration, chef de file for the nomination procedure) and the Legal Service (chef de file for the Court case) the consequences of this judgment and the possible options (appeal, future and ongoing nomination procedures, etc.) There is no need for urgent decisions. Therefore please be ensured that, in the meantime, all HoR will stay in place in order to ensure the continuity of the service. We will keep you informed. ...

This story shows - next to the other scandal of Europe by Satellite how the Department of Communication of the Commission operates and how their Commissioners are often misled in decision making.

4/5 The Monstrous Roaming *Affair*

Mobile telephony is one of the most profitable industries in the world. You can see this from the advertising budgets spent globally and which are in the billions for individual companies. Wherever you turn, from TV and billboards to the neon ads at the airports and even the leaflets distributed during Sunday church services, regardless of faith, you will find a mobile telecommunications advertisement. The profits in the past were huge and they could afford such indulgence.

What is roaming? Roaming is the added incremental costs that a mobile telephony customer pays to enjoy receiving or making calls, sending SMS, and using data when 'roaming' with their mobile in a different country than the one in which the contract was made.

Roaming is also an issue that shapes citizens' perception about the concept of a United Europe.

In a Europe that has a singular, internal market, there should be no roaming costs incurred by consumers – because just like the United States of America, the EU should be considered a single market and a single territory. In the United States, there are no roaming charges from one state to another, even from Texas to Alaska. This is the essence of the "united" world.

Finally, after years of patience, roaming charges will no longer exist within the European Union as of June 2017.

But… there is a problem.

For years, citizens were abused. They were over-charged to receive or make a call from Belgium to Luxembourg or from Italy to France.

And there are laws against this.

Mobile operators, like any other company, are subject to legislation that seeks to protect the proper functioning of markets, to protect consumers, and to prevent corporations from abuse. The European Competition authorities, under the Directorate-General for Competition (DG COMP as it is known in Brussels), are the most powerful authorities in this respect with the ability to levy fines of millions and billions on infringing companies.

In 2004, after continuous criticism against the roaming charges discussed above, from various sectors, DG COMP opened an investigation on the matter of abuse of the market by telecom operators to examine whether there was cartel behaviour, abuse of dominant market position, or a monopoly which was not functioning in the interest of EU citizens. The European Commission claims that the investigations were not prompted by a formal complaint, but started on their own initiative.

DG COMP's findings led the European Commission to initiate formal proceedings against three mobile operators, Vodafone, T-Mobile and O2, regarding their roaming tariffs. Early in 2006, Commission services reached the conclusion that they should penalise the mobile telephony industry of Europe – with some Commission officials at the time talking about billions of Euros in fines.

The upper limit of any fine would have been up to 10% of a company's global annual turnover. Furthermore, for infringements like roaming which was of long duration (more than five years), the fine would see an increase of up to 10% per year in the amount determined for gravity.

Just Vodafone had a turnover of circa €50bn in 2015.

A hypothetical fine could have reached €10bn just for that one company considering the infringement went on for over a decade.

The industry was alarmed. The System was mobilised. When you are the most profitable industry in Europe, you can mobilise necessary forces.

To this effect, it is difficult to understand whether what then appeared as a heroic act of the Commissioner for Communication, Viviane Reding, was indeed a well-staged act. I prefer to think the former is true of Reding's Roaming initiative, but we will never know, as the System is indeed powerful.

Neelie Kroes was not in charge of the roaming inquiry. She was conflicted because she had been a board member of the UK mobile company O2 until 2004 when she was appointed competition commissioner.

When, the Roaming Regulation was launched to progressively eliminate roaming charges (instead of abolishing them), the almost-concluded infringement procedures by DG COMP were cancelled.

On Reding's Roaming Regulation, two Commissioners, the British and the German, opposed the action, but eventually it was passed. When the intention of the Commission to introduce the Roaming Regulation was announced, New Europe wrote an article (27 August 2006) asking why the Commission needs a Directive for roaming when the issue can be fixed by DG COMP without any other complication by imposing a fine (and correcting the market abuse).

The following week, the Director General of Competition of the European Commission, Philip Lowe –now Sir Philip Lowe- replied to New Europe with an official letter to the newspaper. The letter confirmed that an investigation for the roaming overcharging was conducted in 2004 and 2005 and that infringement proceedings were launched against the three companies. The Director General stressed that the infringement proceedings were independent from the Roaming Regulation and the Commission explained to the newspaper that the investigation will be completed regardless of the adoption of the

59

Roaming Regulation and that any companies found guilty would be duly penalised.

"In our roaming charges investigations, we have carried out inspections at the premises of several major mobile network operators and the GSM Association, which is the industry body gathering virtually all operators worldwide. Based on the evidence collected during the inspections and further investigations, in 2004 and 2005, the Commission initiated formal proceedings against Vodafone, T-Mobile and O2 regarding their roaming tariffs... At the time of writing, we are waiting for the final submissions from the companies concerned who have legal rights of defence, which must be respected."

Nice, big words by Philip Lowe. But what happened is that the Commission stopped the roaming competition investigations and cancelled the infringement procedures, even though, the Director-General had very explicitly stated that the Roaming Regulation was "a necessary complement to the application of the competition rules." A complement, but not a replacement.

This was a flagrant violation of Community Law and the elimination of a blow that would have cost the mobile telephone industry hundreds of billions of Euros.

In this way the industry saved tens of billions in penalties, and most importantly, deprived EU citizens of their right to seek damages from the operators for the overpricing of roaming services.

Indeed, when the European Commission finds a breach of the competition rules, victims of that infringement can directly rely on the Commission's decision as binding proof in civil proceedings for damages. European Council Regulation EC 1/2003 and Case law of the Court of Justice (ECJ) both confirm that in cases before national courts, a Commission decision is binding proof that the behaviour took place and was illegal. Regardless of Commission fines to the infringing companies, damages may be awarded to the victims without these being reduced on account of the Commission fine.

It is also necessary to note that under established ECJ case law, the discretionary power of the European Commission is not unlimited, and that a decision to stop proceedings without legal, administrative, or other justification could be subject to investigation by the European Anti-Fraud Office, OLAF, for preventing the billions in fines to be injected into the EU budget.

Indeed, such a decision to stop the proceedings cannot be political under EU law.

In discussing the flagrant cheating of the people of Europe by the System in favour of their mobile telephony "friends" at the time, we understood that the Commission violated all written laws and rules because they did not want to hurt the industry.

The Roaming Regulation was the biggest collective robbery of citizens of Europe with the blessing and the manipulation of the European Commission. It was a robbery that was both immoral and financial.

When New Europe asked why, the Commission spokesperson went on a rampage, suggesting that the question was "ludicrous" and that New Europe's coverage of the affair aimed at selling more papers.

The newspaper you see, in line with etiquette, had sent an email to the spokesperson of DG COMP at the time, Jonathan Todd, to alert him of the topic and matter of the question to be asked. A courtesy, which though not a rule, is more than helpful for the spokespersons to be better prepared to tackle difficult issues and do their jobs.

Not only did Todd attack the newspaper, but he also lied. Despite the European law and precedent explained   above, Todd claimed a fine "would not have had any impact on the consumers that might have paid over the odds…"

It is not often that journalists' questions are met with personalised attacks by spokespersons. Todd, however, chose to do so, despite being met with the highest courtesy a journalist can offer (fair warning).

Personalised attacks are easy, but unnecessary if you have legal basis for argumentation. After all, New Europe did not suggest that Todd's overzealous response was due to an instinctual backlash of having garnered a perhaps overly-close and personal relationship with the Commissioner.

4/6 How the EbS Frequency Passed to Kirmizi Porn TV

Europe by Satellite (EbS) is the TV network of the European Commission and is managed by the Directorate-General of Communication (DG COMM).

On 1 February 2007, the Commission announced that EbS broadcasts would move from satellite Hotbird 7A of the Eutelsat constellation to satellite Astra Sirius 2.

The footprint of Hotbird 7A has excellent coverage in the entire European continent. A dish of 40 cm is enough to enjoy excellent reception. Hotbird broadcasts over 1,000 TV networks and is the most popular carrier for news and entertainment broadcasts.

Astra Sirius 2 is a satellite requiring a much bigger dish, a different orientation and with few commercial broadcasts except for some porn channels. It is used primarily for commercial transmissions, including the Swedish Posts.

New Europe published a series of well-substantiated articles and analysis explaining that the change of satellite for EbS was equivalent to closing the European Community network. As a matter of fact, nobody would ever pay to install a second, much bigger dish, with different orientation with its own LMB and decoder, to watch EbS only. More so, the porn channels were encoded so there would be no additional "incentive" for viewers. EbS, however, could also be watched (edited) in Euronews on Hotbird.

Owned by a group of public European TV networks at the time, Euronews is another "sin" of the notorious Directorate-General of Communication from the European Commission (DG COMM). Since it was established in 1993, the network was heavily funded by the European Institutions and the EU Member States. So far, only DG COMM alone has funded Euronews with over €250m.

The beauty of this pan-European (?) venture is that its controlling majority (53%) and the management were sold to "Media Globe Networks" a media concern owned by the Egyptian tycoon Naguib Sawiris for €35m., in early 2015. Furthermore, in February 2017 another 25% was sold to the American network NBC leaving European public broadcasters with 22%. Therefore, the only European element of the Euronews network is the first component of its brand mane.

It is worth taking note that days after NBC acquired 25% of Euronews stocks (78% non-European ownership), the European Commission (Directorate General for Communication) approved a financial support (grant) to Euronews of € 24,500,000 per year for four years!

I do not wish to elaborate further on the matter because it goes beyond the subject of a book. Indeed, it can well be the content of a dossier with any Public Prosecutor in any of the 28 EU Member States.

From what we perceive, in this Euronews affair, only civil servants were involved on the part of the Commission and no political personnel, as the story goes back to more than a quarter of a century and for such a long period only the administration presents continuity while the political personnel are recycled every five years.

The avalanche of information and analysis in New Europe generated considerable correspondence between the newspaper and DG COMM. Strange (or not strange) enough, in the pressroom of the Commission there was "submarine silence" and our reporters were not allowed to ask questions.

In matters of correspondence, however, DG COMM was very eloquent in writing letters to New Europe to explain that the change of satellite had no real impact in the broadcasts. Of course, this was true, but with a minor detail. EbS was perfectly broadcast on Astra Sirius 2, but nobody could watch it. As a matter of fact, nobody would have ever invested for a second satellite system (dish, LMB, decoder and separate installation) just to watch EbS. What is more, large satellite dishes are even prohibited in most parts of Europe.

DG COMM was very nervous on the matter and one of the letters sent to the newspaper by the spokesperson was sent to the paper in a text file (DOC, not PDF) that included the track changes made by the Head of Cabinet of the Commissioner. As a result, when the newspaper printed the letter with track changes, the spokesperson was dismissed.

Commissioner Margot Wallström, despite the full confidence to her entourage which I described at the time as the Fox and the Cat of The Adventures of Pinocchio, was very worried. We explained to her that the small difference of few degrees between the two satellites is translated into several thousands of kilometres' distance in space. The altitude of civilian satellites is not less than 300kms. Yet, she had so much trust in her team that she did not believe us and refused to ask the advice of a satellite expert of NATO, as we suggested.

The design and materialisation of this superb "patent" was genial.

When EbS signed the first broadcasting contract, Eutelsat was represented in Belgium by Belgacom. Each time the contract between the Commission and Belgacom would expire, it was automatically renewed. When the contract was up for renewal again in late 2006, Belgacom informed the Commission that it was not representing Hotbird anymore and they should be contacting the owners of the satellite (Eutelsat), directly.

The Commission, instead of calling Eutelsat in Paris, claimed that the old supplier (Belgacom) could not provide the service anymore and opened a fast-track tender, a kind of "entre- nous" procedure, and awarded the tender to Astra. How did Astra know of this fast-track tender and Eutelsat not? We have checked and cross-checked, but no one ever explained this to us.

It should also be noted that after the contract with Astra Sirius 2 expired, DG COMM silently, almost like a "thief," moved EbS back to satellite Eutelsat 9A located 9 degrees East and not to Eutelsat 7A located 7 degrees East where from EbS was broadcasting before.

There were two obvious beneficiaries of this change.

Euronews. A TV network, which at the time was abundantly using the broadcasts of EbS, filling most of its air-time for free. Once EbS was not seen by Europeans anymore, Euronews viewers were thinking EbS footage was produced by the broadcaster.

Kirmizicam. This was a Turkish network, which immediately after EbS changed satellite, began broadcasting in the EbS Hotbird 7A frequency (13E 12476/27500H) enjoying millions of high-class viewers. Margot Wallström was so naïve that, despite being handed screenshot pictures showing that Kirmizi cam was broadcasting on the EbS frequency hard porn, she continued to have full confidence in her associates.

By the way, Kirmizicam at the time was one of the top hard- core free-to-air porn channels in the world.

Whether there were other beneficiaries, I do not know and I do not wish to continue with speculations on this subject anymore.

Finally, in the fall of 2007, I was invited to testify before the Internal Audit Service (IAS) of the European Commission on the EbS case. The interrogation lasted four hours and I presented also a 17-page written statement. However, nothing happened.

Omertà, or what?

4/7 The Confession

On the New Europe website, you will find all the details, as it was the only newspaper that published the details of this scandal from the very first day. Brussels media covered the affair rather selectively and mostly under the perspective of the System.

On this matter, the president of the European Commission at the time, Jose Manuel Barroso, was enjoying the support of the System. Not because he was right or wrong. The reason was that after the collapse of the Santer Commission in 1999, following the Edith Cresson scandal, a repetition of a similar scenario after a decade would have been catastrophic for Europe. Moreover, the endemic social crisis in the Union had already taken on financial dimensions and the whole European idea was losing ground.

It was at the start of the summer in 2012 and New Europe was being taken to Court for defamation by the then Prime Minister of Malta Lawrence Gonzi and his Minister for Resources and Rural Affairs George Pullicino. The whole affair had no grounds, as they filed charges against New Europe because Captain Paul Watson, a fugitive activist of "Sea Shepard NGO" had claimed in an interview to the newspaper that "European politicians and especially Maltese politicians are corrupt because they allow illegal fishing of blue tuna." Big deal!

The interview was widely discussed in the Parliament of Malta and Prime Minister Lawrence Gonzi filed charges against the newspaper because a suit could not be filed against Watson, and not for any other reason, but to make a point in the Maltese media.

As summer was just upon us, I decided to start my holidays by driving to Malta to find out more about the case. So, on the way to Sicily, Pozzallo, car ferry to Malta and then who did I meet? I started with the Maltese Commissioner John Dalli.

We had a nice lunch during which I learned about the Maltese political landscape. Then, suddenly, Dalli asked me: "I need a lawyer in Brussels, could you suggest any?" and he added, "not now when we will be back in Brussels, in September."

At the end of August, one late afternoon while driving, I got a call from Dalli. I was returning from Zaventem where I had picked up my lawyer, Ariti Alamanou, who had just returned from Greece. Dalli asked if he could meet me at once, so I drove straight to Berlaymont. When I arrived, I asked Ariti to wait for me, but then I remembered that Dalli had asked me for a lawyer. So, I returned to the car and asked Ariti to come with me. Surprised and bothered because she was not coming from the hairdresser, but straight from her holiday on Corfu, she agreed to follow, noticeably annoyed.

Arriving at Dalli's office, I left Ariti with the Secretary of the Commissioner and entered his office alone. He went straight to the subject. "Do you remember about the lawyer I asked you for in Malta?" he said. "Yes" I replied, "here she is." I invited Ariti into the office of the Commissioner and I left.

Dalli told Ariti that he was under investigation by the EU's Anti-Fraud Office (OLAF) and was very concerned.

In December 2011, Jose Barroso invited Dalli to his office and asked him to stop the "Tobacco Products Directive". Dalli agreed and everybody was happy. However, when Dalli returned to his office, some of his cabinet members did not seem to like the easy surrender of the Directive without getting something in terms of compensation. In cases in which the tobacco industry is involved, our imagination flies and it seems this was the case at that time.

Dalli, apparently convinced by his associates, did not drop the Directive, despite the discussion with his president and the pressures exerted by the tobacco lobby. In March 2012, a Swedish company producing snus, a chewable tobacco, filed a complaint with the Commission, alleging that a close friend of Dalli, Silvio Zammit, who acted as an intermediary, had requested millions of Euros in a bribe for Commissioner Dalli to amend the Directive in order to lift the ban of snus sale in EU. A scared Barroso sent immediately the complaint to OLAF for action. OLAF took the matter seriously, given the gravity of the case involving the reputation of a Commissioner and of the Commission itself.

In late spring and early autumn 2012, John Dalli was interrogated twice by OLAF. Despite that he was offered the opportunity to do it in writing (by correspondence) he preferred to do both interviews live.

In early October 2012, OLAF chief Giovanni Kessler delivered OLAF's investigation report to the Commission. On 16 October 2012, Barroso invited Dalli to his office and told him: "Here is an OLAF report for you in relation to the Tobacco Products Directive. The report says that you did not take any bribe; it says that you did not change the Directive, but it also says that you had private meetings with tobacco representatives and that there are circumstantial evidences you were aware of the discussions between the person you put as your go-between and the snus company for a bribe. Therefore, give me your resignation."

Dalli asked to read the OLAF report, but Barroso refused claiming that it was confidential. This reminds us of the Portuguese Inquisition. Dali, however, asked for one day's grace to consult his family and his lawyer. Barroso handed him a draft resignation and said: "Either you sign this resignation now, or I issue a press release immediately announcing that I dismissed you".

Dalli, however, claimed he had no glasses to read the resignation text. So, Barroso said: "Take it to your office. You have half an hour, either you sign it and I issue a press release saying that you resigned or I issue a press release with your dismissal".

Ariti was in Dalli's office. Returning from Barroso's office, accompanied by three women from the president's office, he told her: "He fired me, please get Basil here, now." Ariti called me and 10 minutes later I was in Dalli's office.

Dalli was sitting in the middle of a conference table surrounded by his team, Barroso's women and Ariti. Dalli was pallid, shocked and holding a pen in his right hand as he looked at the resignation. I asked him, "John, what is going on" and he replied "He asked me to resign". One of the women tried to stop the discussion and told me: "Look Mr., we have no time, my President is waiting for the resignation of the Commissioner". I replied to the woman: "I do not give a ... for your President". Turning to Dalli, I asked him: "John, do you want to resign?" Dalli said "no" and I replied immediately "Then, do not resign."

Dalli asked me why and with a rather strong voice, I replied: "First, because you do not want to. Second, for the honour of your family. Third, for your honour. Fourth, because in Malta you are all in all half a million people and you will not be able to circulate in the street..." And I stopped talking. Dalli continued: "And fifth?" I was rather infuriated and replied immediately without thinking twice as I usually do. "Fifth," I said, "because you will not make it in time to sign, I will cut your hand before."

In the room, everybody fell silent and looked very worried. The scene reminded me of the painting of the decapitation of Saint John the Divine of Michelangelo Merisi da Caravaggio in the Cathedral of Malta where all other prisoners in the painting were looking at the decapitation with perplexed agony.

Dalli took a deep breath, put the pen to the side, started laughing and said: "OK I will not sign." One of the Barroso women said in a low voice: "Commissioner..." and I interrupted, *"Roma locuta causa finita."*

Barroso, before asking Dalli to resign, had gone to Malta to meet with the Maltese Prime Minister and got the clearance to dismiss Dalli. The Maltese Prime Minister agreed with great pleasure because even though they are from the same right wing party (EPP), Dalli constituted a serious political threat for the Prime Minister.

Berlaymont is a close circle where news travels fast. Upon the return of Barroso's women to his office, despite Dalli having not signed the dictated resignation, the Office of the President issued a press release announcing that Dalli had "resigned". This was a lie. Dalli had never signed any resignation.

However, the news that Dalli was asked to quit, but did not resign despite Barroso's announcement that he did, circulated immediately throughout the Commission headquarters. In the next half hour that I stayed in his office, Dalli received on his cell phone six or seven solidarity calls from other

Commissioners, encouraging him not to sign the resignation, for obvious reasons.

Under such circumstances, the dismissal of Dalli would be a precedent for other Commissioners, especially those who were appointed by one government and then the opposition party came to power. First to call was Michel Barnier, the French Commissioner appointed by Nickolas Sarkozy before François Holland came to power. Dalli received similar calls from Antonio Tajani, Stefan Füle and others.

Dalli had drafted a press release on his own and asked his spokeswoman to distribute it, but she refused without a second thought, remaining faithful to the System. So Dalli's press release was distributed to the media by New Europe.

The next morning, John Dalli came to New Europe offices where he granted his first TV interview after the dismissal. As we delayed broadcasting the interview, the Commission's briefing was postponed until the interview was broadcast.

During the briefing, the spokeswoman, Pia Ahrenkilde Hansen, announced that Commissioner John Dalli had resigned. The dramatic performance in the pressroom reminded you of the works by playwright Eugène Ionesco. After Pia's statement, New Europe's journalist Andy Carling asked: "Can you give us copy of the resignation letter because I come straight from New Europe where Commissioner John Dalli is still there and he told me that he did not resign." The discussion about the resignation continued until Pia finally said: "No I have not seen the resignation letter, but I know that there is one."

Next to take the floor was Giovanni Kessler, who explained the OLAF report about Dalli. In this context, Kessler and OLAF can only be criticised for two issues.

Perhaps Kessler should not have appeared in the pressroom. He could not enter into any specific details about the OLAF investigation given the need to protect confidentiality of the case that had, by then, been passed to the Maltese Attorney General. That lack of detail fueled a great deal of misconceptions about the case. And, second, Kessler had had no reason to interrogate Dalli himself during the investigation. However, when I confronted him about it, he told me in his frank style that he took part in the Dalli interviews because, as the head of OLAF, he is responsible for all its investigations and because the matter was regarding a sitting Commissioner and was a high-profile case worthy of the highest-ranked investigators. Makes sense.

Dalli later complained he had not been informed of the OLAF allegations against him, but this was not quite true. He had been interviewed by OLAF several times and been given ample opportunity to explain his position. At no moment in time, however, did he distance himself from his friend who had allegedly asked for a bribe in his name.

Immediately upon the announcement of Dalli's resignation, Ariti suggested to Dalli to write a letter to Barroso to ask him if the dismissal was on the grounds of Article 17 of the Treaty, which gives the President of the Commission the political prerogative to dismiss any Commissioner without explanations. In his letter, Dalli infuriated Barroso as he addressed him as "Dear Jose Manuel" and added that if it were Article he 17 would send his resignation at once. Barroso replied that there was a resignation, not an Article 17 dismissal.

In pre-printing the appeal to the Court, Dalli's lawyers suggested to base the case on challenging Article 17. Ariti, however, disagreed explaining that reference to Article 17 would give the Court the grounds to refuse the trial and put the case in the archives. In this way the Court accepted the appeal.

Ariti substantiated the case by claiming that Barroso violated the Treaty since he did not base his decision on Article 17. In this case, he should have brought the OLAF report to the College, which should have decided collectively whether to take Dalli to the Court of Justice of the EU asking for his dismissal, or not. But he did not. That the Court accepted the case was due to the skill of Ariti, who insisted not to base their case on Article 17 of the Treaty, as it was suggested by the team of legal advisors of John Dalli.

This was the beginning of the end of Barroso's reign. Despite having gained approval from many Member State leaders for getting a third term, the mere fact that the Court accepted to judge the case, was enough to place him out of circulation.

To conclude, I have triggered the whole case by stopping Dalli from signing a resignation.

Today, I confess that had I known then what I know now, I would not have stopped him from signing the resignation. Not because Barroso did the right thing, but because Dalli was deceiving – saying different things to his lawyer and to me from the very beginning. As it turned out, Dalli had been aware of the OLAF investigation concerning him since earlier on. But he had never taken any steps to distance himself from his friend, who had requested the bribe, and by failing to do so, left us all wondering why… If a close friend of yours uses your name to ask for a multi-million Euro bribe, and if you are not involved at all, don't you first of all want to sue this person? Why has Dalli let his reputation become tarnished? Why has he allowed himself to be removed from office without ever speaking out against the friend who allegedly betrayed his trust?

OLAF discovered serious pieces of evidence that make it quite impossible to believe that Dalli did not know of his friend's negotiations with his name. After all, as Dalli himself admitted in the Luxembourg court, he allowed this friend to organise poolside meetings with tobacco lobbyists during his holidays. When you give such friends such privileges, you are putting yourself at great risk…

Based on the "what if" scenario, if I had not stopped Dalli from resigning…

Jose Manuel Barroso would have been re-elected president for a third term instead of Jean Claude Juncker. This would have not been good for Europe.

John Dalli would have become a forgotten face among Maltese pensioners.

As for the Tobacco Products Directive, after Dalli it was watered down (mainly by the European Parliament) and transformed into a harmless piece of legislation for the industry. So, this would have happened in any case.

Finally, there were three protagonists in this whole affair. There was Dalli, Barroso and Kessler. And believe me, I still do not know what to call it. DalliGate, BarrosoGate or what?

Why? Because I still have three questions for which I have not received a satisfactory reply, yet.

Question number one. Did Jose Barroso ever meet (once or twice) with the Manager of Tabaqueira Portugal, daughter Company of Phillip Morris, in Lisbon?

Question number two. Is it possible that John Dalli was not aware that his close political constituent Silvio Zammit was negotiating with a tobacco company, and that they met together, for a bribe, some say as much as €60m?

Question number three. Why was John Dalli infuriated with Giovanni Kessler who drafted a report, which concluded that Dalli did not take any bribe, rather than with Jose Barroso, who has forced him out without having the necessary legal grounds?

4/8 The Court of Justice of the EU

Although it does not look promising, the Court of Justice of the European Union (the Court) is potentially the most efficient protector of ordinary European citizens.

Under the Lisbon Treaty, the Court can sanction Member States that do not fulfil their obligations under the Treaties, at the request of the Commission or of other Member States ('Infringement Proceedings'). In practice despite that all animals are equal, some are more equal than others.

Indeed, according to Commission sources, although the biggest number of complaints arriving in the European Commission concern German violations, very few are investigated. On the contrary, the usual client of the Court is Romania.

Furthermore, Article 267 of the Treaty on the Functioning of the European Union (TFEU) provides that concerning preliminary rulings of the Court must be asked by national courts when the interpretation of EU law is at stake, to avoid diverging national interpretations.

The Court was established in 1952. It is composed of one judge for each of the 28 Member States, directly and unconditionally (that is, politically) appointed by the corresponding national governments for renewable terms of six years. The National Judge may be anything, from a Supreme Court Judge, a lawyer or an apparatchik of the ruling party of his country.

The regular duties of Court consist in judging cases of EU law violations. The basic subject of the Court is to judge any case involving the interpretation of EU law, including cases based on referrals of national judges when the interpretation of EU law is necessary for the application of national law. The latter is the most important function of the Court. It is the duty of the Court to accept and rule in all questions for a "preliminary ruling" raised by any Judge, regardless of grade or position, from any Member State. This is a very strong tool in the hands of European citizens. Indeed, upon request by any citizen, a national Judge may request the preliminary ruling from the Court of Justice of the EU and the Court is obliged to reply. The reply of the Court constitutes EU Law. This is the good part. What's bad, however, is that in most cases, neither ordinary citizens nor civic or other organizations are aware of such a possibility. All rulings of the Court of Justice of the EU, known also as "case law," are officially published and constitute a source of EU Law.

Ordinary citizens can also appeal directly to the European Court of Justice against decisions of the European Commission in cases where they are directly affected ('proceedings for annulment'). For example, in the case of refusal of the Commission to release documents asked on the grounds of Regulation (EC) 1049/2001. This is the good part. What's bad, however, is that in most cases, neither ordinary citizens nor civic or other organisations are aware of such a possibility.

Generally, the Court Decisions are accepted by all litigant parties. However, there are some cases where with some futile excuses the European Commission ignores Court Decisions, which it conveniently renames into "Opinions of the Court." Also, there are cases where big Member State circumvent or violate the EU procedural code to avoid fund recoveries. However, only few big powerful Member States may enjoy such a luxury.

4/9 The European Antifraud Office

Known by its French acronym, OLAF, Office Européen de Lutte Antifraude, is the independent EU authority that fights fraud affecting the EU budget (financed projects, VAT and excise tax) and investigates corruption cases of EU civil servants. OLAF, does not have prosecution authority, as most Europeans believe, but it methodically and silently cultivates such a perception. It is a service of the European Union conducting administrative investigations and can recommend the Commission for funds recovery and in the case, it suspect criminal law violations, it refers the case to the national prosecutor.

OLAF does not have the authority to investigate citizens for any reason except those who are in the payroll of the European Union (i.e. Commission employees) or are beneficiaries of Community money. Indeed, OLAF is only an independent audit service of the European Union.

The powers and the importance of OLAF will be drastically reduced after November 2020, when the Service of the European Prosecutor (EPPO) will start functioning, as it is provided by Directive (EC) 1939/2017.

The European Prosecutor will give an end as to the unclear (to the eyes of European citizens) authorities of OLAF. Indeed, in some cases concerning second class member States with no political leverage in Brussels, OLAF investigators cross-over what are the red lines even for prosecution authorities of Member States.

Only a few months ago, an OLAF investigator, notified to the national research center of second class Member State, that he decided to visit the facilities of the center to audit a certain program implemented three years before. The investigator, informed the center that he wanted to interrogate about 10 researchers. He also asked to make him available two adjacent rooms with a door in between in order to cross interrogate two witnesses at the time, simultaneously but in separate rooms.

Please take note that the program was already audited twice by the Commission, nothing wrong was found, and at the time, the Commission had also congratulated the center.

The center refused to accept this humiliating interrogation procedure and asked OLAF to accept written interviews as it did in the past with others. OLAF refused and referred the matter to the national prosecutor. The national prosecutor made a complete investigation on the matter and closed the file.

4/10 If You Are a "Person Concerned"

When EU financed, or co-financed projects are completed, successfully or not, they are subject to a final audit. In several cases, despite the competent Commission services having even congratulated the actors, auditors may discover discrepancies. Some may be serious, but others are of pure formal nature.

This is the reason that once a project gets EU funding, the beneficiaries must follow instructions about how to complete the various forms required by the programme specifications, to the minute details. Any mistake in completing the forms (i.e. time sheets etc.) may create endless troubles because this is how bureaucrats emphasise their importance and display power.

Therefore, any programme even years after completion, may end up for further auditing by OLAF, the anti-fraud service of the European Union.

OLAF has the power to re-audit a project in-depth and to order the recovery of funds. If the investigation concludes that fraud might have been committed, the case is referred to the national prosecutor for action as OLAF has no prosecution authority.

Theoretically, any EU citizen may be invited by OLAF to testify either as a witness or as a person concerned. The subject matter is presumed mal practices in issues involving EU money, both directly and indirectly. It may be financed or co-financed projects and programmes, VAT, and import duties.

The procedure is quite simple. Witnesses or "persons concerned" who are to be examined will be officially invited to testify. In the invitation letter, they must be informed that they have the right to choose the language of the procedure (any of the 24 official EU languages) and that they must refrain from being self-incriminated. The language is very important and "persons concerned" must chose, for obvious reasons, their mother tongue.

Remember to avoid, either you or your lawyer, any physical contact with OLAF. Everything must be in writing as *"Verba volant, scripta manent."*

If, during the interview of a witness, incriminating elements result from the conversation, the interview will be suspended at once and the witness will become "person concerned". In this case, the content of the interview will not be taken into consideration and the witness will be invited to testify as a "person concerned", in a new interview.

Citizens invited for interrogation may be accompanied by any person of their choice, usually a lawyer. However, anyone of the choice of the "person concerned" can be the accompanying person. The Regulation does not provide for any exceptions.

There are two specific documents which define the procedures of OLAF investigations. They are (a) the "Guidelines on Investigation Procedures for OLAF Staff" issued on October 1, 2013 and (b) Regulation 883/2013. They are extremely important as if the OLAF investigators realise that the "person concerned" or the accompanying person does not master the content of such documents, and might ignore significant provisions in order to "facilitate" the interrogation.

All "persons concerned" who are invited to testify must know that OLAF staff, prior to the opening of the process, must present a written authorisation duly signed by the Director General of the Service. This must state the identity and the position of the investigators, the subject matter and the purpose of the investigation, the legal basis for conducting the investigation and the investigative powers stemming from it.

Such a provision is explicitly stated in Art. 7 (2) of Regulation 883/2013. It is important for any "person concerned" to have full knowledge of such information as it is necessary to avoid self-incrimination and to benefit from the procedural guarantees set out by the law. This includes the principle that OLAF will take into consideration all facts concerning the case, in charge and in discharge.

However, while every prosecutor in every Member State and beyond is obliged by law to take into consideration and investigate any fact presented by the "person concerned" in discharge, is remains at OLAF's discretion whether to examine facts in discharge. This is a serious shortcoming of the content of our democracy. It is something that Member States must change as it is a procedure that concerns us all.

The prior knowledge of such crucial information guarantees citizens that the investigation will be conducted objectively and impartially in accordance with the principle of the presumption of innocence. It is also necessary to decide who, if anyone, will accompany the "person concerned" during the interrogation.

The "person concerned" must never refuse the interview and must go well prepared. He or she must reply to all questions in such a way as to avoid self-incrimination. If there are questions that may lead to incrimination, the "person concerned" must reply either "I do not remember," which is logical as OLAF investigates cases years after their implementation, or "I do not know". If it is this case, he or she may also suggest referring the question to the Agency or the Commission department responsible for the project. Most probably, the middle management officials responsible for the project, at the time of the investigation, would have been moved somewhere else. The mobility principle of the Commission for middle management provides that officials can stay up to five years in the same post and up to 10 years in the same Directorate General.

"Persons concerned" may ask to be interrogated in writing, instead of in person. This is a great advantage as they will have plenty of time to work with the lawyers under easy conditions and consult various records.

OLAF avoids written interviews for obvious reasons. Therefore, they will find several excuses, yet vague and unfounded, to refuse.

However, citizens are entitled to a written interview because it is not prohibited under the rules. As such, they must insist on this all the way through. More so if the person concerned shows fear and uncertainty since a simple interview may turn into a third-degree interrogation.

There are arguments in favour of seeking a written interview. Let's not forget that in the case of Commissioner John Dalli (see chapter The Confession), the dismissed Commissioner was offered the option to be interrogated either in person or in writing. He preferred to be questioned in person. So, if you are refused the written interview, you have to make crystal clear in writing that you do not refuse to be interrogated but for reasons concerning your mental health (stress) you cannot be interviewed in person but that you are willing to take it in writing.

No EU law disallows the written interrogation process and the issue has not been judged by the Court of Justice of the EU. OLAF, however, has often used childish arguments to avoid it.

For instance, they may claim that the spirit of the legislator implies that no written interviews are allowed, more so because this is not mentioned, implicitly or explicitly, in Regulation 883/2013. The reply is that this is a Soviet approach and that in our legal civilisation, whatever is not explicitly prohibited is permitted.

As before the publication of the final report, the "persons concerned" will be given the parts of the report that concern them to comment. OLAF may try to confuse them. They may claim that persons concerned will have the option of a written interview at the end of the procedure. This is true, but this is a different part of the procedure and does not replace the initial interview.

In this context, OLAF will exert pressure, threatening persons concerned that if they do not set an interview date, the procedure will continue without their examination in which case they will have the option to add their comments to the report, at the end of the procedure. The reply of the person concerned must always be in writing and must state that he or she is ready and willing to be interrogated at any time, yet in writing.

As the issue of a written interview is not ruled out, either by the existing legislation or by any Court decision, the issue remains open, in favour of the "person concerned". To this effect, the "persons concerned" and witnesses must remember that OLAF is not a prosecuting body, it is only an independent agency of the Commission investigating possible fraud at the expense of the EU budget and possible violations of EU officials, only. This is the reason the European Union has established the European Public Prosecutor Office (EPPO), which will be operational as of November 2010.

To this effect, if a "person concerned" feels that he or she is in serious difficulty and there are sound elements against him/her, it will be better to avoid any live interview especially if there are other "persons concerned" since it is possible to fall into contradictions during a live interview.

Concerning possible violations by OLAF of the rights of the "persons concerned", the Belgian prosecutor is responsible. In the case of procedural violations, the "persons concerned" can contest the OLAF report before the Court of Justice of the European Union.

Finally, you must remember that your dossier with OLAF was not generated by OLAF but was sent to OLAF by the Directorate General or an Agency from which you were awarded the project.

4/11 The "Auto-Da-Fé" Turned into "Opera Buffa"

I have a friend, who worked more than 30 years for the Commission in transport, and is now normally retired. In the last decade and a half, my friend received several Commission offers for a very convenient early retirement on health grounds, but he systematically refused.

This guy, intelligent to the limits of insanity, had a hobby of taking the Commission to Court. His method was simple. He never used any of the documents he was working on at his office. He was informed of possible Commission wrong-doings from reading national newspapers. Then he was building a file with newspaper clippings and Commission documents he obtained by asking, as an ordinary citizen, on the grounds of Regulation 1049/2001.

This joke lasted for decades. This guy was having fun and the big shots at the Commission in Berlaymont were losing sleep. Eventually, somebody in the Commission had the brilliant idea to find an excuse, any excuse, to fire my friend. So an excuse was invented and my friend was invited to testify as "person concerned" because he presumably had "vested interests in the shipping industry serving passenger routes in the Aegean".

The penalty of such a "crime" was capital as my friend was set to be fired. It was under these circumstances that we met at my house on the evening before the "execution ceremony" to discuss what could be done. At around 7pm (after duty hours), my friend sent an email to the office of the Director General of Administration informing him that he would be accompanied by a person of his choice, named Basil A. Coronakis. A few minutes later, he received a call from his lawyer. "You cannot take Coronakis with you because he is a journalist", the lawyer claimed. My friend replied, "and how do you know about it?"

The lawyer replied that he had been informed by the Commission. So, my friend said, "How come that although I am your client and I pay you regularly you have refused to give me either your mobile phone or your home phone number, even though I have asked you for both, but the litigants have direct access to you? You are fired."

Minutes after the call, my friend received an email from the Commission explaining to him why he could not bring me to the meeting. This time, I wrote a reply to the Commission asking, "Why do you want me to take you to Court for discrimination?" They never replied.

The next morning, just a few minutes before 10am, I arrived with my friend to the Administration building. Present at the meeting were three sitting Directors General, Horst Reichenbach (Administration) Catharine Day (Environment) representing the Secretary General and François Lamoureux (Transport), two lawyers and the court clerks.

Before entering the "court room" I was asked to sign a statement authorising the Commission to file penal charges against myself should I publish any of the content of the session. I signed without reading the statement. Before leaving, I asked for a photocopy of the document I signed.

The "martial court" procedure was rather a "summary." It started at 10.05am and lasted less than five minutes.

Horst Reichenbach opened the "show" asking the defendant for explanations. Instead, I took the floor. "My friend is very touched to see three Commission 'gods' gathering just for his mediocrity and cannot pronounce a word, so I will do the talking," I said.

"The defendant is accused of having vested interests on the shipping industry serving the Aegean passenger routes, yes he does!" All three Directors General remained silent and inexpressive waiting to understand where I was driving the discussion. One of the lawyers, however, happily said, "So you admit it?"

"Yes," I replied, "but I didn't finish.

"As you may know," I continued, "my friend is from Crete and he is travelling with the ships serving the route Piraeus-Crete, often. Since a couple of decades ago in the same route a passenger ship called Heraklion sunk near Falconera rocky islet and 247 lives were lost. As he is a regular passenger in that route, my friend has real interests for such vessels to operate under the best security conditions. Now, hear this. The Directorate General Transport had issued a Directive providing for the training of passenger ship crews on crisis management and crowd management. Such Directive was to be transposed into national legislations by a certain deadline. All countries did this on time, except Greece. The Greek government at the time, wanted to facilitate the enrolment of a political "friendly" shipping company to the stock market. Such training would mean more expenses which would have lowered the trading value of the stocks. However, a couple of years later, a ferry called Samina Express sunk just off the harbour of Paros and 83 people died, just because of the chaotic confusion reigned before sinking as the crew of the vessel, had not been trained as the Directive was not transposed to Greek legislation. If the Commission would have brought Greece to the Court of Justice, after having sent a second warning letter (Reasoned Opinion), Greece would have transposed the Directive, and the sinking of Samina Express would not have cost any human life."

The embarrassment in the "court room" was obvious as no one was speaking and all were looking at their papers except for my friend who was looking at the ceiling.

And I concluded, "I can assure you that if among the 83 dead were any of your children visiting the Greek islands, dear Directors

General of the Commission, by now half of the staff of Directorate General Transport would be deep in jail."

After half a minute of eloquent silence, the Director General of Administration asked if there were any questions. There were no questions and the "trial" was over.

In five minutes, I had destroyed a strategic plan the Commission brains were working for months.

Before leaving I asked to be sent the minutes of the testimony to sign them. I was assured that this would be done in the next couple of days.

While leaving, just in front of the elevator, one of the lawyers handed me a photocopy of the paper I had signed. I returned it to the lawyer without reading and told him: "You are a lawyer and you know that penal charges are filed only when the penal law is violated and not by authorisation. You see, law is common sense. I am not a lawyer but I have common sense."

The next day I called the Secretariat General of the Commission and I asked for the minutes of the meeting, to sign. I received the reply I was expecting, "Don't worry Mr. Coronakis, there is nothing to sign as the Commission decided to cancel the procedure against your friend!"

Eternal principle: kiss the hand you cannot bite!

4/12 The Sinking of Samina Express, 81 Dead

In Brussels, the Commission family speaks of "esprit de corps". In Sicily, for the Corleonesi family, it is called "Omertà." Different names, same concept.

Directive (EC) 98/35, which came into effect in May 1999, provides for training passenger ship crew on crowd management and crisis management.

Unfortunately, the Member State with the biggest merchant fleet in the world did not transpose this Directive into national law within the time limit provided.

Despite the violation being serious enough, as human lives were at the hands of untrained crews, Greece postponed the training, violating the terms of the Directive. The reason is that it wanted a shipping company, close to the then government, not to get into paying more expenses as it was planning to go public and list on the stock exchange.

As the Greek government and other interested parties were lobbying intensively about the matter, the Commission closed not one, but two eyes.

The Directive, which provided crisis and crowd management training, was supposed to enter effect in May 1999. But Greece did not comply. On September 27, 2000, "Samina Express" a passenger ferry servicing the Paronaxia route in the Aegean Sea (Greece), sank outside the harbour of Paros. Despite the fact, the accident happened right off the coast and the weather was not rough, 81 passengers lost their lives in a pandemonium of panic when the ship hit a rock. Most of the crew was going back and forth on the deck asking one another where to go and what to do without any coordination and without providing any help to the passengers.

The passengers panicked and confused started jumping into the sea regardless of whether they knew how to swim while others, seeing that the ship was very near to the port, thought that it was about to dock and went into the garage to drive their cars out. Those who went to the garage drowned in their cars.

Not one, not two but 81 souls drowned in the Aegean, only because the European Commission, for reasons we never learned, despite warnings, did not begin infringement procedure against the Member State.

The Commission, despite being morally responsible and some of its staff having penal responsibilities for 81 dead, did nothing.

The Commission official responsible for Maritime Affairs at the time infringement procedure against the Member State was not launched, was Georgette Lalli eventually appointed to a high (political) post in her country, Greece. Then returned as Director to the Commission, after the state company she was heading in Greece (Cadastre) was fined with 20 million Euro.

As for the families of the victims, who were supposed to be indemnified by the Commission according to Article 288 of the then Treaty, providing for non-contractual responsibility or liability due to omissions or commissions of its staff, the Commission managed to cover the matter completely. It chose not to indemnify the families of the victims to protect its image and its Praetorians.

The then Leader of the Greens Group in the European Parliament, Daniel Cohn-Bendit, formerly known as "Danny the Red" during the May 1968 student revolution in Paris, kept his mouth completely shut during the Spring of 2011 when the matter was very hot. At the time, the shipping industry had managed to keep in its "sensitive" post their favourite Director of Maritime Affairs. Eventually, they managed to be exempted from any pollution tax. Therefore, ship owners proudly stated that their industry "will never be under any Community law".

According to the Cancun Environmental Conference of 2010, if the shipping industry were taxed, it would pay about $4bn per year.

Unrelated, but worth mentioning, is that the shipping industry, especially bulk carriers under convenience flags, is all "offshore" and thus the less-taxed industry on earth. That a big part of their activities involves EU ports (Antwerp, Hamburg, Rotterdam etc.) is irrelevant and within the frame that they "will never be under any Community law".

4/13 Eximo, Small but Beautiful

The Eximo case is a tiny scandal compared to other, grand-style robberies committed with the support and co-operation of the System. Small indeed, as it was less that €25m. However, the Eximo case unveils two interesting facets of how the European Union works in practice.

First, when the nomenclature wants to protect its "friends" and its own "picciotti," it gets its way and succeeds because nothing can stop it. At the time, Eximo received a lot of publicity in New Europe. Two Directors General mainly responsible for the case, Jean-Luc Demarty (then Director General Agriculture) and the late Franz Bruner (then Director General OLAF), did nothing. However, the Commission sent several letters to the newspaper, but without providing any explanation.

Between the "omertà" of the System and the discretionary powers of the Commission, everything is possible. Scandals sponsored by the System, are not a new story. They go way back. The Eximo case, for instance, goes back to 1988 and beyond.

The Eximo case is simple.

A German company, Eximo, in 1988/89 received €24.5m in refunds for the export of skim milk powder from Germany (Member State) to Austria (Member State) and from there to Ukraine (then one of the Soviets of the then Soviet Union). Eventually the skim powder milk returned silently back to the EU. Eximo, however, had received the export subsidy.

The travelling of the dry milk (or rather the travelling only of its documents) raised doubts as to the destination of the product. The then anti-fraud service of the Commission UCLAF (now OLAF) opened an investigation and ruled for total recovery of the subsidy in 1992.

The Commission was not in a hurry to collect the recovery and forgot the internal rules which provide for action within two months. Indeed, the Commission notified the recovery decision to the Member State (Germany), three years after the ruling, in 1995.

The German State did not recover the money immediately as it should have done and Eximo took the case to a provincial Commercial Court of Justice which annulled the UCLAF decision without the possibility of appeal. The Commission was not present at the trial and everyone was happy. Despite the seemingly premeditated negligence, this case also involved a flagrant violation of community law by the Member State (Germany). The German State should have immediately recovered the subsidies illegally granted. This action should have occurred, regardless and in any case before any appeal to the German Court. Indeed, recovery orders by the Commission are based on the principle *"solve et repete"* which means "pay and then protest."

Furthermore, what was this Commercial Court of Hamburg which has the power to over-rule Commission Decisions without appeal? If this were to be a valid procedure, there would be no European Union. Thousands of Courts of any kind all over Europe would be cancelling Commission decisions and that would be the end.

Despite all this, the Commission removed the Eximo case from its irregularities database and stopped asking for any recovery from the German company.

Yes, in the Brussels Wonderland, all animals are created equal, but some are more equal than others.

4/14 The "Thing" and the Flight of Hundreds of Million

The "thing" is an entity called the International Management Group (IMG). By claiming its capacity as an "international organisation", it has collected from the European Commission, through multiple projects, more than one hundred million Euros. While applying for such projects is not illegal and the Commission receives endless applications, it is certainly illegal to disburse funding to ineligible applicants.

The "Thing" was ineligible from any EU financing because it had no status. Indeed, it is a unique kind of creature as it is a non-entity as international organization by EU standards although it has the ability (not capacity) to collect money from the Community budget.

The documents we have in our hands, available on our website, are, the OLAF report which contains concrete recommendations and strongly worded conclusions. The OLAF investigation was opened on 31 January 2012 and was concluded on 12 December 2014.

A 12-page "Note for the file" of the Legal Service, signed by its Director General Luis Romero Requena himself, and which recommends to …disregard the OLAF report. The legal Service was very quick to prepare its analysis, just one month which included the holidays of Christmas and New Year. It should also be noted that the ultra-rapid report, of the Legal Service emphasises on the first page that "This document contains legal advice and is only for the use of the services to which it is addressed. It may not be transmitted outside the European Commission and its content may not be reproduced".

The OLAF investigation established the following: IMG has never presented to the European Commission an intergovernmental agreement setting up IMG as an International organisation. They have only presented an establishment document, which bears no signature of a representative of a government (technically they would need at least two signatures from government representatives of different countries to make the organization international).

To be an international organization you need members. What's more, the 16 countries named as founding members of the organisation had notified OLAF that they do not consider themselves members of IMG as an international organisation.

According to the OLAF report, DG ECHO, the Directorate General for Humanitarian Aid & Civil Protection, did not recognise IMG as an international organisation either during ECHO's funding to IMG or after it. IMG could not provide OLAF with any signed document establishing it as an international organisation, but suggested that the United Nations Refugee Agency (UNHCR) should have its establishment documents in its depository. The UNHCR has not found any such documents. The OLAF report suggests that the Commission services do not disburse further funds to IMG. Indeed, OLAF said, "to stop further disbursement of EU funds to IMG in accordance with applicable EU legislation and contractual rules; remaining commitments amounting to EUR 23,339,508, to prevent any further damage to the EU budget" and added, "to consider recovery of up to EUR 134,403,562 disbursed to IMG."

The OLAF report also says that as the funds were transferred to the accounts of IMG in France this would reveal "indications of possible fraud and associated money laundering".

As IMG had no legal status in France it could not have legitimate bank accounts, which explains why OLAF spoke of money laundering.

The Legal Service, however, on the matter of money laundering said (point 49 of the NOTE): "As to the alleged 'associated money laundering,' in the absence of convincing indications of fraud the Legal Service fails to see how and why the transfer of Union funds to an account in France could in and on itself raise suspicions of money laundering, as those funds did not derive from criminal activity."

Great, as the money did not come from drugs or prostitution, there was no money laundering. As to the fact that the money was going to the bank accounts of a "Thing" which is not eligible to have a bank account, as a non-entity in France, and how this otherwise legitimate money of the EU budget was distributed, the Legal Service, had no idea.

The unwillingness of the Commission to proceed with funds recovery and referral of the case to national prosecutors stems from the fact that several high-ranking officials of the System are responsible for the smooth cooperation with the "thing." Furthermore, some "systemic" Commission officials who were handling the IMG dossiers, after retiring, got well-remunerated employment as functionaries or advisors in the "thing."

Finally, to understand how the System works and protects its people, even though President of the Commission Jean Claude Juncker immediately stopped any cooperation with IMG, some services silently continued to work with IMG. One typical case is the EU Delegation in Serbia, which continued including IMG in its short list for tender award.

On the website of New Europe (www.neweurope.eu) we have published the following documents, should you wish to read the details:

• The OLAF report concerning IMG

• The "Note for the files" of the Legal Service on same subject

• The shortlist of the EU Representation in Serbia including IMG

4/15 License to Pollute

The European Commission's "Roadmap for moving to a low carbon economy in 2050", makes no mention of the maritime industry, despite presently contributing 2.7% of global emissions, which by 2050 will count for something between 12% and 18% of the global total CO_2 emissions. All other transport means, aeroplanes and trucks, are considered and are in line of being taxed or, like aviation, managed under the Emissions Trade System (ETS).

The shipping industry is not included because it has a very strong lobby and good connections in Brussels. It is very profitable (and practically pays minimal taxes, if any) since it transports goods worth over $5 trillion per year worldwide.

To this effect, we read in Lloyds referring by name to the Director of Maritime Affairs of Directorate General MOVE (Transport) of the European Commission. "We need him [the Director of Maritime Affairs of the European Commission] to [stay there, in that position, and] work on our files. In particular, the tonnage tax and the possible inclusion of shipping within the EU's greenhouse gas emissions trading scheme."

The good Director remained there as Director of Maritime Affairs of the Commission, "untouchable" for some 15 years. It should be noted that the position of Director of Maritime Affairs is categorised under the classification "sensitive" (for obvious reasons). The maximum time spent in a sensitive post is five years, not one day more and this is a rule. The fact that the rule has been grotesquely violated, simply demonstrates that such rule is applied "a' la carte." There have been numerous stories in the press, as well as discussions in the European Parliament, but with no results. Two interesting facets of the efficiency of the ship owners' lobby.

"Greenpeace," the famous global watchdog of the environment, despite awareness and presumable interest in this kind of problem, has never ever raised a question or touched the subject despite being very well informed.

However, in February 2017, the Parliament voted that international shipping will be incorporated into the EU Emissions Trading System (EU-ETS) starting from 2023 if a measure is not introduced by 2021 in the framework of the International Maritime Organisation (IMO). The IMO roadmap has a two-staged approach, with an initial strategy to be decided in 2018, and a final plan to be adopted in 2023, considering real emission data that will start to be collected as of 2019.

4/16 The Others

There are several other EU institutions, satellite organizations and Agencies. Their number is not quite clear as any time a "need" is emerging, a new organization is born out of the non- where and lost in the outer space of the Commission constellation.

The European Court of Auditors is supposedly the "watch dog" for all European Institutions. But this is true only in theory. In practice, auditors are appointed one from each Member State and do not necessarily originate from the auditing authorities or even auditing firms in their home countries.

There are two Committees set up to represent citizens. These are the "Economic and Social Committee" (representing civic organisations, chambers etc.) and the "Committee of Regions" (representing local administrations such as regions and municipalities). Despite their significant costs to the Community budget and their minimal impact for the cause of "Europe," they are still useful to Member States as they provide a valuable psychotherapeutic effect for many national "second class" politicians or political aspirants.

The European Union has also over 50 formally autonomous "Agencies" specialising in various activities. It is difficult to give a specific number as some operate almost silently, while their number is growing gradually, depending on specific expediencies of the System.

Of course, there are also certain very useful EU-wide Agencies such as the European Union Intellectual Property

Office (EUIPO) in Alicante, Spain and few others. However, a significant number of entities provide only complementary work and should be absorbed by the central Commission services.

Agencies are based in Member States throughout the European Union, many in provincial cities to serve specific tasks. Unofficially they supervise sensitive issues between the Member State and the System. Some Agencies constitute a political reward to a specific Member State for its role on a specific issue, usually of sub-regional scope in nature.

The most important role of the Agencies, especially the newly formatted, is hiring personnel from the back door that would be difficult to hire centrally. Then, the "chosen" ones are silently moved to the Commission.

RISE AND FALL
OF AN EMPIRE

5/1 It all started here

The origins of political Europe go back to the Athenian Democracy of Pericles. Democracy derives from the rule of Demos, not Republic, the Latin term originating from "Res Publica," the public thing. The Athenian Democracy was where the state and religion were two separate authorities. Although the state was not completely secular as the priests were respected and accepted in performing their religious ceremonies. Most of the city-states (Polis) had no separation between the "sacred" and the "profane" and they did not have an official religion.

However, this ideal balance was upset by the Christians and to European (and not even all Europeans) it took twenty centuries to come back to square one: a state without an official religion. And if the concept of the official religion of the state was abolished, in many countries, like Poland and Ireland, religion, although not even official, has a major role in the everyday life of people.

Europeans share common values, Greek philosophy and Roman law.

However, the key philosophical and political concepts of the Athenian Democracy are worth keeping in mind if we want to sail in calm waters. Those who had debts they could not repay, likely became slaves and after a period of slave work they could buy back their freedom. Furthermore, there was no racial classification of immigrants, black, yellow, white and the like. They were all "outsiders" who could become Greeks by participating in the Greek culture, or if not adapted, they would remain "barbarians" (incomprehensible speech, "bar bar"), another Greek invention. This is interesting. If only we could partially assimilate this concept today, Europeans are all those participating in the European culture.

It is worth devoting a few words to the Parthenon, the Greek monument, which belongs to humanity. Besides harmony and beauty bears also an eternal political message.

Pericles came to power in Athens (461 BC) with a populist campaign (free access to theatre plays etc.) and ostracized Cimon – the leader of the aristocratic party – under false accusations that he was linked to Sparta. In Athens, such accusation was something comparable to "extreme right" "fascist" "racist" etc. today, leading to a kind of Pavlov reaction from the public. To celebrate the victory of democracy, Pericles asked the Athenians to build a temple on the Acropolis of Athens. The Ecclesia of Demos (the then-Parliament) initially refused the project for budgetary reasons. However, Pericles insisted and, even though he was very tight-fisted (although also very rich), he offered to build the temple with his own money and give it his name, the Temple of Pericles.

The Athenians, a jealous society, reconsidered their decision and finally approved the funding and for purely political reasons used free labour in building the Parthenon (no slaves were used) to give a special political connotation to the temple project.

At that time, in the middle of the Acropolis of Athens there existed another temple, built by the Pisistratus dictatorship, which ruled the previous century. The Athenians then said, OK, let's demolish the temple built by the dictatorship and build our Parthenon in its place. Pericles told them no, we must first build a retaining wall and fill it with earth to create a completely new space and build the Parthenon over there. In this way, we will leave the Pisistratus temple intact and future generations will see exactly what democracies can do and compare it to what dictatorships have done. Today, the temple of Pisistratus no longer exists because it was built with cheap material and did not resist the passage of time. On the contrary, the Parthenon is still there and will be there forever.

The political message is important, but it is not all. Contractor Kallikratis, sculptor Phidias and architect Ictinus built the Parthenon. When the project was finished, the Athenians realised that the three gentlemen had rather overpriced the project and all three were exiled to Pyrgos (West Peloponnese, south of Patras). There, they convinced the authorities to allow them to build a better temple, which they did in mountainous Olympia. There, they built the temple of Epicurus Apollo, like, but aesthetically superior, to the Parthenon. When they finished the project, all three were too old to be brought to the court on similar charges and the temple was so beautiful that they let them go.

However, speaking of the Greeks, we should not forget that in the Athenian Democracy, where political freedom and freedom of speech were invented, no one was ever persecuted for his ideas. No one, except one who was sentenced to death and executed: Socrates, the greatest philosopher of all times.

Nobody is perfect...

5/2 The Endless Cold War

The defeat of Germany and Japan 1945 signalled the end of the Second World War giving room to winners to sort out their differences.

George Orwell was first in 1945 to use the term "Cold War" in an article, which referred to a future nuclear stalemate between superpowers. On 22 February 1946, George Kennan, then an officer at the US Embassy in Moscow, sent an 8,000-word diplomatic dispatch, known as the "long telegram," to the US State Department presenting his views on the Soviet Union and suggested the possible policy options for America in its relations with the Soviets. Since then, the "long telegram" remained the most influential policy paper (it was seen as the source of America's "Containment Policy") for the United States until the end of the Cold War.

The Cold War between the Democratic West, and the Autocratic East started with the "long telegram" and formally ended in November 9, 1981 with the fall of the Berlin Wall. Subsequently came the collapse of communism and the dismemberment of the Soviet Union.

The Cold War ended with clear winners the Democratic West but left behind deep political anomalies which marked the future of both conflicting parties. The Autocratic East, abolished the socialist base of its economy, abolished the communist structures and created a new clan of rulers, the Oligarchs. In their majority, they are former party apparatchiks who before becoming owners of privatized state companies, where the managers appointed by the communist party in the same companies. Therefore, the system turned from a socialist autocratic system into an autocratic market economy wild-west style.

The Democratic West suffered the consequences in two different ways.

In the United States of America, the Cold War was turned into the "hunt of communism" staged by Senator Joseph McCarthy. The use of demagogic and exaggerated mostly unsubstantiated accusations on presumed Communist subversion, maintained high tensions all over the nation neutralizing any Soviet propaganda attempt. Consequently, the economy, was not influenced at all by the Trade Unions. The economy under no distortive constrains was developed in pure market economy terms. In this context, however, the American society remained way behind in matters of welfare. As the Cold War required highly sophisticated handling, in the United States the two alternating power ruling parties had silently agreed to leave matters of foreign, defense and security policies with the Administration and exert only political supervision. The rest, economy, agriculture, industry and the like, remained the exclusive prerogative of the politicians. That is why often in State and Defence, the Secretaries, not to speak of deputies, originate from the ranks of the Administration. In this context, while Democrats and Republicans keep silent in most serious matters such as the engagement of US in warfare all over the world, they fight like dogs and cats in domestic matters such as Medicare.

Western Europe was in the front line of the Cold War sharing boarders with the Communist bloc was the direct target of the Soviet Communist propaganda. Particularly influenced were lower income classes, intellectuals and artists. The first were building hopes for a redistribution of the wealth. The others, being sure that Communism would be never established in their quarters, were generously sympathizing the left to build admirers and clientele.

The impact for Western Europe was diametrically opposite. Europe, under the Communist threat, which never really existed, overdid it with granting excessive rights that the economy could not sustain in medium and long term, to white and blue collars in matters of health care, pensions and trade unions. Such concessions, led to today's socio-economic crisis which the European Union is unable to address.

The Cold War was a merciless propaganda conflict, which contaminated the mindset of societies involved, limiting political choices and inspiring social stratifications based on extreme political believes. The spirit of the Cold War was, "either you are with us, or you are against us." The Soviets were aiming the lower income classes of Europe and all kind of intellectuals with one and only target, America. The Western bloc were targeting Communism also with one argument, freedom.

The Cold War inspired fear and uncertainty in both sides resulting to stable political situations, convenient for both sides. The Cold

War secured peace from the end of WWII till today for one simple reason. The mutual distrust between the two parties was securing fair and sustainable agreements in all relational facets of both sides. From the exchange of spies in Checkpoint Charlee (Berlin) to the barter agreements between countries of the two blocs providing for the exchange of equal value products. Typical was the trade of fresh agricultural products of the European South against heavy agricultural and industrial machinery from the Communist bloc.

Politically, in Western Europe the anti-American Communist propaganda was very efficient as the Soviets had excellent know-how and endless resources. Individual countries had no capacity to challenge the Soviets. Consequently, the result was to generate in Europe a wide spread anti-American climate infusing a deep anti-American temperament. In this the Soviets were extremely successful.

Indeed, although the United States after the war fed Europe and the Marshall Plan helped Europe to rebuild its industry and its infrastructures giving room to the post-war European economic miracle, Europeans were in their majority anti-American. Ambiguity, yet real.

Today Europeans and Americans are into serious troubles. The USA is facing an extended economic crisis, but it will make it as its economy, thanks to the Cold War, is based in simple healthy market economy grounds.

In Europe the crisis is global, affecting all facets of life, and has a strong social character as it is based on austerity. Europeans are seeing Germany as responsible, which with its superior influence, imposed Europe-wide austerity. As a result, as the working class cannot handle more than one "class enemy" at a time, the anti-American climate turned into anti- German. Indeed, when a flag in symbolically burned in a leftist demonstration it is not American any more but German.

However, the Cold War never ended, Russians who are very active in "political communication," (this is the politically correct term a la mode for propaganda), are rather successful of reversing the anti-German climate, which is real, to anti-American. Whether it is merit of the Russian capabilities or of the senseless idiosyncrasy of Europeans, it remains to be seen.

And while Europeans must deal with unprecedented situations that the collective leadership of Europe does not have the capability to handle (immigration, refugees, unemployment), we are in the mid of a new Cold War of which most of us have no idea. The United States against Germany as the latter refuses (for pure economic reasons) to diversify its energy suppliers and stop purchasing Russian gas.

5/3 From the Treaty of Rome to EU-15

After the Second World War, the French wanted some control over the steel production in the Ruhr Valley to prevent Germany from diverting steel into German arms production. This is why European Steel and Coal Community (ECSC) was established in 1951 with the Treaty of Paris by Belgium, France, West Germany, Italy the Netherlands and Luxemburg.

The European Union was founded in 1957, primarily for political and military reasons. It aimed at securing peace in Europe, especially between France and Germany.

Initially, under the name of the European Economic Community (EEC), the European Union was established by the same six states, which signed the ECSC Treaty. On 25 March 1956, the Treaty of Rome was signed. It entered in to effect on 1 January 1957. Since then, the European Union has been expanding with the addition of new Members, all of the traditional Western European bloc, reaching the total of 15 Members by 1 January 1995. East Germany was annexed to West Germany on 3 October 1990.

The substance of the EEC Treaty, and what followed, was to fulfil the desires and the hopes of the European people, to preserve peace and work for prosperity and a better life. To this effect, the European venture was successful. Since the Treaty of Rome, Western Europe has been living the longest period of peace in its history. Indeed, not a single bullet has crossed the French-German borders since the end of the Second World War, except for hunters' bullets. It should be noted that casualties in the First World War were 18 million and over 60 million in the Second.

Common interests in business and finance unite peoples better than military treaties. The key to success of the EEC Treaty was that although in essence it was an armistice treaty, it worked since the very beginning as an economic association based on common financial interests.

The establishment came shortly after the end of the Second World War and as France was the undisputed leading power among the six, insisted that the three basic European institutions were based in three French-speaking cities. The European Commission was based in Brussels, a French-speaking city within the Flemish-speaking Flanders region; the European Parliament in Strasbourg (France) and the Court of Justice of the European Union in French-speaking Luxemburg.

Similarly, in the context of the preservation of the French language, culture and geopolitical influence, the French put up a good fight in the early days of the United Nations and accordingly the Economic and Social Council ECOSOC/ UN rotates annual sessions between New York and French- speaking Geneva.

The Treaty of Rome signifies the end of Western Europe as a continent of continuous local wars and the establishment of Europe as a common house of peaceful growth, encompassing most Europeans in their cultural and religious diversities.

As the unification of Europe was building momentum in the minds of the people, the European Union began to enlarge with the addition of new Member States. Most of the new members, so far, share the same democratic, social and religious values.

5/4 The Intermezzo Between Rise and Fall

Following the liberation of Eastern Europe in late 1989, the Soviet Communist system as we knew it, finally collapsed. Consequently, Союз Советских Социалистических Республи, *(Soyuz Sovetskikh Sotsialisticheskikh Respublik a.k.a. CCCP or the Union of Soviet Socialist Republics, USSR)*, consisting of 15 Member States (Soviets), disintegrated in 1991. The Commonwealth of Independent States (CIS) was born in an effort by the Russians to maintain the Soviet Union by re-inventing "the wheel," under a different name. This attempt, however, lasted for less than two years.

After the Soviet collapse, 15 new independent states were born. Russia is one of them, clearly the bigger and the real Soviet successor state. This final dismemberment signalled the end of the Cold War between the United States and the Soviet Union, which had begun in 1946.

This open, yet restricted, rivalry between the two nuclear superpowers maintained the highly efficient "balance of terror" and was primarily based on mutual distrust.

The Cold War greatly influenced European decision-making about the formation of the European Union. Europeans were convinced they were permanently living under the threat of Communism and such a perception was a decisive factor in most European policy issues. In this context, NATO was perceived as the shield protecting Europe from this communist threat. As it would later be proven, the threat was only a communication tool of convenience, but very few were aware of this at the time. This knowledge was limited to the White House and the Kremlin. It was this mutual mistrust that maintained peace between the two superpowers and their satellites, as it was a healthy base to reach durable agreements in any field.

Mutual mistrust is the key to success for every deal. Europeans believed in the communist threat and developed European policies, accordingly. The Cold War left the Europeans with a Soviet phobia. Of course, the large Soviet "defensive" deployments in East Germany since the end of World War II were so big they could not easily be disregarded.

It was under the influence of such a syndrome that the European Union took the almost suicidal socio-political step of the Big Bang enlargement launched in 2004. The enlargement incorporated into the European Union the former Communist states of Eastern Europe.

Today, the European Union is struggling with the biggest crisis in its history. It is called the "economic crisis," and it is also a very convenient term for the European leaders. Even though the crisis is manifested in the economy, it is socio-political and only as such can the European Union deal with it. If it is considered economic, the interests of bigger Member States will prevail over the rest, and the crisis will continue to deepen.

The Big Bang enlargement did not serve any of the European strategic goals. On the contrary, it accommodated American geopolitical interests. By trapping nine former Communist states (East Germany, Czech Republic, Hungary, Poland, Slovakia, Slovenia, Bulgaria, Romania and Croatia), mostly USSR satellites, and three former Baltic Soviets in the EU (and NATO) it secured that they would never join Russia to remake the Soviet Union. Unless...

The Big Bang enlargement was one of the motives of our socio-political crisis. The other reason, equally important, was the repeal of the Glass-Steagall Act of 1932 by US President Bill Clinton in 1999. This Act was preventing the banks from using insured depositories to underwrite private securities and dump them on their own clients. The repeal was the result of a compromise; repeal, versus the acquittal on all impeachment charges for the President. Bill Clinton was impeached because of his extra-marital activities with a White House intern. However, a deal was reached and the impeachment process was never concluded. Bill Clinton remained President and signed the repeal of the Glass-Steagall Act.

The repeal of Glass-Steagall Act of 1932 and the Big Bang enlargement, which served exclusively the goals of the Atlantic Alliance and brought into the Union 11 former Communist states (plus East Germany, which was united with West Germany in 1990), signified the end of the European Union as it was conceptualised by its founding fathers.

5/5 The Lost Opportunity

The Second World War and the subsequent Cold War gave birth to strong statesmen in Europe, leaders who could handle any situation and any crisis, capable of driving their peoples to peace and prosperity. All these leaders were the make of the ongoing confrontation and fighting.

They were personalities like Charles de Gaulle, Winston Churchill, Alcide de Gasperi, Robert Schuman, Jean Monnet, François Mitterrand, Helmut Kohl and Margaret Thatcher.

The change came in the 1980s, during the years of the transition. I remember, in the then Davos symposia, the perplexity of the outgoing Communist leaders – characters like Wojciech Jaruzelski of Poland who could not understand what was happening in Europe. They were losing ground like falling stars, yet they were living in their own world.

The transition from the 1980s to the 1990s brought a new breed of dynamic leaders to the former Communist countries while a new species of leaders emerged in the traditional West. As confrontation had come to an end, the new leaders were the product of PR agencies and the European Union passed from the hands of the leaders of conflict to the leaders of compromise.

The Soviet Union was essentially dismembered on 26 December 1991, signifying the end of the Warsaw Pact (the Communist military alliance equivalent to NATO), COMECON (the EU's Communist trading bloc doppelganger) and of the Cold War.

All of a sudden, the world became unipolar, with one and only superpower: the United States of America. While Russia emerged as the biggest and strongest former Communist country, it suffered nearly total catastrophe under the eight years of Boris Yeltsin's rule.

Those eight years were the time slot when America had a chance to lead the world. At the time, America could have claimed and won leadership roles in science, technology, medicine and space, becoming the undisputed leader of the world, for a long time. But America wasted this opportunity. Instead it preferred to declare wars in the Balkans, followed by the wars in Afghanistan and Iraq a few years later.

What were the odds that America could remain in first place for more than a few years? Not bad. First, the Clinton Administration ended its term with a budget surplus meaning resources were available for investment in technology, health, infrastructures and increased foreign aid, so-called "smart power." Russia's demographic and health services situation was desperate after the collapse of the Soviet Union, on top of the war in Chechnya and related domestic terrorism. But instead, Washington took the September 11 attacks as the call to find new enemies everywhere and focus on a new militarised global posture.

Under the George W. Bush Administration, America attempted to maintain its positioning as the only superpower in a unipolar world based on its military. This perception only lasted a short time since Russia and China retuned to superpower status in a few years and resumed their international roles. Thus, the world stopped being unipolar. America is still the leader of the world, but with shorter distance from the second and the third. Indeed, at the end of the day, US nukes can destroy Earth several times over. Russia and China can do the same trick fewer times, but one time is enough.

In 1999, after eight years of continuous decay and humiliation, Vladimir Vladimirovich Putin emerged as the new leader of Russia. This new leader was a former KGB agent, and at the time of his election to the position of Prime Minister, the then-US Secretary of State Madeline Albright expressed her satisfaction as "finally (after Yeltsin) she could negotiate with a strong leader, someone we are able to do a deal with."

Yet, all in all, Vladimir Putin did not prove himself to be what Madeline Albright thought he would be. Meanwhile, the United States lost, at least in that round, the opportunity to lead the world peacefully. America opted to invest in the military, to force democracy onto a few select dictatorships, and the world became multipolar, again.

Certainly, the European Union suffered the biggest collateral damage of this policy turnaround.

5/6 The Devastating Big Enlargement

The enlargement of the European Union with 12 former communist countries was the major failure of Europe. This failure will be one of the fundamental reasons for the collapse of the European Union, if it ever occurs.

The devastating enlargement started with the re-unification of Germany on 3 October 1990. At that time, almost overnight, the then (EU Member State) Federal Republic of Germany (Bundesrepublik Republik Deutschland BRD) commonly known as West Germany, annexed the (formerly Communist) German Democratic Republic (Deutsche Demokratische Republik, DDR) commonly referred as East Germany. To be fair to history, it was an annexation, not "unification," as the Federal Republic of Germany incorporated the German Democratic Republic without changing its name, currency or anything else.

At the time, no EU Member State reacted when Chancellor Helmut Kohl ruled that one BRD Mark was equal to one DDR Mark. This was a financial blow to the European Union but no one dared to react as the political act of the annexation was the biggest bloodless victory against the Soviet Union ever, which formally dismembered itself just a year later 26 December 1991.

Although there is no evidence whatsoever, this great bloodless achievement of the West could have been the result of possible "under the table" transactions between Chancellor Helmut Kohl and the last First Secretary of the Communist Party of USSR Mikhail Sergeyevich Gorbachev. This may explain why the CDU (the Christian Democrat party of Germany) donation scandal uncovered in late 1999 never ended up in Court. Indeed, during the Cold War and the first years after, the dominant religion in Europe was the intellectual and political defeat of Communism. Therefore, whoever contributed to this, even by unorthodox means, was a hero.

The anti-communist cult continued for over a decade and on 1 May 2004 the European Union enlarged by granting full membership to another eight former Communist countries. They were the Czech Republic, Estonia, Latvia, Lithuania, Hungary, Poland, Slovakia and Slovenia (plus Cyprus and Malta, two small western countries). The "crime" against the European Union and the people of Europe was extended in 2007 with the accession of Bulgaria and Romania and was concluded with the inclusion of Croatia in 2013.

Yes! The EU's enlargement with 12 former Communist countries (East Germany, above eight, Bulgaria, Romania and Croatia) was a cardinal obstruction against European integration and the ideals behind it. The why, is quite simple.

Only the US benefitted, in terms of its geopolitical confrontation with Russia, by the EU's absorption of the 12 former Communist countries. By enlarging the EU-15 to 28, Europe trapped 12 former Communist countries in the Western partnership and stopped them from joining the reconstruction of the new Soviet Union (or its rough equivalent) under Russia, either as Member States or as satellites.

Europe had no practical benefits from this massive expansion. It gained no political power, as the Union has no common foreign or defence policies. Furthermore, in matters of Internal Market, the benefit was bigger for the newcomers rather than for the old Member States. The perception to connect NATO to EU membership was groundless and naïve. These two international organisations have nothing in common to justify this perception. Indeed, it is only the participation in the Atlantic Alliance that keeps these countries from re-joining the new Soviet Union in the making, not EU Membership.

It should be noted that half a century of Communism has become part of the DNA of all, no matter whether ruling or ruled. This cannot be erased by a Commission Decision.

All eleven former communist countries were enrolled first to NATO and then became Members of the European Union.

Looking from the interest point of view of the EU, common sense says simple things.

Once in NATO former Communists were practically dominated by western forces which replaced the Soviet troops of the Warsaw Pact. Therefore there was no need to enrol them in the EU. To "cement" them in the new western alliance, NATO membership was enough.

The difference between NATO and the EU is that in NATO countries are substantially under the undisputed supreme command of the United States of America and no country dares to dispute or negotiate any NATO supreme command (USA) decision, even minor.

In the EU, all countries have a voice and are theoretically at the same level of all others. The difference between theory and practice is that old Member States are conscious of their size and situation thus understand that although all Member States in the Union are equal, some of them are more equal than others. In the case of former Communist new comers, take this equality verbatim and believe that they all are equal.

The conservative and heavily unionised Western Europe is now facing tough competition from countries that are part of the single market yet without serious trade unions, with low or no minimum salaries, extremely low taxation, in a not-yet-regulated environment. Taking advantage, not only of the single internal market, but also of the free movement of people, the European Union has been flooded by cheap labour. These are workers who will take jobs for much less pay than the prevailing minimum European wages and (mostly) without any social security coverage. As such, they take the jobs away from the locals, who in turn collect unemployment benefits from the Member States.

Furthermore, the cost of helping the new EU Member States to reconstruct their social structures and modernise their economies is enormous and has deprived the EU-15 of the means for the deepening of the European Union. Funds that would help the European South reach the levels of the North were absorbed to repair damages of half a century of communist rule in 11 new Member States, plus East Germany, which was annexed to the founding Member State Federal Republic of Germany.

In this way, the former Communist countries entered a rapid growth period with the funds of traditional EU Members. And all this at a time when their citizens could not expect more than what they had during the communist years.

Today, the situation is quite clear and only those who are short-sighted cannot see it. The EU former Communist countries are on the path of hard market economy growth. East Germany is a case a part, which explains the other side of EU's decay. With loose rules, low tax rates and easy tax administration rules, which makes doing business easy, without tough labour laws and with businessmen ruling as kings, the former Communist countries in Europe are flourishing. In the not-so-distant future, they could even leave Europe proper behind.

Why? Because Europe proper was left with the labour unions and tough state mechanisms tilted against any private initiative and robbing our youth of their hopes and dreams. Europe proper was left with over-regulation, over-taxation and austerity, which led to depression and the systemic bias against any initiative for growth and innovation, as individual profit in Europe proper is becoming a sin.

This is seen, but not discussed by anyone (it is obvious why). In the case of East Germany, it unconditionally joined the European Union some five years before the other Communist countries. The EU and West Germany generously supported it. However, among the former Communist states that became full EU Members, East Germany remains one of the least developed and much remains of its Communist past. The reason is that West Germany imposed to the newcomers its rules of development. Indeed, with inherited communist mentality, over-regulation, over-taxation and not government-controlled trade unions, there is no chance for growth.

Therefore, if the European Union is ever dismembered, the first to leave will be the former Communist countries, which need more room to breathe and grow after their transition to market economics and rudimentary democratic rules. Once disassociated from the European Union, the former Communist countries will likely join the new Soviet Union in formation under Russia. The irony will be that Western Europeans will realise that this new Russian Commonwealth will be an association of free market countries with its biggest enemy being any form of Communism while in Europe proper, after a few years, everything will be dominated by the state and governments will vary from neo-Communists to the Far Right.

5/7 The Commission from the French to the Germans

Since the establishment of the European Union, France was the leading Member State. Among the six founding members, France was on the winning side of the war. The others were either losers or too small to claim anything. France was the big player and ruled up until recently.

In 2004, Jose Manuel Barroso was appointed President of the Commission as the third choice among the candidates. He was elected President in the third round, upon the recommendation of the Greek Prime Minister Kostas Karamanlis and the support of Germany and the US.

In that moment, the rule of Europe passed into the hands of the Germans. During the first Barroso term (2004-2009), the President did a good job. He accommodated all Germans demands on matters of policies and funds distribution and gave extra powers to the administration, which he managed to populate in key positions with Germans and German-friendly executives. That was a blow to the underbelly of Europe. Indeed, the Administration took advantage of this opportunity and began to further consolidate its own rule, under the shadow of the German interests.

With such a record, Germans granted Barroso a second term (2009-2014). In the middle of his second term, however, Barroso showed signs of autonomy from his patrons. The reaction was immediate. His trusted Head of Cabinet (Portuguese) Joao Vale de Almeida was transferred to Washington DC as head of the EU Mission in the United States. He was replaced by the German Johannes Laitenberger, one of the close associates of Angela Merkel.

Despite having announced his intentions for another term, the European People's Party, refused to nominate Barroso for a third term. This was on the pretext of the rather unorthodox dismissal of the Maltese Commissioner John Dalli, who ended up before the EU's Court of Justice.

In the Juncker Commission, Head of Cabinet of the President is an extremely sharp, capable and ambitious German, Martin Selmayr, who is close to CDU.

The position of the Head of Cabinet of the President of the European Commission is the most powerful position in the Brussels complex. He is the real ruler next to the System and depending on the extent of the authority granted by the President can be more powerful than the President himself.

In the case of the Juncker Commission, President Jean-Claude Juncker has divided almost the entire gamma of his authorities between the first Vice President Frans Timmermans and his Head of

Cabinet. The President has kept under his direct control only major political issues such as the Transatlantic Trade and Investment Partnership (TTIP) while he personally keeps open communication lines with the political groups.

The leading role of Germany in the European Union is further reinforced by the decision of the people of Great Britain to withdraw from the European Union (Brexit).

5/8 Forty-Five Years of UK Membership

The United Kingdom joined the European Union in 1972 because it had run out of colonies. This explains the colonial terms of the association. This explains why the UK, contrarily to all other Member States was getting money back (abatement). This explains why the Commission services despite audits rarely was recovering any funds from the UK.

And, last but not least, this explains why the EU was never allowed to set its own foreign and defence policy. Colonies do not have their own foreign and defence policies. It is the metropolis, which does that.

The economic damage to the European project of almost half a century UK membership is enormous. Only in the year 2015 the annual "rebate" to the UK from the Community budget was about six billion Euro (€6bn). And this "rebate" the so-called "abatement" obtained by Margaret Thatcher in 1985, goes on every year since then.

But the damage was not limited to the "abatement" rebates. Brittan took great advantage of the various Community programs and co-financed projects as the UK (and a couple of other Member States) were never subject to any real audit.

Not many years ago the then Commissioner for Agriculture Marian Fischer Boel, during a cabinet meeting, ingeniously asked, "Why do we always catch the same Member States with their hands in the cookie jar" and got the amazing reply, "because we do not audit the others."

AGRI.H.1	- 1 -	FEOGA Déc. 2003/ 481/CE

DÉCISION DE LA COMMISSION

du 27 juin 2003

relative aux conséquences financières à appliquer dans le cadre de l'apurement des comptes des dépenses financées par le Fonds européen d'orientation et de garantie agricole (FEOGA), section «garantie», dans certains cas d'irrégularités commises par des opérateurs

United Kingdom

Case number (internal reference number MS)	Amount (in £)	
UK/1978/011	2.942,00	Dans des cas similaires le montant a été pris en charge par le FEOGA
UK/1985/001	229.948,00	Le bénéficiaire final n'a jamais été identifié
UK/1988/025	1.064,00	
UK/1989/166	4.995.290,00	Bénéficiaire sans moyens
UK/1990/070	33.830,00	Liquidation

The dialogue was reported at the time by New Europe and the spokesperson service of the Commission denied with a long letter. Point is that the newspaper got the information on condition of anonymity from one very reliable executive who was present in the meeting.

However, the Commission never gave a satisfactory reply as to why the Commission in its College Decision of July 27, 2003 in writing-off several millions of Euro to be recovered from the UK, included cases where "the final beneficiary was never identified." All such cases were silently closed, instead of being referred to the prosecutor.

The responsibility of the cancelled recoveries concern the Member State, not the beneficiaries However, the financial damage was the less.

The UK was not part of the Economic and Monetary Union (Eurozone), did not participate in the Charter of Human Rights and was not part of Schengen zone.

Furthermore, the UK always opposed the deepening of the European Union by adopting common foreign and defence policies. To this effect, it boycotted the establishment of the European External Action Service (EEAS). As eventually could not block it, got control of it by a "hostile takeover" at the making of the new service, by forcing the appointment of the first Commissioner in charge while populating the new service with British diplomats.

5/9 Hotel California

Hotel California, you may check-out, but you never leave....

So, seems to turn the Brexit. The Brits democratically decided by clear majority to leave the European Union, but they do not want to leave. Hotel California syndrome.

The Brexit was anticipated in my first book "The Deep State of Europe" (April 2016) and our predictions were well substantiated by the content of the book. The United Kingdom, voted to leave the European Union despite the great benefits it enjoys because the subjects of Her Majesty simply do not trust the European Union. The United Kingdom whether we like them or not, is the most democratic country of Europe and the Brits do not accept to be ruled by a non-elected Administration without any kind of legitimacy in the context of lack of transparency and lack of accountability. This is the quintessence of the Brexit.

On June 23, the people of Great Britain voted to withdraw from the EU. Their decision was accepted with relief by the collective leaders of Union. The next day, the Presidents of the Commission, the Parliament and the Council, hours after the German Economy Minister said that the UK is out of the EU and there is no way back, said the same. Whatever it means.

Since then, the Brits are looking for ways to avoid or postpone forever to leave the EU, but the Germans are determined to get them out. However.

Technically, the UK is out of the EU, as it notified to the Council that it has activated Article 50 of the Treaty. Then there are procedures to follow and in two years' time, by March 29, 2019, should be completely out. Therefore, unless something spectacular happens, the UK will be gradually ousted from the EU by the Commission under the pressure of various Member States. Germany, those closed to German interests and those who are waiting from some of their nationals to take important posts that will be liberated by the outgoing Brits, especially in high positions.

After the referendum, the British employees of the institutions are massively applying to get Belgian citizenship as they live in Brussels for years and they can apply for it. However, it may not be of great use for their careers, since Belgians are already well represented in top positions.

The exit of the United Kingdom from the European Union, may pass various kinds of adventures but the result, which in the first reading appears unavoidable, in a second reading seems to be unpredictable.

Geostrategic interests prevail over the economies and the democratic desires of the people. Europe without the UK will be economically but also politically dominated by Germany.

Since a few years, a Cold War, silent but very tough, is undergoing between the United States and Germany. The reason is that Germany is exclusively buying its energy supplies needed to operate its heavy industry in the form of gas from Russia. This means injection of cash in the Russian economy something that is against American strategic interests. Americans repeatedly invited the Germans to diversify their energy supplies but the latter refused categorically since the price for equal thermal value of oil to gas is two to one. Deadlock.

Germany always had relations of understanding with Russia. The notorious Ribbentrop-Molotov Treaty before the second world war is indicative of the potential relations of the two countries. A Brexit, would facilitate German-Russian relations, and would make Germany driven Europe vulnerable to Russian pressures which would certainly aim at the neutralization of NATO and the Finlandization of Europe.

Americans, despite US President Donald Trump is flirting with Russia for business reasons and geopolitical considerations versus China, will never allow this to happen.

121

5/10 The Ukraine Crisis and the New Cold War

The crisis in Ukraine has been steadily developing, just under the radar since the collapse of the Soviet Union in late 1991. The country's first president, Leonid Kravchuk (1991-1994), came from the ranks of the old Soviet Communist Party, but was not necessarily pro-Russian.

These early years of Ukraine's independence came at a time when Russia had enough major internal problems of its own to not be concerned that Moscow had any nefarious or neo-imperialistic designs that would challenge Ukraine's territorial integrity or even call into question its right to exist as a sovereign state.

The new government in Ukraine's capital Kyiv was, itself, both read for ready and very enthusiastic about securing a lasting independence. The European Union could have played a decisively influential role in determining the geopolitical future of the country but it, instead, opted to abstain.

The European Union missed an opportunity to achieve for Ukraine a status of neutral independence of the type that we saw established by Finland during the Cold War. Known as "Finlandisation", this allowed the small Nordic country on the Soviet Union's northern border to maintain its full sovereignty in exchange for not challenging its far more powerful and larger neighbour in the realm of foreign policy. Creating a similar model for Ukraine would have been fairly easy during the first years following the collapse of the Soviet Union.

This was a grave mistake and a major missed opportunity on the part of the European Union, but the System has neither the experience or the knowledge of geopolitical strategy, particularly in regards to the former Soviet Union. All that it knew - and continues to know, in great detail - is how to manipulate the smaller Member States and "provincial" politicians in favour of its patrons.

As time passed, Russia slowly re-emerged as a world power and the Ukrainian issue took on a more strategic East-West dimension as tensions between the Kremlin and the West began to worse. Once Moscow was on the mend and ready to re-enter the game of big power politics, the window of opportunity to further integrate Ukraine gradually closed.

Immediately after the collapse of the Soviet Union, Ukraine found itself flooded with nuclear weapons from the time it hosted the bulk of the USSR's strategic rocket forces and also continued to host the Russian Black Sea Fleet in Crimea. Ukraine gave up its nuclear weapons in 1994 as part of the Budapest Memorandum signed by the Russian Federation, the US, UK. China, and France, which included security assurances against threats or the use of force and guaranteed the territorial integrity and political independence of Ukraine.

The move successfully removed Ukraine's nuclear arsenal, but question over the vast Russian Black Sea Fleet based in the Crimean port of Sevastopol remained unresolved. The pipelines crossing Ukraine from Russia to Europe were and continue to be the property of Russian companies that are either private or partially owned by the Russian government - which is an important element to consider.

Russia still supplies Europe with one third of its natural gas needs and in the wake of the gas crises of 2006 and 2009, Russia and Germany built one more pipeline with two parallel routes, one of which is the so-called Nord Stream, which fully bypassed Ukraine for Germany, Russia's best customer in the EU.

European geopolitical interests came too late to save Ukraine. In November 2004, the pro-Western Orange Revolution stripped successfully overturned a rigged election won a pro-Russian oligarch, Viktor Yanukovych, and handed it to the staunchly pro-EU Viktor Yushchenko, who took over on January 2005. Yushchenko's Orange Revolution co-leader, Yulia Tymoshenko, later became the first woman to serve as Ukraine's prime minister from January-September 2005, and again from December 2007-March 2010.

Early in January 2009, for purely commercial reasons, Kyiv stopped Russian gas transit to Europe. The suspension resulted in serious damages to nearby Bulgaria, which was completely dependent on Russian gas. The damage caused by the supply cut also affected other former Communist countries in Eastern Europe, as well as Germany.

It seems that officials responsible for parallel gas transit, by pure coincidence, were simultaneously replaced by both Moscow and Kyiv. As a result, certain types of gas flows, in addition to regular supplies, were suspended until the new people would find the proper modus operandi.

Representatives of the two governments flew to Brussels to negotiate a new deal. Ukraine sent Deputy Prime Minister Grigory Nemira and Russia dispatched the Chairman of the Duma's Foreign Affairs Committee Konstantin Kosachev. At the time, both visited New Europe's offices and in separate interviews, explained that the deal was reached easily and the gas flow was resumed immediately. The agreement was signed in Moscow by President Vladimir Putin and Ukraine's Prime Minister Yulia Tymoshenko just a few days later on 18 January 2009.

The ease by which the deal was closed was characteristic of how good the climate was at the time between all the key parties involved, as the flow of gas supplies restarted two days before the agreement was actually signed. When Putin and Tymoshenko met at the Kremlin, Putin asked Tymoshenko what she would like to drink, she replied "Water", to which her host responded, "With or without gas?" Not missing a beat, Tymoshenko replied, "With gas, of course".

The pro-Russian Yanukovych orchestrated a remarkable turn around of his political by making an unexpected comeback in the 2010 presidential election – a mere six years after being ousted from power following his attempt to rig the vote in 2004. In an election that was deemed fair and transparent by the Central Election Commission, Yanukovych easily defeated a weakened Yushchenko after the latter got himself bogged down in a serious of power disputes with his former Orange Revolution ally and prime minister, Yulia Tymoshenko.

By August 2011, Yanukovych had Tymoshenko arrested on trumped-up charges of abuse of power for the conclusion of the gas contracts with Russia in 2009. She was later sentenced to seven years in prison and was not released until February 2014, only hours after Yanukovych fled Ukraine during the height of the Euromaidan Revolution.

Yanukovych downfall during the 2013-2014 Euromaidan Revolution that took place in central Kyiv's Independence Square were markedly different from the bloodless Orange Revolution a decade earlier. The daily clashes between the pro-Western protestors and Yanukovych's praetorian guard, known as the "Berkut", resulted in more than 100 deaths, mostly between 18 and 20 February 2014. The Euromaidan Revolution resulted in the removal of the democratically elected, but largely unpopular, Yanukovych, in favour of a series of rapid changes to Ukraine's socio-political system, including the formation of a new pro-EU interim government, the restoration of the previous constitution, and the call to hold impromptu presidential elections within months.

European leaders and the US often encouraged the Euromaidan protests by dangling the EU carrot of "integration". But neither of the two were willing to fully commit to supporting a robust EU-backed reform process that would leave the notoriously corrupt Ukrainian judicial and political systems fundamentally overhauled. The events resulted in the successful overthrow of Yanukovych, but also left Ukraine embroiled in a war against pro-Moscow separatists in the country's eastern Donbass Region, and the loss of the Crimean Peninsula less than a month after Yanukovych's ouster.

Putin moved quickly to pounce on the weakness of Ukraine's interim government – which was bitterly divided between pro-European democrats, ultra-nationalists, and oligarchs – by invading and annexing Crimea (although he calls it something else) and to provoke turmoil in eastern Ukraine through the effective use of online propaganda and fake news that fanned the flames of separatism with the mostly Soviet-nostalgic working class.

The Kremlin refused to recognise the new interim government, calling the revolution a "coup" and initiated a not-so-covert invasion of Crimea. After an internationally unrecognized referendum that was overseen by the watchful eye of the Russian Armed Forces and Moscow's security services, Russia signed a treaty of accession with Crimea in March 2014 and later absorbed the peninsula into the Russian Federation.

Though Yanukovych was considered corrupt and followed Putin's suggestions, the new government of Petro Poroshenko is also seen as corrupt and bitterly divided. The sad story of Ukraine is a story full of European mistakes as there have been no clear EU plans to resolve the crisis. The European Union encouraged an undemocratic, revolutionary change of an unpopular government, but did nothing to provide for a controllable succession scheme.

The Ukraine crisis has ultimately triggered a new Cold War in Europe that is now rapidly unfolding and based on both traditional and new techniques. Indeed, besides the developing "balance of terror," a combination of nukes with well-served propaganda, newish weapons that are being employed include sanctions, cyber-warfare, terrorist threats, as well as massive traditional and new media campaigns targeting a global audience.

This new Cold War goes far beyond the Crimea issue. It is an ongoing and unseen confrontation between the United States and Germany. Under Gerhardt Schroeder's leadership (SPD, 1998-2005), Germany attempted to set its bilateral accord with Russia, as it is dependent on Russian gas. The United States is against any such move and managed to block the deal, while pushing the basic American position that Germany must stop buying natural gas from Russia. For Germany, this is practically impossible because it is the Russian gas arriving to Germany through Ukraine that fuels German industry. Replacing gas with oil is out of the question for German economy for simple reasons of cost.

This explains the ongoing invisible Cold War between the US and Germany, which is likely to be diffused and may well pool in this logic the entire European Union. Indeed, to a growing extent, the latter is under the controlling influence of Germany.

Following the election of US President Donald J. Trump, there were deep concerns in Kyiv – which later proved to be untrue – that the new administration in Washington would pursue a more pro-Moscow policy towards Ukraine and lift the US sanctions against Russia. However, in February 2017, White House spokesman Sean Spicer said Trump expected Russia to return Crimea to Ukraine, which Russia flatly rejected. Consequently, with the sanctions still in place and with the new Cold War in full swing, the future of Ukraine remains unclear.

5/11 The Emergence of the New Political Order

Post-war democratic Western Europe has developed into two main political streams, confined between the neo-Nazi fascist ghosts and the Iron Curtain. These were the Christian Democrats and the Socialists. Both political families started by sharing similar values in matters of human and civil rights and democratic freedoms. Over the years, both followed the same principles, though with slight differences in matters of social welfare and the conception of the free market's role.

As time passed, the two families evolved from belligerent opponents to blood brothers.

Consequently, the ideological gap between the two families has been fading-out with the passage of time and both parties started making compromises on matters of principle. Today, social and market policies are quasi-similar in the two families, while both agree on laws that curtail political freedoms.

In Europe proper, back in the old days, nobody could arrest and detain you just on suspicion of a crime. You were always entitled to be questioned in the presence of your lawyer and nobody could enter and search your home without a court order. That was in the past in the decades of the 1970s and 1980s when European Union citizens enjoyed real freedoms.

Over the years, from there we somehow got here. Although I have said it before, I will repeat it because *"repetitio est mater studiorum."* Today, anybody can be arrested as a terrorist suspect and be detained without being formally charged and without access to lawyers and family for years. At the same time, the authorities can enter and search the home of any "terrorist suspect" any time, unannounced, using force, without a warrant or even the presence of a prosecutor. If, during the search, they find any cash or undeclared precious items (jewels, paintings, etc.) you will be accused of money laundering, unless you have solid proof of the origin of this cash and proofs that the money you purchased the valuable items was declared in your tax statements. This is the typical Stalinist justice concept where the defendant must prove his innocence. Yet it seems that we have not yet reached our limit.

Our society is divided on this new reality. The eldest take this gradually changing situation, including more restrictions, for granted. Elderly citizens do not react anymore because the "Woodstock Generation" is ageing and "Danny the Red" of May 1968 wears his reading glasses as a decent former Member of the European Parliament and studies the new generations' of activists.

Another reason they do not react could be because they are happy and satisfied with what they achieved in their life or because they are too old to react. Perhaps they have reached the stage of pessimism, being convinced that no matter what they say or do their world would never change.

Wrong. The world is changing because people change their minds. This is what our youth believe.

Young people, the well-educated and unemployed, now total over 25 million in the European Union. They will bring about the change we need. If the conservative society detests change, then it must keep the youth busy by giving them jobs.

Young people trying to do something to survive difficult times feel that the fast rise of Europe's democratic deficit, under the cloak of combating terrorism and money laundering, is prohibiting any creative development. Our youth has nothing to do with terrorism and they have nothing to wash except their underwear. The only things they are looking for are jobs and freedom. This means deregulation, a word that ruling administrative elite considers blasphemy.

One more factor is also driving people to extremes. It is the continuous wave of immigrants and refugees that is altering the social, cultural and religious identity of Europe. In the years to come, the problem will negatively impact the daily life of most Europeans before we see any improvements. This situation, if not addressed, will favour political groups campaigning against immigrants and refugees.

Immigrants have taken unprecedented risks in a furtive effort to reach Europe for a better life and they are determined to get it. This new situation, which is associated with increasing criminality and sharply increased security troubles from terrorists penetrating together with immigrants and refugees, is fuelling xenophobic predispositions. The issue of disorderly immigration to and within Europe, politically favours the extremist political and social forces.

This reality, together with the crisis in Europe, which from an economic problem has become social, political and endemic, is driving ordinary citizens (especially unemployed youth) to look for political alternatives. We have seen that recently in Italy and Slovenia while similar situations, bottom-up changes, are fermenting in other countries such as Hungary and others.

This emerging new situation, which the old ruling class erroneously is labelling as far-right extremists, are neither far-right, nor neo-left. It is the new political order in Europe and its number one characteristic versus the old and is acquiring momentum. To paraphrase Abraham Lincoln, it is the "government of the Citizens, by the Citizens, for the Citizens".

THE DARK SIDE
OF THE NOON

6/1 Complexity and the European Union

The European Union is a typical complex system. It consists of diverse, interdependent, interconnected, adaptive entities. They are the Member States, which display a significant degree of adaptability as they respond to global and local influences in their own self-organised processes. Complex systems are unpredictable and can trigger large events.

This is our potential problem.

A country is a complex system, financial markets are complex systems and so are ecosystems. This is also the case of the European Union.

Complex systems are remarkably robust, as the European Union is. Complex systems can produce amazing novelty. Look at the astonishing progress achieved in European research in the last decade. Complex systems can also survive after experiencing large traumatic events. We experienced the large trauma the European Union has suffered to-date with the integration of East Germany. The Union adapted to the new situation smoothly, survived and maintained functionality.

The Enlargement with 11 former Communist states is even a larger trauma, too large, which is still in progress. Where it will take the European Union, nobody can know for sure, but only guess.

The latest large traumatic event is the decision of the people of the United Kingdom to leave the European Union. No matter if, when and how it may practically happen, the EU has already suffered a serious political trauma.

Emergence is a fundamental property of complexity producing self-organisation. In the case of the European Union this principle has been violated. The peoples of Europe did not bring gradual bottom-up integration, but unification came, and still comes, through a top-down methodology that imposed strict discipline. This discipline, affecting all facets of the life of ordinary people, is designed and exerted by non-elected senior staff, top Commission functionaries, who do not respond to any public scrutiny. In the eyes of ordinary Europeans, such administrators are parasites. At the end of the day, the parasites will kill the host as they are looking only after their own puny self-interest. However, no parasite can survive long with a dead host.

Complex systems do not obey laws dictated by Treaties and Regulations. Complexity is a theory and has its own basics ruled by nature. If the basics are not met, any complex system will sooner or later collapse, under uncontrolled bottom-up emerging phenomena.

So, that is where the European Union, as a complex system stands but cannot stand in this way for long. With the years and the zeal of its self-produced leadership, it became an inflexible solid complex system, very large, which has deviated from the basic rules of complexity.

There are many facets to the way the European Union has grown and developed, some going against the natural laws of complexity. All top-to-bottom imposed rules by an autonomous, self-reproducing system, which is not the result of a natural process, that is elections, go against the principles of complexity, and go against the laws of nature.

Today's European Union is moving along two parallel lines.

The first is the apparently democratically adapted rules. Yet Germany-forced, common currency and the labyrinth of laws, which over-monitor and over-regulate the everyday life of citizens, is not very democratic.

The Second is that Europe has been self-trapped in its own rules. The world has embarked upon a new course. The grandeur of China, locomotors of the US economy is fading out, and the emerging markets are sharply declining. In this context the European Union entered into a spiral deflationary depression, which led to the destruction of values and very high liquidity in the hands of few. Moreover, the solid productive forces of the Union, young people with hopes and innovative ideas, have been driven into an induced coma.

Under these circumstances, the European Union is being navigated without a pilot into bottom-up developments, which may be triggered by a random event. Worse still is that our highly sophisticated European Union leaders who master laws and treaties, relax like castrated fat cats next to the fireplace and have never heard of complexity in their life.

6/2 The Melian Conference, and the Commission

The Melian Conference is the name given to the dialogue conducted between Athenians and Melians during the Peloponnesian War some 2,400 years ago, as reported by Thucydides.

The Peloponnesian War was the first real world war in human history. It lasted 29 years and was fought on three continents, Europe, Africa and Asia, involving the biggest part of the then- known western world. The war was fought between two city-states, Athens and Sparta (Lacedaemon) and it was also the first civil war in history. All combatant parties were speaking Greek.

As Europe enters a phase of rapid decay affecting its values and principles any random event could trigger unprecedented bottom-up developments. Thus, it is worth taking notice of this historical dialogue. The Melian Conference, is similar to the dialogue conducted today, in several occasions, in this case between the European Commission and some class C Member States.

Politically, Athens was the great liberal state of Pericles preaching and trying to impose democracy and freedom across the world. Sparta was a military state where everything was owned by the state and everybody was ready to sacrifice themselves for the state. Under these circumstances, Sparta was the first communist state in human history and, among others, was the inspirational model followed by Karl Marx.

Melos (a.k.a. Milos) is a small isolated island in the western Aegean, which had a loose association with Lacedaemon, but had no participation in the armed conflict because it had no army to offer and was far from any theatre of war.

In the summer of 431 BC, an Athenian armada of 20 warships under Admiral Alcibiades sailed to the island. Upon arrival, the Athenian Ambassadors asked to meet the local authorities offering to speak either before the public or in private. The Melians opted to have a closed-door debate in the Ekklisia tou Demou (Parliament). The Athenians accepted and clarified "we will do the talking and if you have something to say, you can interrupt and then we will continue."

The Athenians started by giving the Melians an ultimatum: peacefully surrender and agree to become their slaves or be destroyed (killed). The Melians initially argued that this was not just. The Athenians replied that Melians could not talk of justice, as they did not have equal power to support it. The Melians then proposed to the Athenians to become allies, but the Athenians refused, explaining that they had to go back to Athens with a clear solution.

Then the Melians reverted to their last argument that if the Athenians had killed them and they themselves had lost the war, their enemies would not show mercy on them and would kill them all.

The Athenians concluded: "We do not care what will happen if we lose the war. All we care about is that we have to go back to Athens with solutions as elections there are due soon."

The Melians finally refused, the Athenian Ambassadors left and the fleet of Alcibiades carried out a siege of the island. After two years under siege and isolation, the Melians opened the gates of their city. The Athenians walked in with no resistance, killed all the men and sold all women and children in slavery. After this very democratic solution, the Athenians sent 500 Athenian immigrants to Melos.

Ever since then, nothing else has happened to that island, which is in the middle of nowhere, with no visitors and few tourists. Today, Melos is considered the only place in Greece where one can find true Athenians – the direct descendants of the Athenian Democracy of Pericles.

It is worth noting, however, that after 29 years of battles in three continents the Peloponnesian war was not won by the mighty Athenian democracy, but by the communist Sparta.

The Melian Conference, ceteris paribus, is exactly the pattern of the dialogue conducted on every occasion between politicians and businessmen from small Member States and the Commission. Either you agree, or we will destroy you!

6/3 Who Rules the European Union?

Until the Brexit referendum, politically, the British and the Americans had the biggest say in how the European Union is ruled. Financially, the Germans are in command.

In business matters, American interests are predominantly taken care of by the British. Also, France has a big say in EU affairs and enjoys a fair share of the overall business. Indeed, Germany, France and until the Brexit referendum Britain together constituted the three main players, which along with the European Commission formed the deep state of Europe. These key players decided, after granting certain, rather minor, concessions to less important Member States. They decided for and on behalf of, half a billion Europeans, "in the name of the Union."

The Germans are the economic overlords of Europe. For more than a decade, they have kept the European Union under a regime of tight austerity, with the only beneficiary being the German economy and the victims being all European citizens, Germans included. Germany is abusing its leading economic role and the System manage to keep the Union under its strict financial control.

Brexit, has created the conditions for a reset of the roles in ruling Europe. After Brexit, the leverage of the United Kingdom is gradually declining, as bottom line in life is that everything is politics. Whatever you do, whatever you do not do, whatever you think or pursue, is politics.

Politically the UK is out of the EU and the USA is alone. However, Brexit turns to be like Hotel California. You may check-out, but you never leave. Indeed, politics is politics and business is business.

Washington DC and London have set up a well-proven mechanism and are still using it to maximise both political influence and business results. To this effect, Anglo-Americans with their soft-power structures are highly efficient.

For years now, a section of the British Chamber of Commerce in London runs a service that supports American and British companies doing business at the EU level. This includes co- financed projects in Member States, EU tenders and all EU programmes. This service was also highly influential in shaping new EU legislation.

In this context, the Brussels British Permanent Representation is still actively involved. It is the Representation (not the UK Embassy to Belgium), that represents Britain in the System and knows the appropriate contracting practices and procedures.

There are standard weekly meetings taking place at the British Permanent Representation with (British and Irish) selected, most seconded, EU officials. Their agenda usually has two items: EU legislation under preparation and business matters.

Many of the British functionaries working for the European Commission originate from the British civil service. Once hired by any European institution they do not resign from their service. They maintain the post and they remain part of the hierarchy. They are treated as being active; they get their promotions, but are not paid a salary.

The issue of EU legislation in the making is worth looking at. When the Commission is beginning to prepare a new law, (Regulation, Directive, Decision or whatever) the competent service in the respective DG undertakes the preparation of the draft law. In discussing the matter within the Unit, officials are often trying to avoid taking on such an assignment because it requires hard work and can be very boring; at least this is what people tell us.

In this process, it often occurs that in the team in charge of drafting the new law, a Brit is offered to consider the subject and present a draft to the team. From then on, the assignment is reported to the regular meeting with the UK Delegation, which forwards the matter to the London Chamber of Commerce. The latter prepares the draft law, which, via the same route, returns a few days after to the Commission. Certainly, in drafting new laws both the Secretariat General and the Legal Service are involved, but the key element remain the initial British contribution.

I remember in the 1980s that the Department of Agriculture (DG AGRI) was working on a Regulation concerning olive oil subsidies. At the time, the British government presented a proposal, which was including, besides olive oil, seed oils as well. The Commission rejected the proposal. A decade later the same issue was discussed and a new law proposal on the same subject was launched. The proposal was carefully prepared by the Commission and was the same proposal presented by the British government, 10 years before.

An interesting facet of this discussion is the officials' category of the Expert National Détaché (END) or Seconded National Expert. Such personnel act often as the Trojan Horse. When Neil Kinnock was the UK Commissioner for Personnel and Administration in the Prodi Commission (1999-2003), the British government proposed to the Commission a simple experimental project aiming at educating British civil servants. The purpose was to detach for a short period several British civil servants in the various Commission departments with ordinary assignments so to become familiar with the EU. The "experiment" was based on two letters exchanged between the UK and EU and since then the whole matter has been forgotten.

Silently, temporary detachments became long-term and the small number of detached UK nationals is continuously growing. The beauty of this invention is that when other, less important Member States are proposing to detach one of their civil servants to Brussels, the Commission, most of the times, invents nice ways to refuse.

Brexit or non-Brexit the British structures are all over Brussels and it will take decades to eradicate if the System, for its own protection, does not invent the way to keep them. The more so, that in a second thought, such structures may well constitute the basic cell of organized resistance to the total domination of Europe by the Germans.

It is very important to understand the decision-making process in the European Commission because ultimately it shapes the future of Europe but also daily life of ordinary citizens. An understanding of how power is possessed, gained and exerted in the Commission is necessary to change things. This understanding will show you how you can make this superb powerhouse of Europe work in the interests of the Member States and their citizens.

If a Commissioner from a small Member State wants one thing accomplished and the System does not, the will of the System will prevail and the Commissioner will observe silently, without participating at all.

Roughly, and taking out the *"s'il vous plaît"* type ornaments, a hypothetical dialogue between the Commissioner and his Director General (a "systemic" career functionary, different nationality of the Commissioner) goes like this:

"Commissioner, here is the final text of the Directive that the Services have prepared on exempting ship-owners for the next 50 years from paying carbon dioxide tax. Please sign to be included as Point A in the agenda of this week's College."

"No, dear I disagree. We have to tax all transport means, including shipping, as we already did for trucks and aeroplanes."

"Dear Commissioner, you do not understand, the draft proposal has been fully cleared by the Legal Service and is already approved by the Secretariat General.

If we propose dear Commissioner what you suggest, it will be against the rules. Please sign as we have to meet the deadline of next Wednesday."

"No Director General, I insist."

"Very good Commissioner, then since you want to act against the rules (note that the word rules, not law, is used here) you will take full responsibility, so you must sign this act of refusal, right away."

It must be added that all this "process" is oral and most part of it is conducted through third parties. That there are more recorders in the Commission buildings than in the Sony shop in Japan is what many believe, axiomatically. However, none of such devices are run by Commissioners.

This is it. So far, I have never heard of a Commissioner who dared to sign such a paper or had the courage to say to his Director General, "Just get the hell out of here and send in your number two." The point is, however, that Commissioners do not really know what powers they have. Indeed, if ever a real dispute occurs between the Commissioner and his Director General, the latter will never win. Commissioners with rare exceptions, however, never bring a confrontation to extremes.

6/4 The Grand Bluff, the Decision-Making Process

The way European laws, affecting every-day life of half a billion citizens, are tabled and approved, is a state-of-the-art procedure that even the classiest dictators would envy. Everything looks legal and democratic, but with a twist.

The European Parliament, the supreme political body of the European Union, directly elected by the citizens of Europe, has no right to introduce legislation. The legislative initiative is the monopoly of the Commission.

On the contrary, Europe's draft legislation makers are solely the functionaries of the European Commission who, I repeat as *"repetitio est mater studiorum"* have neither political, nor moral legitimacy. Moreover, it has happened that many laws were drafted in certain capitals and were brought to Brussels in the suitcases of seconded officials.

If draft legislation is substantially changed by the Parliament or the Council of Ministers, the Commission has the right to withdraw the proposed law. In this case, after some time, the Commission brings back the law for approval, same content with different wording, and repeats the procedure until the law is passed as proposed. These are the nasty details.

The System has invented a long, complicated scheme of procedures with alternatives and shortcuts. In this way, while it makes essential decisions for new legislation unilaterally, everything looks legitimate and democratic.

Recently, the Commission introduced the so-called "Impact Assessments" of their proposals where social, economic, competitiveness and environmental effects of the proposed law are considered. Basically, the services do the job. Sometimes the Commission buys specialised reports as guidelines to compile the Impact Assessment. However, the latter is exclusively drafted by the services and approved by a Commission-dedicated board. Besides spending funds for no reason, the Impact Assessments serve exclusively to add legitimacy in a bluff claiming to be an open democratic process.

In real terms, decisions are made by the System without any input from the citizens or their representatives through a complex labyrinth, which very few can perceive. The final act is staged in the European Parliament where new legislation is approved.

In this process, all players are happy and satisfied. The System is "democratically" getting approval for whatever it wants. The various noisy citizens' organisations that participate in the party are happy because they can prove to their co-nationals how important they are in the governance of Europe. This constitutes a good reference for pre-election campaigns. The European Parliament also gets a chance to underline the importance of its work and existence, while several of its members take the opportunity to communicate to their national constituents how important they are and how important their input in Brussels is for Europe.

If it were only so...

As for the substance of the adopted legislation, it does not really matter, as it did not go through any real scrutiny. The essence of this process is that it happens the way the System wants. In this context, the great no-nonsense is the "Impact Assessment." It is the evaluation of the draft legislation by external, independent experts, to check if the positive aspects of the draft law prevail over the negative. As it happens, the "Impact Assessment" is always in favour of the draft legislation, as suggested. As to the (well-paid) "independent experts," they are carefully chosen by the System with supposedly "objective" and "meritocratic" criteria.

At the same time, the democratic deficit of Europe is growing and the invulnerability of the System is further consolidated.

What makes the decision-making process significant is that despite the fact everything is arranged beforehand and very little changes during the procedure are made, if any, the process itself is a very live activity involving many people. Yes, we are talking of class C role actors on the political stage but this is somehow enough to justify their role and their salaries.

6/5 The Classification of Member States

Member States are virtually classified along certain criteria and this classification defines how much leverage each one has over the European Institutions. The classification of Member States is one of the "unwritten" rules of the System.

The first criterion is the political importance of each country. Second is its role in international affairs, its financial strength, its military capacity and the size of the country.

The net financial position of each Member State vis-à-vis the Community budget is also important.

Member States are divided into net contributors and net receivers, depending on what is the difference between what a country gets in the form of Community payments in EU programmes and co-financed projects and what it contributes to the Community budget.

Germany, France and still the UK are the top three Member States, which unquestionably dictate their wishes to the Commission and the latter, like a good wife in an Arab harem, satisfies their wishes cheerfully and willingly. The top three are the Class A countries. The position of the UK is politically declining, after the Brexit referendum, but this has nothing to do with Commission's operations. The UK is present all over with several sitting Directors General, staff in key positions and omnipresent, in one way or another, in all Cabinets.

Class B countries with more limited leverage are the three big Catholic countries, Italy, Spain and Poland along with the three Benelux countries (Belgium, The Netherlands and Luxembourg).

Class C countries are the rest, the remaining Member States with very little leverage, if any. With them the Commission feels uninhibited in exerting power and treats them as little better than tin soldiers.

6/6 The Rule of Law

The European Union has a wide variety of legal schemes under different tags, which have so far produced over 110,000 pieces of legislation, all binding for EU citizens and superseding national legislation, even national constitutions.

The various legal schemes include Treaties, Regulations, Directives, Decisions, Recommendations and Case Law that are decisions of the Court of Justice of the EU, as well as many other types of rule under various labels. All of this information can be easily retrieved from the Commission's website, with few exceptions.

In addition, this corpus of legislation is so overwhelmingly numerous that it is practically impossible for ordinary citizens to make use of it. Furthermore, certain pieces of legislation including College Decisions are hidden and not available to the public as they are supposed to contain "sensitive" information concerning specific commercial interests. This is outrageous, but it happens when special benefits are granted to "friendly" companies and the Commission does not wish Citizens to have knowledge so that others could benefit as well.

One typical example is Commission Decision 9418 dated Monday, 17 December 2012. It provides for the reduction of the recovery from €70m to €9.6m from the (French) *Centre National de la Recherché*

Scientifique (CNRS). This decision was meticulously kept confidential for years (until New Europe forced its disclosure) to avoid that other companies may benefit. If this is not Dictatorship of the Administration, what then Dictatorship is?

Making things worse, the Commission, according to the expediencies of the case, is also producing legal opinion papers often contradicting each other on the same subject. The problem is that in most cases the concerned Member State, company or citizens, has no actual idea of the previous interpretations in similar cases and is limited to claim back home that it was defeated with dignity.

A prominent example is the South Stream case. The Commission, in a Legal Opinion and Services Opinions, stopped it while accepting for the same reasons North Stream II. They are both pipelines. North Stream (I and II) is transporting gas from Russia to Germany, while South Stream was set to supply gas from Russia to Bulgaria and Greece. This kind of unfair behaviour does not happen every day, but it does happen, not too rarely, for very serious matters.

The Treaties are the legislation that has total democratic legitimation, being adopted by the European Council (the assembly of the Prime Ministers and Heads of State of the European Union and ratified by the Parliaments of all Member States). The Treaties define the moral and legal principles of the European Union, forming what is practically the constitution of Europe and its amendments.

The "Treaty of Rome" (1957) established the European Economic Community (EEC). The real purpose of the Treaty of Rome was to secure long-standing peace in Western Europe, and to this effect the European Community has been an unprecedented success. From that point on, how a peace agreement, a kind of upgraded and flowery armistice agreement, ended up becoming progressively a tool for ruling half a billion Europeans by a non-elected nomenklatura, is something to be seen and debated by all of us, but primarily by the political elite ruling Member States.

These were followed by the "Merger Treaty" (Brussels, 1965) streamlining the European Institutions; the "Single European Act" (The Hague, 1986), establishing the single market and the principle of the qualified majority of the Council to make it harder for individual countries to veto legislation; the "Maastricht Treaty" (1992) introducing the European Monetary Union (Eurozone); the "Treaty of Nice" (2001) reforming the EU institutions; the Treaty on Nice (2001) upgrading EU institutions and last but not least, yet very theoretical, the "Lisbon Treaty" (2007) supposedly making the EU more democratic and more efficient in order to better address global problems.

The System has intelligently managed to introduce endless rules under various schemes, in many cases overlapping each other with slight differences, for which depending on the case, the System gives different interpretations. For this reason, the European Commission has a Legal Service, a Directorate General directly under the President with more than 150 lawyers (Agents) while every Directorate General has its own legal team, each one with several lawyers and jurists.

The result is that when a dispute arises between the System and a non-privileged Member State, the System wins because it has superior knowledge of the law and the Commission may always appeal to its 'discretionary power".

Indeed, the lack of substantial knowledge in Member States is an important element in dealing with the System. Recall that in many cases, handlers from national administrations visiting Brussels do not even know the difference between a Directive and a Regulation.

It is practically impossible to defeat the System in legal or administrative grounds. It has deep knowledge of European law and has mastered the art of manipulation. The System's know-how and its technical expertise are unbeatable.

Under these circumstances, what is missing is a "codification" of the labyrinth of EU laws. "Codes" would improve transparency, legibility and legal certainty. They would also contribute to "better law making" – something that the Commission "wants" to promote. However, the Commission services, which spends billions of Euro in futile exercises every year, systematically avoid any discussion of globally codifying EU legislation across the current 'silos' corresponding to the turfs of the different Commission directorate generals. For obvious reasons as knowledge, is power.

Codification occurs systematically. However, only within the portfolio of each directorate general. For example, data protection and consumer affairs are handled by DG Justice and the relevant directives are not consolidated with those depending of DG Grow (such as the Services Directive) or DG CONNECT (Electronic Communications Services).

6/7 The College

Theoretically, and to a large extent also practically, the ultimate level of power in the European Commission is the College: the collective body of 28 Commissioners. Since the May 2014 European Parliament elections, European parties nominate their candidates for Commission President and the winning ticket wins also the President who is (formally) validated by the European Parliament through a "hearing" process. The College meets every Wednesday and its decisions are EU law. During the Strasburg week of the European Parliament, the Wednesday meeting of the College takes place in Strasburg.

Except for major political issues, the last word lies with the President of the European Commission, who after informally "consulting"

- on sensitive issues - the big Member States and the Member States concerned, conveys his thoughts to the College and the latter adapts to the political reality. Equally important is the role of the Head of Cabinet (Chief of the Office of the President) who in practice is the number two in the European Commission. Sometimes, and in certain matters, depending on the personality of the President and the issue, the number two becomes de facto the number one. We have seen this in the past, in the case of President Jacques Delors and his Head of Cabinet Pascal Lamy.

President Jean Claude Juncker has for the first time appointed several vice-presidents, all coming from small countries, to dilute the responsibilities of the President and render the decision-making more collective.

Given that for all practical purposes the European Commission is the government of the European Union, the President of the Commission corresponds to the Prime Minister of Europe, while, his Head of Cabinet is the Chief of Staff. The Commissioners are Europe's Ministers. Until 1974, Commissioners were addressed "Monsieur le Ministre." The practice, not the rule, was that they had previously served as Ministers in their countries and the President of the Commission had served as Prime Minister in his country. By the way Jacques Delors, twice president of the Commission, had never served as Prime Minister.

Every Member State appoints a Commissioner. The term of service of the Commission is five years. The President of the Commission, in consultation with the Member States, distributes the various portfolios. Every portfolio corresponds to a Ministry and is called Directorate General.

Once a Member State nominates its Commissioner, the appropriate Committee of the European Parliament screens the Commissioner in a three-hour process called a "hearing." Once the Commissioner is approved by the Parliament, he or she is no longer is a representative from the Member State of origin. After the hearing, the Member State cannot withdraw its Commissioner, even if the government of the Member State should change.

Only the President can remove a Commissioner on the grounds of Article 17 of the Treaty. However, this prerogative of the President has not been tested so far. Indeed, even President Jose Manuel Barroso, when he unilaterally decided to dismiss his Health and Consumer Protection (Maltese) Commissioner John Dalli (16 October 2012), despite the government of Malta plead in favour of the dismissal, did not dare to cite Art. 17. Obviously because in the Barroso Commission at the time there were several strong Commissioners originating from Member States where the governments had changed (i.e. France, Michel Barnier, Italy, Antonio Tajani and others). If Jose Barroso would have dismissed Dalli on the grounds of Article 17, he was not sure how the other Commissioners would have reacted.

Since the first Barroso Commission (2004), all Commissioners are based in the Berlaymont Building the headquarters of the government of Europe in Rue de la Loi 200, at Rond Point Schuman, in Brussels. The building hosts the President of the Commission and his Commissioners and their teams. In addition, the Berlaymont structure is the home base for the Press Service (spokespersons), the Secretariat General and the Legal Service.

For the period 1999-2004, when Berlaymont was under refurbishing (because of asbestos used when it was built), Commissioners and their Cabinets were stationed in the central building of their respective Directorates General. There they had direct contact with their services and could follow-up on important issues efficiently. In practice, they could call and have immediately in their office any staff member of their DG. For that short period, the Commission was much more political as Commissioners (the political leaders of the Commission) were in daily direct contact with their services. Today, Commissioners consult mainly with their Director General. All other contacts with any staff member are rare. Indeed, if for any reason the Commissioner or his team wants to be briefed on any issue, the Cabinet must ask for, only through the Director General. The European Commission services occupy more than 80 buildings in Brussels, and the Commissioners, working and living in a "golden cage," have difficulties to visit their services unless accompanied by the Director General.

This relocation into the most luxurious headquarters of Europe has practically deprived the Commissioners of many practical political powers, which were transferred to the System. Indeed, in a private lunch with one Commissioner earlier this year, he confessed, "how can I control my Directorate General? I have in my office, under my direct control, less that 20 people and my Director General, that I did not appoint, and I cannot replace, controls 2,000."

Finally, it must be underlined that the College is meeting every Wednesday noon and has many characteristics of a public relations exercise rather than a real substantive meeting of the Ministers of Europe. Everything discussed and decided Wednesday in the College was already discussed two days before (on Monday) and mostly agreed by the Heads of Cabinet.

The procedure is quite simple. Every Monday, the Directorates General concerned, submit their proposals for the College to the Heads of Cabinet meeting. Each case is discussed by the Heads of Cabinet and if they all agree on the proposal this is countersigned as "Point A" and is approved by the College without discussion. Cases where no agreement among the Heads of Cabinet is reached are countersigned as "Point B" and the College takes the final decision, after discussion. However, this rarely happens.

This intense bureaucratic process, we are told, "refines and facilitates" the work of the College so the Commissioners can get things done efficiently. Critics might call it little more than a rubber stamp for the prerogatives of the System.

6/8 The Cabinets

Each Commissioner can have a team of up to17 members to assist in all operations. This team includes functionaries, assistants, secretaries as well as a driver for the Commissioner. This is it.

Theoretically, all members of the team are to be chosen by the Commissioner. In practice, most of the staff is selected by the System, making support and control of few political appointees much easier. This happens in the case of a Commissioner from one of the new Member States and who has been appointed for the first time.

The Head of Cabinet (HoC) is the "alter ego" of the Commissioner and can fill in or replace him/her in all occasions. In the great majority of cases, the HoC has more real power than the Commissioner because this person is the top "systemic" element in the Cabinet. Unless the HoC has been appointed by the Commissioner.

However, one of the "unwritten" laws of the Commission, and one that is often violated as it is contradicted by the "written" law was until Juncker has abolished it, was that the Head of Cabinet of the Commissioner must be of a different nationality from the Commissioner and must be a permanent official of the Commission. For the position of the Head of Cabinet and other positions in the Cabinet, many apply simply by sending their CV to the Commissioner. However, the selection is usually done with the assistance of the Secretary General, the Director General of the Directorate General (department) of the Commissioner, the Head of Cabinet of the President and sometimes even the President himself. Formally, there is a written rule (introduced by Jean-Claude Juncker) that either the Head or the Deputy Head of Cabinet may be of the same nationality of the

Commissioner. However, ordinary Commissioners are "advised" to be limited to choose the Deputy Head.

The Commissioner is bound to place in his/her Cabinet up to six Administrator (functionaries) level team members (not more). Not more than two of whom can be outsiders. Also, a total of three or four Assistants (secretaries, drivers etc.) are allowed to be of the same nationality of the Commissioner.

It is important to note that the Directors General of the DG of new Commissioners are appointed based on rotation, by the previous administration, under the outgoing President, a few weeks before the change of the Commission. As the outgoing Commissioners care only to secure positions for few of their friends, it is the System that controls the rotation of the Directors General. This appointment is for five years, which means that new Commissioners find the Director General of their DG already sitting in his/her post and immovable for five years.

So far, in only a very few cases, a new Commissioner could change his Director General, which means that despite the internal rules, it is possible.

The Commissioner's Cabinet is the organ, which manages all interactions with other Cabinets and the Services. The Head of Cabinet is the absolute ruler of that organ. He/she is the one to dictate policies and procedures, in theory upon orders of the Commissioner, in practice upon instructions from the System.

If someone in the Cabinet dares to oppose the System and inform the Commissioner on sensitive issues directly, that poor soul will be ousted from the "inner circle" and at the first occasion will find he/she has been transferred somewhere to work on logistics.

The Cabinets are the launching pad for young and ambitious Administrators (functionaries) to become part of the cadre of Patricians of the System and thus secure a brilliant career in the Commission.

6/9 Plebeians, Patricians and the Praetorians

There are about 25,000 civil servants (plus another 7,000, temporary staff under different forms of contracts) working for the European Commission. A third of them are Administrators (AD), the officials formulating policies and taking decisions, the remaining being Assistants (AST) who are performing auxiliary tasks. In addition, there are 6,000 and 3,500 employed by the European Parliament and the Council, respectively.

The European Commission is a democratic institution where all staff members are equal. Yet like in George Orwell's book Animal Farm, some animals are more equal than others.

The Administrators are the important ones and they can be divided into two big categories: The Patricians and the Plebeians.

The Patricians, a troop of about one thousand, are also split into the Patricians proper (senior executives) and the Cadet Patricians who are the young Administrators serving in the Cabinets.

Patricians proper range from Heads of Unit, included, until the top civil servant positions, those of Directors General and the Secretary General of the European Commission, who is also a civil servant. In the US Administration, this would roughly correspond to the Senior Executive Service (SES), the top rung of the career Federal executive corps, or flag officers in the military, excluding the very top rung.

The very top positions - Secretary General, Directors General and Deputy Directors General - are politically assigned with the tacit agreement of the Member State of the country of origin, the President of the European Commission and the relevant Commissioner. This practice is not all that different than the United Nations, but as usual, the more powerful Member States clearly dominate. To a certain extent, this is also valid for the positions of Directors for which Member States often intervene, discretely.

Apparently, in appointing the top positions of the Commission, the "kingmaker" is the President of the Commission and his Head of Cabinet. This is correct, unless any of the Class A or B Member States express a wish. If this happens, then the President of the Commission wears his technocratic hat and *"Roma locuta, causa finita."*

Cadet Patricians are those Administrators working in the Cabinets for the first time.

Every Commissioner has eight Administrators in his/her Cabinet. Most of them are coming from the System, while some are coming from the country of the Commissioner and serve under direct contract. These assignments terminate at the end of the Commissioner's term.

Those coming from the System, in the last six months of their five-year term, work closely with their superiors in the Commission to secure a good onward position (theoretically a promotion for the good work done in the Cabinet), after leaving the Cabinet and in view to become Patricians proper, instead of returning to the ranks of the Plebeians.

For those coming from the System, finding an "after Cabinet" position is something that they are silently working for, from the first day they get into the Cabinet job, which is their first "big break." Even worse in the context of the same ambition, is the case of the outsiders brought in by the Commissioner – those who intend to land a permanent job with the Commission. The Americans call this phenomenon by its real name: political appointees "burrowing in" to the civil service. In Brussels, those individuals are the first who will sell out the Commissioner to the System for a job offer, without second thought.

The struggle for an "after Cabinet" position is done in a discreet manner in the first four and a half years of the Cabinet mandate, but it becomes obvious during the last six months of the mandate when in the Commission, except for routine tasks (payments to Member States etc.) has almost nothing else to work on.

The post each candidate will get in the top positions of the "system" depends entirely on how "cooperative" he/she was with *"la maison"*, the "house", during his/her post in the Cabinet. It means how much the candidate, on crucial issues, where *"la maison"* had a different opinion versus that of the Commissioner, succeeded in intelligently cheating/undermining his/her Commissioner and without this being understood, managed to satisfy the System. This, however, is not manipulation it is truly Brussels' art.

Finally, attention should be given to the Praetorians. They are "la crème de la crème" of the Patricians. They are a small number of functionaries, ready to voluntarily help Commissioners, Ministers, Prime Ministers and Administration officials from Member States. Their help seems genuine and for someone to whom Brussels is "terra incognita" they appear as the "Deus ex Machina." Indeed, they appear at the last moment and with the "right" advice and connections help to avert a major catastrophe. The Praetorians are the most-dedicated members of the System and are those who are waiting patiently for the victim to reach the stage of desperation and to step in at the right moment as "el Salvador" to offer a nice well-decorated package with the solution that the System wants to give.

6/10 Corruption, Good-Looking, Legal and Systemic

Corruption is a perennial social phenomenon, directly related to power. The principle is simple, old and clear. Power corrupts and absolute power corrupts absolutely. The power of the Commission is absolute. So is the corruption.

The difference, however, between conventional corruption and the Commission corruption is that the former is illegal and selective while the latter is legitimate and generic. We will define this unique type of legitimate corruption as "systemic corruption."

"Systemic corruption" is different than conventional corruption and has its own characteristics. It is horizontal, vertical and... official. It applies to all and, most importantly, it is legal.

Where the types of corruption, illegal and legitimate, meet, however, is in the results. In both cases, the legal framework is violated.

As the System is sophisticated and *"comme il faut,"* so is "systemic corruption." It is not as grotesque as in some Member States (i.e. cash in brown bags), but there are a few exceptions concerning mostly staff members coming from the south or new Member States.

Corruption is an intrinsic element of human nature and whoever believes that a good salary is sufficient to win over human nature is wrong. You simply cannot ignore human nature. Still, a very good salary, maybe even an unbelievably generous salary bundled with the threat of losing it, is sufficient to restrain nature, meaning to abandon the traditional method of the classic envelope or brown bag with cash. This method of cash distribution does not work in

156

Brussels. Conventional corruption in the European Commission is a very rare phenomenon.

Then, what the hell is this thing we call Brussels "systemic corruption" and is it legal? It concerns all grade AD functionaries (Administrators) and consists of a combination of an extremely lucrative salary with generous fringe benefits linked with the fear of being side-lined, demoted or even fired. This would be equal to economic and social death.

The Commission is comprised of about 25,000 permanent employees, of which one third Administrators (AD) and the rest are Assistants (AST). Those who are potentially corruptible are the Administrators, who take decisions with financial impact.

In theory, Commission decision-makers are all untouchables as they have a very good salary. In practice, they are all corruptible as they all are already recipients of the "bribe" regardless of whether they have violated the rules or not.

What is the "bribe?" It is the exceptionally high salary, with generous fringe benefits (compared to similar positions of the administrations in Member States). More so, it is only subject to EU taxation, much lower than national tax rates. This exceptionally high salary associated with the "discretionary powers" of the Commission, which essentially provides guaranteed juridical and administrative immunity for any violation, administrative, civil or even penal, done in "the interests of the service" is the "bribe." That is why this "bribe" is of a particular type and is legitimate.

Salary, discretionary powers and fear are all legitimate (?) elements, which may lead to illegitimate side effects.

The superior (a supervisor) of the alleged transgressor defines the "interests of the service," and this is where it normally stops. About the possible penal violations, the Belgian authorities are technically responsible in this area, but they must first ask the Commission to lift the immunity of the functionary in question. This never happens unless it is the Commission itself or a major political party that has triggered the case and has a special political reason to do it, going beyond the facts and the substance.

A Director General gets roughly, 18,000 Euros per month, a Director earns about 14,000 Euros and a Head of Unit can take up to approximately 12,000 Euros, depending on his/her grade. The grade of Heads of Unit varies from AD5 to AD13. The salary of € 12,000, which include the expatriate allowance (the Belgians do not get) is paid to Heads of Unit with grade AD13. It should be said that salaries for newly appointed staff are lower. On top, medical insurance including dentists, eyeglasses and therapies are added.

All this money is net in the employee's pocket and may not be taxed by Member States, as taxes (12%-42%) were withhold by the EU budget! Why, this withhold taxes are not paid to the Member State of origin of each employee, is something I cannot understand. This is something Finance Ministers of Member States should pay some attention. However, EU staff pay taxes on savings. For the Member States, the European Union is not an international organization and thus it does not come under the Vienna convention.

As the System is not subject to any real control, with such kinds of "bribes" and the minimal threat of firing for professional decisions associated with the unlimited immunity provided by the superiors, the System can practically do everything: from tender awards management and fixing of tender specifications all the way to manipulating Complaints and ignoring Decisions of the Court of Justice of the EU.

It should be noted, however, that in the Commission, as in all good "houses," there is order. This institutionalised Commission "bribe" though generic and applicable to all Administrators favours mostly the big and influential Member States. It may also favour the political (and potentially other) interests of the very big shots of the System.

For all others – countries, organisations and individuals, the EU law is applied, strictly and severely, and without exceptions. In practice, all others fry in the same pan.

6/11 Omertà

If you ask those familiar with the System to describe the European Commission in one word, most of them will say "omertà."

A basic principle of the US administration is that information should be released "on a need-to-know" basis. In Brussels, the principle is that "information should not be released, no matter what." In Washington DC, the Freedom of Information Act is respected and observed no matter what, despite the high costs of additional legal staff. In Europe Regulation (EC) 1049/2001 on "Access to Documents," it is violated in every possible way and with the catchall explanation of personal data protection and protection of commercial secrets. The System does not release any information, no matter what, that will let citizens get a sense of how "dirty" the System is and how it hides and covers up illegalities which vary from simple misinterpretations of EU law to serious economic crimes.

If what I describe in chapter "The Audit of the European Science Foundation" had occurred in any Member State not one but many would be deep in jail. In the capital of Europe, however, the protagonists of this science fiction story are still sitting in their seats enjoying the lucrative salaries paid by EU citizens. There you will see two original pages of a (cancelled) audit and the same pages as released by the Commission supposedly covering sensitive information referring to personal data and commercial secrets. In reality, the Commission covered the evidence of the loot!

It is worth noting is that in this case which involves, among others, a sitting Director General, nothing has happened for more than one year because the System wants the case hidden under the carpet.

In Brussels, like in Japan, nobody with inside information speaks, thus it is hard to get any information about anything. More so, if it concerns the System and its omissions and commissions. This explains why the secret services of major powers try to establish relations with extra-institutional centres with access to the inner circles of the System such as journalists and lobbying agencies employing former high- ranking Commission officers.

The issue of "omertà" is a serious limitation to the transparency of the European project and it adds much to our growing democratic deficit. Indeed, when important financial interests of certain companies (not all) are at stake, the Commission goes as far as to refuse the release of information, even to the Court of Justice of the EU, claiming such information may cause real harm.

In 2006, a European citizen who felt offended by the fact that the European Commission refused to grant him access to documents on an EU co-financed project, took the Commission to the Court of Justice of the EU asking for the release of the contracts on which the co-financed project was executed. The Court asked the Agents (lawyers) who defended the Commission to present the documents to the Court for the judges to decide if the documents could be released. The Commission informed the Court that its auditors visited the premises of the project beneficiary, and explicitly asked for the contracts and sub- contracts of the project. The Commission was stonewalled by the company despite the fact the company had benefitted from the Commission with funds amounting to €250m. The company simply refused to release the contracts claiming that it did not have them. The auditors returned to Brussels and no follow-up was given to this crazy situation.

If the company were not originating in one of the three Class A Member States, things would have been different. To start with, the Commission, upon the refusal of the release of the contracts and subcontracts of the project by the beneficiary, would have demanded total recovery of the €250m. Then, it would have sent the case to OLAF (the anti-fraud service of the European Union) for further investigation. In this specific case, OLAF, under German administration at the time, was aware of the Court Decision but did not bother to investigate. The fact that the company concerned was German was only coincidental...

In matters of "omertà" there is no significant qualitative difference between the "honourable societies" of South Europe and the System.

When Salvatore Riina, also known as Toto, La Belva (the beast) and U Curtu (the short one) the notorious "capo dei capi" leader of the Corleonesi family was put on trial in Palermo, he proudly refused to reveal information to the Court. This is "omertà". After the trial, Toto returned to Poggioreale penitentiary, in Napoli, in chains and his orange prison uniform.

Under analogous circumstances, after the Commission refused to a citizen the release of certain documents of a co- financed project which received a €250m grant, the latter took the Commission to the Court. Like Toto, in the context of the Brussels systemic "omertà," the Commission representative when asked by the Judge to present the documents to the Court refused, although it goes beyond any logical doubt that the Commission was in possession of such documents. Contrarily to Toto, however, who is still in Poggioreale serving a life sentence, the good case-handler took the train to Brussels and happily returned to his residence in Woluwe-Saint-Lambert.

Another element of the "omertà" is that, by Staff regulation, the System has established a perfect "reign of terror" among employees of all grades. Indeed, Commission personnel are legally prohibited from disclosing any information received in the line of duty. This provision is binding for life.

Not many years ago, a Commission official wrote a letter to the then-Secretary General of the European Commission asking permission to inform the Belgian Prosecutor about a case of possible fraud committed by the Department of Regional Policy, involving a major co-financed project in a Member State. Fraud is not an administrative violation, but a criminal act. The Secretary General replied that it was not necessary to inform the Belgian Prosecutor, as the "service" would be investigating the matter. The "service," however, never moved forward and the case was closed by the Secretariat General and OLAF. The latter (then under German administration) had opened an investigation, but then closed it with no reasonable explanation. Tell me about "accountability…"

Under the circumstances, it is worth mentioning what MEP Paul van Buitenen told to Deutsche Welle, on April 2, 2007:

"The European Anti-Fraud Office (OLAF) has had success in combating external corruption in the member states, but it is in the internal cases where it has found problems. Working with the EU authorities makes it very difficult to proceed in an investigation.

OLAF's independence exists only on paper.

Every time the committee is approached about corruption, it promises to improve the situation. But then a new case arises.

We must decide if we are to continue with the European arrangement. If we do, then we must also create these democratic structures at European level. Otherwise we should revert to allowing the national authorities and parliaments to take over the controlling functions again. But now, as it stands, everything goes wrong.

Things have got even worse. There is now a regulation which supposedly protects the so-called whistleblowers which makes officials

believe that they can uncover scandals. But in reality, if one does
this, is are destroyed. So the regulation does not work."

6/12 The Pilot Fish Eating
from the Sharks

In ancient Athens, Prytaneion was the place where citizens
with a significant contribution to the City could eat for free,
upon a decision of the City Assembly (participatory democracy concept, all Athenian citizens over 18 were voting),
known as the Ecclesia of Demos.

Among those "fed by the Prytaneion" were retired politicians and
personalities with exceptional contribution to the society. Among
others, to realize the spirit of this gesture, was the case of the "mules
of Parthenon." The marble used for the construction of Parthenon,
was pure white marble produced in the queries of Penteli, a mountainous suburb of Athens some 12 kilometers from the rock of Akropolis of Athens where Parthenon was built. The Parthenon marble
was carried by mules from Penteli to Akropolis. Upon arrival in
Akropolis, the mules were fed and then returned to Penteli to sleep
and start the next day carrying new marble for the temple. The mules
were used to the travel schedule and were going back and forth in
the same trail without any escort, for years. When the construction
of Parthenon finished, the mules continued to walk every day the
same trail without carrying any marble and were "fed in the Prytaneion," until they died.

The System has its own "citizens" with significant contribution to the "house." They are also fed for free by the Prytaneion of the Commission even after they retire in the form of consultants or "consigliori," like the "mules of Parthenon."

Today, "free eating" citizens can be found in NGOs, consultancy firms, media and other "charitable" institutions that are getting significant amounts and support from the System in a rather privileged manner. Others, not part of the inner circle of the Sublime Port, are excluded.

Quite possibly, it is not coincidental that in many of these, let's say, "privileged organizations" retired EU officials have been employed in various capacities. In some cases, such officials were owners or partners, in other cases, they served only as consultants.

Take one specific case for example. From all the 28 Member States, there are 30 or 40 big companies offering digital services. Of these, only two or three Brussels-based companies win most of the Commission tenders. Only a small part is assigned to companies based in other Member States.

There are two reasons the System is paying hundreds of millions every year for useful, but also useless, projects and to a small number of specific beneficiaries.

First, it is not their money, but the money of others. Second, by "feeding" them regularly, the System has built an army of mercenaries protecting it from intruders. Furthermore, in such privileged relations, no one can tell what other fringe benefits may eventually exist. The more so that nobody can guess the real dimension of reciprocity.

This becomes obvious in the pressroom of the European Commission. When a "difficult" situation is anticipated to arise, questions are given only to journalists considered to be "Commission friendly". In this way, they can use up all time that logically would be devoted to the "difficult" subject. The end of the story is that no time is left for embarrassing questions coming from other journalists.

All such questions are being methodically discussed ahead of time between the competent spokesperson and the "journalist" who will make the "tough" questions on this very hot topic.

As for the journalists of the big media networks, they are usually briefed before the official briefing and are also given or promised some exclusive story on another subject to make them happy and keep them quiet for the day.

Still, the way in which Commission money is donated to its "chosen" has a legitimate "look." Always, the money, little or big amounts – it makes no difference, is given through tenders. With one detail, often tenders are "photographic," that is the tender specifications are describing only one bidder. A second detail is that if such tenders were issued and allocated in any Member State the way the Commission does, the officials responsible for the "photographic" tender would be thrown in jail and their political boss would be, at the very least, banned from politics for the rest of his life. A typical case of "photographic tender" is documented in chapter "The Cancelled Tender."

The System is supporting certain organisations, not only by announcing "photographic" tenders and grants, but sometimes it does this in a very grotesque manner. There are cases where the Commission even promotes certain brands.

6/13 The Cronus Syndrome

Cronus (Saturn in Latin) was the son of Gaia (Earth) and Uranus (sky), and ruled together with his sister Rhea after he cut the testicles of his father. Cronus used a sickle given to him by his mother who had her good reasons. According to the myth, Cronus would have had the same faith of his father, to be betrayed by his children. Therefore, Cronus was systematically devouring his children upon birth.

So does the European Commission. With the 2001 reform, the notorious Neil Kinnock Administrative Reform, staff of the European Commission was reduced by 5,000 and salaries were scheduled to be gradually decrease. In 2016, the cumulative (gradual) salary reduction reached 30%. Several other benefits enjoyed by the EU staff were also curtailed. Despite that, employees of EU institutions, remain the best civil servants. Reductions and cuts, concern only those appointed after the Kinnock reform came into effect.

The reform introduced extensive outsourcing. This is done by private, mostly British and American companies, as well as through new Executive Agencies employing few Commission (permanent) employees and several hundred contractual agents.

In 1975, Great Britain became a Member of the Union and imposed a change in the pension scheme of all EU Institutions civil servants. The European Commission's employee pension fund was absorbed by the Community Budget, which since then provides for the pensions of the staff. The System did not react.

The question is quite simple. If, for any reason the European Commission collapses overnight, hopefully impossible yet not improbable, who will pay for the pensions of the retired Commission employees? Obviously, the Member States, but certainly at the same level of national pensions.

There will be two large categories of people affected: those who will lose their pension and those who will be losing their job and their pension prospects. The worst-case scenario is for those who are close to retirement and have a small or serious health problem.

Those losing their job most probably will remain unemployed except for those who will take a political position in their Member State of origin or will land a position of a high-level expert in their national administrations. Yet out of the 25,000 people permanently working with the European Commission, not to mention the European Parliament and the Council, a maximum of 5,000 will be settled in this or some other way.

The others would have to arrange something. Probably, a position in the government of their country of origin with a salary of that position that is, depending on the country from 3,000 to 8,000 Euros (before taxes). The private sector may pay more, but not much more. However, the working requirements, for middle positions, are very demanding.

What is the moral lesson of our working, hopefully groundless yet not improbable after the Brexit referendum, hypothesis? It is that the System does not care for its "children." Before the interests of the big Member States the devoted and respectful "children" of the Commission are just orphans.

6/14 Getting a Job in the Commission

The System is totally independent and self-reproducing, very similar to an hermaphrodite organism. In fact, it has all the characteristics of a single-cell organism.

The Commission, like other EU institutions, hires (does not recruit) personnel in two ways: either through internal vacancy announcements, or by opening a specific post to external candidates based on a list of selected candidates following an open competition.

Internal hiring is relatively simple. The position is announced internally and candidates express their interest. The Personnel Department of the relevant DG evaluates the CVs, interviews selected candidates, and the job is done. Employees with lower grade usually apply for such positions, to get to a higher grade. Frequently, this is one of the ways for the System to upgrade its "patricians." There is also the possibility of appealing the hiring decision in the European Court of Justice. The beauty of this whole exercise is that the System, if not happy with a Court decision, will just ignore it.

Outsiders who wish to work for the Commission have two options. To be hired either as a contractual agent (a temporary position) or as permanent staff.

Getting a contractual position with the Commission is easy if you have the right connection. The procedure is simple. One must upload a CV to the relevant database of the Commission. It is easy as there is an application form to fill out on the designated website. When a department, unit or whatever really needs someone for a specific job/ project and for a determined timeframe, it seeks out the applications under a totally transparent procedure.

The contractual agent must be chosen only from the relevant database. It does not matter if you have a Nobel Prize in Economics and the services are looking for an economic analyst. If the Nobel Prize laureate's CV is not in the database, the person will not be considered. Of course, nobody can guarantee that any person will be considered for any job once he/she is registered in the database (including the Nobel Prize laureate). The candidate will get the job only if the department, which needs a contractual agent, chooses him. This is life. Sometimes qualifications and availability is not all that matters.

If you have a friend, relative or whatever and a temporary position opens in his/her department, you are duly informed in time by your friend, and then you carefully fill in the form on the website to get registered in the database (everybody can do this). Then your friend will do his/her best to select you for the job and that's it. You can stay there for up to six years. Once you are there, you can participate in the procedure below and work on getting a permanent job.

Similar, but a little more complicated, is the procedure for getting a permanent job with the Institutions. From time to time, the Commission announces its intention to hire a small number of staff members for the coming year. The number may vary according to the projections made by its personnel gurus who look at the number of staff retiring/departing and calculate the new hiring needs of each Institution.

Once the number of new hires is decided, a competition is opened for every EU citizen to participate. Then a series of tests follows, most of them relatively easy. Indeed, there are a couple of books to read, common things one learns in any college that if memorized will provide an excellent chance to pass the test.

Only those who pass this process can be included on the "reserve list." What is the "reserve list?" It is an alphabetical list of those who have passed the tests. When the time comes for a DG to hire someone permanent, they consult with the "reserve list" and select.

To this effect, it is not uncommon to see that the son of a high-ranking official in the Commission is hired in one DG, of course, not related to the father. Then the daughter of another high-ranking boss is hired by the DG of the father of the first candidate. After a couple of years, within the internal hiring system, some positions open and the "exchange" takes place. If look at the carefully personnel hired by EPSO and their blood relation with "gods" and "semi-gods" of the Commission, in the last couple of years, then you will understand exactly how fair is the process.

On a parallel track, we see the selections of stagiaires (interns, trainees), young people who come from all over Europe to get a paid (or unpaid) specialization course in the EU services for short period (5 months), normally after university. Also in this case, there is an online application based on the CV and a large competition, which allows the inclusion of successful candidates on a list called the "Blue Book." Then the various departments chose their stagiaires, at will, from the Blue Book. This is a procedure, which leads to selection of well-connected, though less qualified, candidates who are chosen at the expense of applicants with postgraduate and PhD qualifications. (although the percentage of PhD is progressing among trainees)

The latest joke is the agency set on purpose to hire personnel. Is called European Personnel Selection Office (EPSO) and is headed by a …British. Why it is a joke? Because not few of the EPSO appointments, are annulled by the Court of Justice of the European Union!

GET TO KNOW EUROPE

7/1 Better than Товарищ Nikolai Ivanovich

If Nikolai Ivanovich (Bukharin), one of the founding fathers of Soviet propaganda, Editor of Pravda and Izvestia, were alive today and watching the Department of Communication of the European Commission (DG COMM), surely, he would be jealous. Undeniably, his work, as well as the work of his colleague Vladimir Ilyich (Lenin), looks grotesque compared to the state of the art "political communication" of the European Commission.

"Communicating Europe" is supposedly the System's most important task, but in practice it is the opposite. Not to communicate Europe. Everything is pre-set. What to communicate, how to tell you one thing and let you understand another, what to hide and how to do it. Manipulation of perceptions is a cult in Brussels and this is the context and the essence of political communication.

The System, to maintain control over half a billion people, has concentrated its efforts in two directions. They are both based on two essential elements of human nature: lack of sufficient knowledge and fear. Citizens do not understand the European Union because the truth about it is well-hidden. Consequently, they are afraid of the Union because they do not know what it is and thus they do not know how to handle it. The average citizen does not care about the Union because nobody ever told him/her what it is. The System works to keep citizens far from that knowledge.

People are terrified of what they do not understand. That is why people are afraid of God. Furthermore, people do what they do either from fear or for pleasure; there is no third option. European citizens behave the way they behave from the fear of the unknown.

The System is keeping citizens distant and in the dark. It works to keep them Europe illiterate. This is particularly true for middle level civil servants and ordinary businessmen who, if the Union had educated them, might prove to be troublemakers and demand a voice. So, it has set up the perception that merciless audits, penalties, fund recoveries and the threat of the national prosecutor is looming just around the corner. The System keeps citizens far from the light, constricted at the bottom of the dark cave of Plato.

In matters of working with the European Commission (funding, EU law enforcement etc.), the System, especially for class C Member States, has framed a kind of reign of terror by keeping the fear of sanctions in the public eye. This implies "economic and social death" so most entities and citizens opt to stay far from the "monster."

DG COMM, is the most unethical segment of the System. The staff is very well paid and enjoys special privileges such as close relations with media and political leaders in Member States and beyond. Its personnel are unconditionally faithful to the inner circle of the Commission.

Their task is to turn truth into lies without lying. The job is difficult and requires sophistication and extensive know-how. Bukharin and Lenin, not to mention Goebbels, had armies of theoreticians, academicians and agit-prop experts helping them. The task was relatively easy as they were addressing illiterate peasants and ordinary citizens in the context of an absolute dictatorship. The Commission is more successful than Bukharin and Lenin, with fewer people, while addressing intelligent, educated citizens in a supposedly democratic setting. They are *"la crème de la crème"* of professionals, true masters of strategic communication.

Every day, the Commission has several stories to sell and DG COMM must prepare the narrative and handle the management of perceptions. The System decides and DG COMM implements. It decides which stories will be opened to the public, which will not, and which will be hidden or distorted.

To summarise, while DG COMM is good in manipulations, in turning lies into truths and it also very professional in character assassinations (with others' money you can buy everything), has no real communication know-how. Indeed, the Commission spent many millions to communicate to the Brits that they had to stay in the EU and it gloriously failed.

7/2 Truth Well Hidden

Hiding the truth is the most important task for he Communications Department of the Commission (DG COMM), as there are facts and details citizens should not know. For instance, I was told of a fantastic story about something that happened a couple of decades ago to an Agent (lawyer) of the Commission who was to deliver penalty notices amounting to a total of €10m (ECU at the time) to five companies.

They had violated competition law having formed a cartel in their sector. The Agent of the Legal Service, took the five penalty notices, put on his black suit and began the deliveries. Out of the five "beneficiaries" of the penalties, one company could not afford it and went bankrupt.

Two paid immediately, one went to the Court of Justice of the EU where it lost the case and ended up paying. The fifth did not pay.

Why did the fifth company not pay I cannot say for sure. However, what I have heard from Brussels sources is a nice explanation, which "se non e vero, e ben trovato". However, as the Commission is not famous for being generous, unless it had a reason not to claim the penalty, it could well be "vero."

The Agent went to the fifth EU law transgressor to deliver the penalty notification. He was well received and was offered coffee, which he refused. However, the host insisted and the secretary brought a coffee and a glass of water. The Agent, ignoring the coffee, opened his briefcase and presented the penalty notice together with a delivery receipt. He handed the documents to the person concerned and kindly asked him to sign.

The host disregarded the receipt, gave back the notice to the Agent, pulled a nine-millimetre calibre from his desk drawer, pointed to the head of the Agent and very softly said: "If you please, eat it, drink your water and then go back to Brussels with my regards." When you have a 9mm under your nose, believe me you eat everything. At least the good Commission Agent was offered mineral water (sparkling) to... digest it.

The System decided to forget the penalty and disregard the incident, as if it never happened. The reason is simple. The Commission was afraid that by punishing the violator it would have set a "bad precedent" for repetition of similar reactions in various cases, in other countries. Similar situations, some of which resulted in even physical injuries of the auditors in South Italy, occurred during the audits of olive trees and hard wheat subsidies. All such incidents were silently closed.

This could be one extreme case. However, if you look around, you will discover many cases of citizens' tough reactions to audits, especially in the case of agricultural subsidies. Indeed, most audits of this kind were concluded in local restaurants offered by the cooperative of the area and there were cases where the auditors determined to audit, were "convinced" to abandon the idea. Also, these kinds of incidents are hidden and do not get any publicity. The System protects its image and reputation.

However, there are cases more serious that the Commission is hiding from citizens and this is every day practice. Legitimate decisions which are taken to favour one specific concern, which in most cases is mentioned by name, are kept secret. Even College Decisions are kept confidential. The reason for hiding such personalized decisions, although legal, is that other concerns in similar situations should not know in order not to take advantage of such benefit.

That is why sometimes when people refer to the EU call it Yevropeysky Soyuz.

7/3 The Management of Perceptions

The priority of DG COMM and the Spokesperson Service is the manipulation of the pressroom briefing. This is very important, as the place is full of journalists, not all of them "System friendly." Furthermore, all press events are broadcast live (with a certain unreasonable time lag). This is done by the Commissions' TV network Europe by Satellite (EbS). Private networks also do live broadcasting, but only on rare occasions when there is enough of a special interest to send a camera crew.

Briefings are pre-set. Journalists who will be allowed a question are usually arranged with the spokesperson service and everyone is happy. The System allows and promotes only the questions it wants, while there is no time for other unpleasant questions or non-friendly journalists. Simply, once the pre-agreed questions are finished, the spokesperson on the floor says, "so far so good, have a good day" and leaves from the back door, just behind the podium, no matter how many journalists are raising hands with unanswered questions.

Questions on major policy matters are discussed with major media in advance and they are quite open. Therefore, the dialogue is smooth. Deals among big players are easy and simple. I give one thing to you, you give one thing to me, and we are even.

The Commission does not allow questions that are embarrassing for the System. Journalists who are given the floor are aware of this. They do not complain, however, as they are systematically given exclusive and important scoops, in fair distribution among "System-friendly" media.

Other journalists do not have the chance to ask questions, unless they compromise with reality. If the situation gets out of control, for one reason or another, the spokesperson in charge takes the question and says: "I have to check and will come back to you with an email" and then leaves. The email reply will be general and vague and the issue will never be raised again in the pressroom.

Journalists from Member States visiting with national politicians are not a problem for the System as they are pre-selected for the trip. Questions are usually limited to the purpose of the official visit and possibly to current affairs in the Member State concerned. The visit is concluded with a joint press conference of the visiting Head of State and the President of the Commission or the visiting Minister with the competent Commissioner. The event takes place in a mini- pressroom known as "Press Point" on the ground floor of the Berlaymont building. The event has a luxurious look and is broadcast, live or the same evening, by national networks to much satisfaction of the visitors. As to what is spoken at the press conference is irrelevant, as everything is pre-set.

In general terms, this is the way of communicating Europe to the citizens. With the Spokespersons Service and the pressroom of the Commission, the System manages the perceptions of half a billion Europeans.

An equally important task of the noble institution is to methodically misinform opinion leaders and decision makers in Brussels, in cases where the System decides to destabilise national governments. If national governments of small Member States are not cooperative, the Commission has ways to destabilise them. From merciless and unjustified audits to selective flow of information to Commission decision-makers channelled from the inner circle of the System, and nasty articles in national media routed in off-the-record diners of the Representation staff with selected journalists.

The Commission maintains offices in all Member States called Representations, which file to Brussels a brief daily report (usually one page) summarising the main themes of national media. It is a kind of brief clipping service. Logical as it is necessary. The Commission should know what national media are reporting, especially in matters concerning the European Union. The added value of such contributions, however, is very limited.

Yet, such otherwise innocent reports are CONFIDENTIAL and are selectively distributed within the Commission only. The government services of the Member State concerned do not have access to such reports. This is ridiculous because what is the European Union? A Union of States and the Commission with its extensions should be their Coordinating Secretariat. The Commission is not a political entity that is democratically elected by the people of Europe. It is an appointed administrative body and that is it. The fact that it has managed to become the overlords of the European Union is something to seriously consider and seriously address.

Why Representations behave in this way is simple. Heads of Representation are an integral part of the System. They are confidentially instructed by the Commission, DG COMM in this case, about which media to use (pro-government or pro-opposition) according the country and the relation of the System with the current government. The fact that the Commissioner of the country has a say in the appointments in the Representation of his/her country has little impact. Commission employees of all grades are first faithful to the "House." Motherland comes second.

One flagrant example is the FLASH REPORT from Athens, dated 10 January 2008. It reproduced information from opposition papers criticising the then government (which the System disliked and contributed to destabilise and overthrow). The document was prepared by the Head of the European Union Representation, who the System was keeping in Athens in violation of a Court of Justice of the EU ruling for his removal. Title of the Commission internal (confidential) report was, "SEX LIES and DVDs" with similar content. The report, which is not reporting what national media say but is criticising a democratically elected government of a Member State, was prepared by a "mujahideen" of the System and was never notified to the government concerned, as it was classified CONFIDENTIAL. Why it was confidential is known only to God.

Like this, there are thousands of reports from the 28 member States. These reports aim at building the image of national politicians in the way the System wants to support or degrade them. This is a subtle, yet efficient, way of intervening in domestic affairs of Member States.

Kassandra's NOTEBOOK

NE 764, January 13 - 19, 2008

Kassandra@neurope.eu Fax.+32 2 6390839

Liars, Bias and Disinformazia

We present this week the Internal Document of the European Commission Flash Report number 50417 of December 17, 2007. The report was filed by the Representation office of the Commission in one of the 27 Member States and concerns domestic political affairs of the Member State. The report was secretly handled by the Commission and was not notified to Member State concerned. We have in our hands many similar reports and to give an idea as to how the Commission is handling highly sensitive issues concerning the private facets of life of political officials in Member States we also reprint the title of another report, sent from the same Commission's Delegation, on January 10, 2008.

Representation in Greece
FLASH REPORT
Athens, 17/12/2007
Internal document 50417

EUROPEAN COMMISSION
DIRECTORATE-GENERAL COMMUNICATION

Ref. No. D21607

REPORT FROM ATHENS
RESIGNATION OF EMPLOYMENT MINISTER
Ioanihnos PAPADOPOULOS

Summary: Another headache for the government. The Employment Minister has been obliged to resign, following multiple allegations of wrong-doing in his private life. The new Minister is Ms Palli-Petralia, former Minister of Tourism. The government claims no changes in its policies regarding the reform of the social security/pension scheme, despite the widespread negative reactions of the public and the media.

The Commission's Delegation report lied in presenting the resignation of Employment Minister Vassilis Magginas . The writer of the report claims that Mr. Magginas "has been obliged to resigned." The truth is what Mr. Magginas stated, that he resigned on his own initiative, for reasons of political sensitivity.

Representation in Greece
FLASH REPORT
Athens, 10/01/2008
Internal document 50468

EUROPEAN COMMISSION
DIRECTORATE-GENERAL COMMUNICATION
Made-Madeleine ICANTELOPOULOU
Ref. No. D/282

REPORT FROM ATHENS
"SEX, LIES AND DVDs"
Ioanihnos PAPADOPOULOS (signed)

This is the title of a recent Commission's Delegation report. Regardless the fact that it does not reflect the Commission's position on the matter, the Commission disseminated the report confidentially to selected high ranking officials without denying thus damaging the image of the government concerned among the services, without the government of the country having the minimum knowledge of what is said behind its back. This is the usual way the Commission is formulating the climate among the services, thus damaging or upgrading at her will, the political image of member States.

The re-birth of Stalinism

These reports are supposed to be press reviews of local media. Yet, they are not, because in no place is a reference made to specific media and no names of journalists or analysts are mentioned. The reports, at least in the case of Athens, include the opinions of the head of the local Commission office, exclusively reflecting the views of the opposition parties and serious lies, as well as misleading conclusions based on imaginary analysis. The report damages the image of the Member State among Commission services, without the Member State having any knowledge, thus undermining its negotiations with Commission services. This methodology - for the defendant not to be informed of what and by whom he was accused and to be sentenced *in absentia* in secret trials - was used only by Stalin in the 1930s and by the Holy Inquisition in the Dark Ages. In our case, in the 21st Century, an anonymous, accountable-to-nobody low-grade civil servant has the power to compromise the efforts of a senior Member State of the European Union, without the Member State having knowledge by whom and of what it was accused.

Spying instead of working together

With such a Stalinist methodology, relations for Commission and Member States, instead of being smooth, cooperative and complementary, became inimical, hostile, and, for no reason, competitive. This is the real problem and it implies that the role and the methods of such offices should be redefined. The role of Commission offices in Member States is not to spy on governments but to communicate Europe to EU citizens. We should not forget that if the Constitution failed to be approved in France and in Holland that it was mainly because the corresponding

EU Representation offices, instead of communicating Europe to the citizens and by talking to the media about the Constitution under referendum, were using their efforts and resources toward other activities, probably similar to those of their colleague in Athens.

The Greek Connection

To implement the picture of the Athens case, we have to add that when the Athens post was opened three years ago, from six or seven applicants, the Department of Communication produced a short list of three candidates called for an interview. The man who got the job was third on the list and was included because the Department of Communication decided - after 27 years - to downgrade the requirements of the post. Indeed, Mr. Papadopoulos at the time was grade A5 (upgraded from grade B). Until then, the post required an A3 grade or better. It must be added that the chosen candidate has strong friendship ties with the wife of the Director General and the Deputy Director General of the Department of Communication. Politically, the candidate was supported by the Greek Socialists, which explains why Commissioner Margot Wallstrom did not satisfy the request of the Greek Commissioner to make the appointment on the basis of merit. This also explains why the Commission's Representation office in Athens informed Brussels last summer that Commissioner Stavros Dimas (who although he had a completely curable, routine retinal detachment problem and

was immobilised only for a couple of weeks), was about to die. Commissioner Dimas was very much upset when he was informed by several sources in Athens and Brussels he was about die. The appointment of Mr. Papadopoulos was presented to Commissioner Margot Wallstrom as a unanimous decision of the service, but at the time she intelligently passed the initiative of the appointment to Administration Commissioner Siim Kallas.

The *Omerta* Syndrome

Unfortunately, the Department of Communication is not the only service the Commissioner has to deal with and impose its political presence on a techno-structure based on a *sui generis omerta*. What is to blame for that? The most important, in our view, is that the Commission, although it behaves as if it is the government of United Europe, is only a Secretariat of the Council because it exerts no political power. President José Barroso is a good, intelligent politician and was a good prime Minister. But he proved to be a good Prime Minister because he was leading a government where all the members were of his choosing and he could replace any of them, at any time. In a few words, he could rule on the basis of political discipline. What options does President Barroso have in Brussels? He did not choose any of the Members of what is euphemistically called "The Barroso Commission." Each of his Commissioners was appointed by a different European government representing different political parties and now has any reason to fol-

low any political discipline. Mr. Barroso has a given College of all colours, right, left, and centre, and cannot fire any of them.

The Power Elite

That is why the executive, the techno-structure, is arbitrarily assuming political responsibilities and trying to secure powers to which it is not entitled by usurping them from the politicians. The Brussels techno-structure takes advantage of this basic shortcoming and has silently been transformed into a "power elite" working behind the scenes, deciding many important issues of daily life for the ordinary people of Europe, without any of them having any knowledge or any possibility to oppose or negotiate what happens. Indeed, the lack of a political Commission has given the opportunity to the administration to interpret, instead of enforcing legislation. The sociologist C. Wright Mills has depicted this phenomenon very eloquently:

The "power elite" is composed of men whose positions enable them to transcend the ordinary environments of ordinary men and women; they are in positions to make decisions having major consequences. Whether they do or do not make such decisions is less important than the fact that they do occupy such pivotal positions; their failure to act, their failure to make decisions is itself an act that is often of greater significance than the decisions they do make. For they are in command of the major hierarchies and organizations of modern society. They rule the big corporations. They run the machinery of state and claim its prerogatives. They direct the military establishment. They occupy strategic command posts of the social structure in which are now centered the effec-

tive means of power and the wealth and celebrity which they enjoy.

All this comes to a logical consideration: how and why the European Commission is legitimised to spy on Member States. Why do the Member States not get copies of such espionage reports to defend themselves from possibly false allegations submitted by low-ranking employees who, for their own reasons, may feed the European Commission with bias and lies? Why are the member States not given the benefit to defend themselves from the disinformation of any potential Mr. Papadopoulos, who, hiding behind the secrecy of Commission documents and the coverage of their supervisors, can influence the relation of Member States and the Commission on the basis of lies? All over Europe there are another 26 potential Papadopouloi, spying daily on the governments of the countries who host them. The unveiling of this deplorable Commission report presented in *New Europe* is an opportunity for President José Barroso and Vice President Margot Wallstrom to review from a zero base the role and tasks of the Commission's Representation offices in the European Union capitals and build better and more sound relations with Member States, based on transparency, frankness and truthfulness, and not on lies and practices which remind of the notorious *Komityet Gosudarstvennoy Bezopasnosti* (KGB). Thus, the role of the Commission's Delegations in Member States cannot be similar to those of Embassies in foreign countries, as the Commission claims (Commission's briefing January 11, 2008) in order to justify the regrettable performance of its Athens subsidiary. Member States are not foreign countries and Delegations in Member States have nothing to do with foreign Embassies. Indeed, I don't think that Commissioner Margot Wallstrom would be particularly happy to find out one day that the activities of the Commission Delegation in Stockholm and those of the American Embassy in Teheran are similar.

FLASH REPORT
To realize how the Commission services work to undermine the credibility of certain Member States, we have to notice that the notorious report was internally distributed on January 10, 2008 and the day after, January 11, it was leaked to London's **Telegraph**. The British newspaper printed a story with the same content and used the very original title of the report of Mr. Papadopoulos, **"SEX, LIES and DVDs."**

7/4 The Cancelled Tender

On 19 June 2013, the Directorate General of Communication of the European Commission (DG COMM) issued a tender with the imminent deadline of 16 August 2013. The tender, PG/2013-9/A6 DG COMM A6 was called for the creation of an "independent trusted site" dedicated to "provide news," yet matching "the political priorities of the EC agenda." The tender detailed how the organisation had to justify the inclusion of every story to Commission officials.

In midsummer, the European Commission asked serious media groups, to prepare quotes for a tender providing for the organisation of a multilingual, multimedia news service based in 10 languages. No serious organisation could prepare such a tender in such a short time (less than two months). And more so that in midsummer all major enterprises in Europe operate with skeleton staff.

Unless the "cards" were stacked, and they were. The tender was "photographic", that is it was written so only one organisation could meet all the requirements.

This is proven by the fact that after a letter I wrote to the then Vice President of the European Commission in midsummer, the tender was immediately cancelled. Where is the scandal? That the tender, was cancelled without any explanation or excuse and nothing followed. The issue was not referred to OLAF, the anti-fraud service of the Commission, and not even an internal investigation was launched. The tender was cancelled on a simple complaint and nothing happened afterwards. This is the accountability of the European Commission.

On July 9, while I was in Corfu on summer vacation, I got a call from a friend who sent me the link to the tender documentation. He ingenuously said, "This is for you, go and take it." I checked the tender specifications and called him back. "This is not for me. This is for ….. and I gave him the name of the company, photographically depicted in the tender terms of reference. Yet I will cancel it." My friend said, "Dream on."

Same evening, looking at the call for tenders and knowing the integrity of the then Commissioner in Charge of Media, Viviane Reding, who was also on vacation at the time, I wrote her a letter bringing to her attention the following.

Dear Vice President Reding,

At a time of austerity why is the EU planning to spend £2.75 million a year on a news service? No, dear vice President, to the EU "Pravda".

We read on page 2 under the heading Objective and Context of the tender, "EU affairs are not under-represented in printed and digital media," as the tender PG/2013-9/A6 claims in its introductory statement (&2, p. 3). As with this tender "the European Commission wants to create an online media dedicated to provide news etc.," and as the subject of the tender is only digital (not print) media, we wish to underline the following.

(1) We notice at least four digital media platforms with original news and news analysis, specializing in EU affairs all four with excellent Google and global Alexa rank high have the following traffic, according to Alexa, (July 5, 2013): New Europe (neurope.eu) 53,437 Euractiv (euractive.com) 85,119 EU Observer (euobserver. com) 110,206 European Voice (europeanvoice.com) 285,943

Under the circumstances, the claim that there is not a specialized platform is demonstrably false. Therefore, why does the EC not offer independent support to existing independent media?

(2) The claim that the Internet is increasingly trusted would be worth a close examination. The idea that people trust the Internet more is dubious, perhaps they trust media organizations on the Internet more. However, what is certainly true is that citizens trust the EU increasingly less. This is an argument for the EU to stay out of news gathering, selection and reporting.

(3) The Commission suggests various cutting edge reporting methods, which are actually being regularly used by existing Brussels media, blogs, integrating social media, live blogs and so on. 50% of content will be 'harvested' from 'trusted sites.' Could the EC define what is exactly a 'trusted site'? Can they list some untrustworthy sites?

(4) It is hard to see the 'independence' in the tender when it is the EC that has financial and editorial control on news released.

(5) Choosing articles because they match the "political priorities" of the EC agenda is an attempt by the EC to take over and control independent reporting. Furthermore, reports to the EC must contain "a justification of the choices made," which is not really compatible with independence.

(6) The Elephant In The Room: How exactly is a EC news website going to attract visitors in significant enough numbers across the EU? Likely Reaction: It is not hard to see how this will play in the Eurosceptic and independent press in view of the European election of May 2014: 'EU pays millions for Pravda, diversify the present EU-affairs propaganda news.'

(7) Finally, as we think it is not necessary, we do not wish to comment on the specifications of the tender as well as to issues relating to the EU subsidization of activities competing free media enterprises in times survival of independent media is an extremely difficult endeavour. Indeed, among the criteria for participation the call for tenders provide, "Ability to deliver creative and innovative solutions. As evidence, he will provide a list of 2 to 5 projects carried out in

the past five years, for a minimum value of 2 million €, showing at best his capacity in European journalism."

This provision and the fact that the services required by the tender are already produced only by a specific company under other economically supported activities (most by the Commission), indicates that the tender specifications are "photographic" for the specific company which I am sure you yourself can pronounce without second thought.

Under the circumstances, we wish to invite the European Commission to revoke the above tender.

(signed) Basil A. Coronakis

The vice President was quick to respond to our complaint and cancelled the tender. To this effect, we received from the Director General of DG Communication, the letter (printed at the end of this story) announcing, the cancellation of the tender, without providing any further explanation.

So far so good. Viviane Reding was informed and cancelled at once a photographic tender, but what was the follow-up on this matter?

NOTHING!

No one was asked to give explanation and no report from DG COMM was sent to the investigative authority of the European Union OLAF.

In any Member State, at least five or six civil servants would be called to testify before the prosecutor and a couple of them would be fired and sentenced to jail while the minister in charge would have resigned. In Brussels, nothing happened and business continued as usual. And then you wonder why Euroscepticism is growing.

At the time of the cancelled DG COMM tender, Martin Selmayr was Head of Cabinet of Commissioner Viviane Reding (in the Juncker Commission Head of Cabinet of the President).

EUROPEAN COMMISSION
DIRECTORATE-GENERAL COMMUNICATION

Director-General

Brussels, 24/07/2013
COMM/A6/LB/Ares(2013)

Mr Basil Coronakis
CEO
New Europe Media Group
96, Avenue de Tervueren
1040 Bruxelles
Belgique

BY EMAIL
coronakis@gmail.com

Dear Mr Coronakis,

Thank you for your letter of the 9th July 2013 addressed to Vice-President Reding, who has asked me to answer on her behalf.

The Commission decided to cancel the call for tenders for the development, implementation and management of an Online Media on EU Affairs. A notice to this effect has been published in TED, the online version of the 'Supplement to the Official Journal of the European Union' dedicated to European public procurement.

http://ted.europa.eu/udl?uri=TED:NOTICE:235140-2013:TEXT:EN:HTML

Yours sincerely,

Gregory Paulger

Annex: Martin Selmayr, Head of Cabinet of Vice President Viviane Reding.

Commission européenne, B-1000 Bruxelles / Europese Commissie, B-1000 Brussel - Belgium. Telephone: +32 2 299 11 11
Office: 56, Rue de la Loi 06/007. Telephone: direct line +32 2 299 94 34

http://ec.europa.eu/dgs/communication
e-mail: gregory.paulger@ec.europa.eu

ANATOMY OF THE LOOT

8/1 Structural Funds, the Rape

Structural Funds are aimed at the development of public infrastructure in Member States and at promoting economic, social and territorial cohesion. In matters of allocating funds, the procedure is relatively simple.

At the political level (i.e. the government), the three big players, France, Germany and the UK, the System informally decides how to split the big projects. This concerns more than half of the co-financed projects every year. It is the money part that returns to the big three and to some others, as political money, safe and clean. All other sources of political money in Member States such as bribes from arms purchases and the like are highly risky and have nothing to do with EU funding.

Only Brussels money is safe. Brussels funds, originating from Member State contributions, are transferred to large contractors doing over-priced projects in Member States. From there, money from over-charging together with profits return to the contractors and the loot is distributed, as agreed.

This state-of-the-art operation is locked from any further controls by the audits implemented by the System.

Look for instance at this:

OLAF, the anti-fraud Service of the European Union, investigated a case of a "non-entity", a "Thing" that claimed to be an international organisation. OLAF, based on documents presented by the "Thing," concluded that this non-entity was not an international organisation, and as such it was not eligible for funding. Details on the "Thing" case are in chapter "The "Thing" and the Flight of hundreds of million euros." In brief, the "Thing" had received the money in a bank account in France (some €135 million only from the Commission). OLAF concluded that since the money was transferred to a bank account of the "Thing" in France (the "Thing" was registered in Serbia and had nothing to do with France), "this reveals indications of possible fraud associated with money laundering."

On this specific matter, the Legal Service of the Commission, in an obvious effort to cover-up the case in order not to expose "colleagues" who are part of the System's inner circle and were involved with the in the case, issued the following opinion on 16 January 2015:

"As to the alleged "associated money laundering," (i.e. claimed by OLAF) in the absence of convincing indications of fraud the Legal Service fails to see how and why the transfer of Union funds to an account in France could in and of itself raise suspicions of money laundering, as those funds did not derive from criminal activity." (Legal analysis No. 2015/199435, paragraph 49 by the Legal Service of the European Commission, on the OLAF investigation OF/2011/1002).

Of course, the legal opinion of the Legal Service signed by the Director General himself, did not say anything about where was the money transferred after it was disbursed by the Commission to a French bank account, (which as such is not justifiable in the first place), Where it was channelled after the transfer to the French bank? Who got what? Why and how? The Legal Service did not bother to ask those questions.

But let's stay on the subject. Once Structural Funds are allocated and major projects are assigned, the System often decides which company will take each project and the services are orally informed.

An example of this routine is given in the next chapter, "The Athens Airport Robbery." In a closed-door meeting of the College, it was decided that the two major projects for Greece would be assigned: the construction of the airport would go to the Germans and the construction of the metro with its extensions to the French.

Immediately after, the Cabinet of the German Commissioner informed the Director General of Regional Policy (Structural Funds) what the decision was. He further said that Germany thinks that Hochtiev AG was a very good company to be assigned the project. The information was passed discretely, by word of mouth, to the competent department and a functionary travelled to Athens and informed, always by word of mouth, the Minister of Public Works. After a nice dinner with fresh fish in Piraeus, the functionary returned to Brussels happy, as all was set as agreed.

The Director General knew that if the would have disagreed with the choice presented to him by the Cabinet of the German Commissioner, in the next change of Directors General, if not before, would be given retirement with Article 50 of the Staff Regulation. His services understood by following the wishes of the boss everything would go smoothly and that they would be covered in case of Complaints. They also knew that disobeying would signify the end of their career.

The Minister of Public Works in the Member State was aware, that by following instructions, they would be left a small amount of the money allocated for the project, usually from 20% to 50% to distribute among local subcontractors to do the job, while in case of Complaints he would be covered by the System. The Minister also knew that in the case of refusal, it was highly likely that the application for assistance for building the new airport would be rejected, while the Department of Regional Policy of the Commission would have sent its auditors to audit some past project and recover a few hundred million.

The Minister also knew that biggest part of the funding was not paid to the subcontractors who did the job, but was taken by the initial contractor. That part of the business will never be audited, by anyone.

8/2 The Athens Airport Robbery

The sad story of the construction and management of the new Athens International Airport Eleftherios Venizelos is not a scandal. It is a crime that led to the requiem of a country: Greece.

Indeed, if the construction of the airport was paid at real cost, charges to passengers and airlines would be among the cheapest in Europe (today they are among the most expensive). Thus, tourist arrivals in Greece would be at least double and the economic catastrophe of the country would have been avoided. It is as simple as that.

The construction of the airport, one terminal, two corridors and 114,000 m2 of cheap construction (passenger building and airplane depot), which under normal conditions in the year 2000 would have cost no more than €250m, was invoiced at €2.25bn, of which little more than one billion was a loan from the European Investment Bank. That loan, which was not needed, had to be repaid with interest. The difference between the real cost (which probably was even less the €250m, because the contractors were paying very cheap local sub-contractors) and what appeared to be the cost of the airport in the papers, little more than €2bn, was the loot.

As a result, airport taxes (to depreciate the €1bn loan received from the EIB) have been, since 2000, among the highest in Europe. The airport taxes amount to €35 per passenger (passenger charges) plus on average €10 per passenger extra charges to the airlines. This gives a total of €45 per passenger, compared to €12 per passenger at the Madrid airport, Barajas.

This is the crime against Greece, which instead of welcoming 20 million tourists per year would have at least 40 million. And, given that tourism is the main industry of the country, the catastrophic crisis of the past six years would have been avoided or at least manageable.

The story is sad and reminds me practices of Cosa Nostra.

On 15 March 1996, the then Greek government (Socialist administration under Prime Minister Costas Simitis) filed the final (revised) application for Cohesion Fund assistance under Council Regulation (EC) No. 1164/94, asking for a grant of €250m for the project of the construction of the new Athens International Airport at Spata.

The first page of the Application for Assistance by the member State Greece, says: The Cohesion Fund: Application for Assistance. Organization Responsible for the Project Implementation: Athens International Airport S.A., Suite 815 Divani Caravel Hotel, Athens.

"Athens International Airport SA" (AIA) is a profit-making enterprise without serving any public interest. It was formed by the partnership of a German joint venture (45%) and the Greek state (55%). That AIA is a private law company, as it is explicitly stated in its bylaws and in article 12.2.6 of Greek Law 2338/1995 which ratified the airport development agreement as well as by two Greek Court Decisions (No. 6190/97 and No7144/99) which ruled that AIA is a private law enterprise.

Indeed, five members of the nine-member board of the AIA Company are not appointed by the Greek state which controls its 55% but from the minority shareholders who control only 45%. The minority shareholders (German joint venture) appoint the management of the company. This is an exception that is against Greek and Community corporate laws, but which is valid because tailor-made Greek Law 2338/1995 ratified it.

In the Cohesion Fund Application for Assistance, under "Organisation Responsible for the Project Implementation" and "Organisation to which Payments are to be Made" the Greek authorities clearly indicate "Athens International Airport SA" (AIA). Profit-making companies not serving public interest cannot be direct beneficiaries of assistance, but only indirect. This means that between the government of the member state, which gets the EU Funds for a project, and the investor who ultimately benefits from such funds, an intermediate authority to make partial payments and control and audit the progress of the project's implementation were to be established. As it was not, the Commission should have returned the application to the Member State, asking them to indicate the intermediary (state) authority. But it did not.

On the contrary, on 23 May 1996, the College (the body of the Commissioners) approved the €250m grant by Commission Decision 1996/1356 (final). In page 8 of Annex I of such Decision, says: "Authority responsible for the implementation: Athens International Airport."

The Decision was signed for and on behalf of the College by the then Commissioner for Regional Policy, Mrs. Monika Wulf-Mathies (a German, appointed by the SPD Socialist party). The Commission accepted the application as it was and simply falsified the nature of the private company and upgraded it to "authority" (state entity) removing from the title of the company the letters SA, thus changing the real status of the airport company. In this way, the Commission did not only entrust the EU grant of €250m at member state level to a virtual Authority but it entrusted to it the entire project of €2.25bn, which was almost exclusively public money (EU grants, Commission recommended state guaranteed EIB loan of €1bn and €300m national grant) to the same "Authority."

Finally, although requested on the grounds of Regulation (EC) 1049/2001 on Public Access to Commission, Council and Parliament Documents, the Commission refused the release of the final technical report on the reception of the project and it did not reveal the Authority, which endorsed and accepted such a report.

Can you guess why? In practical terms, the Commission, in clear violation of Community law, entrusted a private profit-making company not serving public interest to act as (1) employer (AIA), (2) contractor (the German mother company which is managing AIA) and (3) implementing Authority in one of the biggest EU- funded European projects, thus holding at least three capacities. This unprecedented act was committed by the Santer Commission and enjoyed the political coverage of the Prodi Commission, and of President Romano Prodi himself.

In the past 15 years of operation, the profits of the Athens Airport are estimated around €6-7bn which include over €1.5bn VAT that the company refused to pay to the Greek government since it began operations in the year 2000. And all this even though operations of the Athens International Airport, are not exempted or derogated from VAT payments (Council Directive 2006/112/EC of 28 November 2006).

As for the construction costs, considering buildings of 114,000 m2 (covered) at €500 per m2 (maximum for the year 2000, the land was already given planed by the state, two corridors of 3km each at €2m per kilometre, plus €20m parallel (simple) roads, plus lighting two corridors maximum €10m, plus the control tower another €10m, plus contractors' profits, the entire bill comes to about €250m. This compares to the total cost of €2.25bn.

Finally, the Airport Company built six grand department stores between the two corridors, at 2 km from the terminal. The land was part of the expropriated land (Art. 17 of the Greek Constitution) for building the airport. According to same article, expropriated land cannot be used for other purposes except for the reasons cited in the expropriation. Therefore, all big stores where built illegally, without a building permit.

Furthermore, same on land expropriated under the same procedure, the Airport Company build a huge exhibition centre, the biggest in Greece.

To summarise, while the cost of the Athens airport, did not exceed the amount of €250m, thanks to "creative patents" of the European Commission the amount that was paid was €2.25bn. As a result, passengers pay the highest airport fees in Europe reducing permanently the tourist potential of Greece at least to one half.

8/3 Programmes, the Looting

The difference between Structural Funds and the various Programmes is simple and clear. With Structural Funds, serious amounts of EU money is channelled into the pockets of people who shouldn't be receiving it. Yet, at the end of the day, an infrastructure project is done and the Member State, even if the project faced serious cost overruns, gets something: a highway, an airport, a railway, something real and tangible, which is useful to the society and improves the life of ordinary citizens.

Infrastructure projects last and remain for future generations even if during the implementation of the project, the budget was overspent, and bribes were flying in all directions.

The "beauty" of EU's Programmes is that all money allocated, billions of Euro every year, is spent with little (if any) benefit to society, through procedures that benefit only a few. Indeed, the beneficiaries are certain types of "qualifying" organisations, such as universities, select municipalities, research and various centres, friendly NGOs as well as the Commission staff managing the funding.

Beneficiaries get the money not because they necessarily have the top scientific capacity, but thanks to the ability they have developed to handle complicated (and mostly useless) bureaucratic procedures and formalities and to fill in the application documents adequately. You may have two or three Nobel Prize winners on your team but since in your 600-page project proposal you couldn't comply with the formalities and you are not among the "chosen ones" you will be disqualified.

Hence, it is necessary to hire a group of so-called "experts" to write the proposal. Such "experts" have in fact as sole expertise their knowledge of the Commission's bureaucracy. It is not rare that they also have the proper contacts among Heads of Unit and Case Handlers.

As to the benefits for the Commission staff, it is mostly about justifying their otherwise useless existence and building a nice career with all the "goodies:" great tax-free salaries, fringe benefits, friendships and power. In Napoli, they claim *"u cummana è meglio che fottere."*

There are several EU Programmes worth several billion Euros each, such as Horizon2020, LIFE, INTERREG, MOBILITY, MEDIA, ERASMUS, COSME etc., but still very few people can effectively participate in most of them with reasonable chances of being selected. Information is available in huge quantities, but it is vague and only those specialising in bureaucracy, and with some links to the System can decipher the terms and compete successfully.

In the past, projects used to be assigned in proportion to Member States size. Under such practice, local authorities were inviting national calls for tenders and assigning the various projects of the specific Programme. The various Commission departments in charge were limited to doing the audits.

However, using various arguments, like the fairy-tale that in Member States there is corruption while in the European Commission there is none (!), the System managed to obtain responsibility for the allocation of these funds under its jurisdiction. Thus, with the exception of media and Erasmus, Member States are excluded from the process of distributing the funds to beneficiaries. Now, this privilege was transferred to the Commission services and the money is distributed to the "chosen" few by the Commission. And, no matter whether the playmaker of this loot is i.e., a Head of Unit in DG Energy who managed to build his own "kingdom" within the System maintaining his (sensitive) post for decades or a Commission Delegation, it makes no difference. It is the Commission in its entirety that European citizens consider responsible for the loot.

It is also worth mentioning that in the context of taking over the distribution of funds for Programmes, the System has created numerous "Agencies" scattered throughout the Member States and in some cases, they handle significant amounts. This was a particularly intelligent move because in this way the "indigenous" believe that by hosting an Agency, they might influence the audits. This isn't true, however. Agencies are the "long arm" of the Commission, achieving things that the Commission cannot do itself, while having only therapeutic effects in Member States.

The Commission controls everything. It decides on the project parameters, issues the calls for tenders, assigns the projects, subcontracts the projects monitoring and auditing etc, But most importantly, it is never held accountable.

It is a common characteristic of all Programmes that many of their elements leave ample room for arbitrary interpretation. Procedures are very complicated and lengthy, with a long time span between the proposal presentation and payments. In this way, while awards are limited to a small number of candidates (among them the various projects of each Program are assigned on… rotation), transparency is far from being served.

A second equally important characteristic of all Programmes is that once a call for proposals is issued and an ordinary potential beneficiary decides to participate and submit a proposal, if rejected, it will never be told the reasons for rejection but they are told what they have to improve. In addition, there is no way to appeal a rejection decision. Such management practices were widely in use in the past only by the Soviets.

It is worth noting that despite the fact the EU has 28 Member States, a large part of each Programme, sometimes more than half of the Programme's funds, ends up being awarded to beneficiaries originating from two or three countries only. For example, 60% of LIFE projects are awarded to Spanish and Italian organisations! The reason might not be unrelated to the fact that in the Commission's LIFE units Spaniards and Italians occupy the most crucial positions. However, the three ruling Member States, in particular Germany, are not left behind as their companies have branches or subsidiaries all over.

All Programmes are characterised by unprecedented levels of useless bureaucratic procedures, many reminiscent of the good years of the Soviet Union. As a result, nobody cares about the specific projects' results and nobody ever asks if the project had any significant impact on society. Usually, once completed, the projects are closed in a file cabinet and forgotten forever.

In fact, their only utility is in certain cases for the beneficiaries of the project, and not for the society. For example, a University lecturer who happens to be a project's scientific director will benefit from one or two otherwise meaningless scientific publications (papers) presenting the project's results. Such papers will be added to his CV and will certainly boost his scientific career. Furthermore, he will be able to favour some of his associates by enrolling them in the project thus offering them the possibility to be paid twice (University salary and project fees) for tasks they were routinely doing during their academic assignments.

All EU-funded projects require beneficiaries to offer their "own participation," i.e. an amount that the applicant must contribute to cover part of the costs. In practice, most beneficiaries effectively cover their "participation" through their own staff costs, by simply "exaggerating" their occupation in the project in the compilation of their employees' time sheets.

On the Commission's side, they care to award the projects to their usual "customers" and make sure that the bureaucratic procedures are carefully observed. In other words, nobody cares for the substance of the projects, nor assesses the utility of such spending to the people.

The real utility of the projects is that the System in its various forms and ramifications (Commission Units and the Executive Agencies) through a highly sophisticated and demanding bureaucratic methodology, distributes money at will to "selected" recipients. As for the real impact of this huge investment, most of those projects have no commercial value and very limited possibilities of surviving in a private market environment.

To summarise: "Programmes" are a classical European Commission-style mechanism to distribute money to the "usual clients". Thus, a whole community of academics, consultants, experts etc. live off this money.

The Commission is so tightly closed that "outsiders" are discouraged from participating. Why would they bother to participate when they know in advance that the rate of acceptance for a proposal is less than 10% (i.e. less than 10 out of 100 proposals will eventually be financed), and that a handful of countries will get 60% of that money?

There is also a full arsenal of bureaucratic controls, based on an absurd system of "regulations", that only few know how to handle. The purpose here is to "feed" an army of experts: consultants specialising in writing proposals, others specialising in evaluating proposals, then others who perform "monitoring" on behalf of the Commission, and finally those who can interpret the regulations. And on top of all those come the auditors, in diverse varieties: those specialising in auditing projects, those who audit the Commission officers' work, and those performing "ex-post" audits... It is a full army of people totally useless, just as useless as most of the projects themselves.

If you're still not convinced, just ask the Commission what percentage of these projects' findings end in some way in the real economy, in the market – half of them? 20%? 10%? No, not at all. The proportion of useful projects is just not published, and for a good reason because it's in the range of statistical error.

8/4 The Audit of the European Science Foundation

Many of you, when getting a project financed by the Commission, might think you have conquered the world. But at the end of the project, although the Commission congratulates you for the good work and you work fervently to apply for the next project, the audit comes.

It is the moment that you start to lose your sleep. The audit, if you are not one of those described in chapter "Programs, the Loot," certainly will find something and this will be only the beginning of your tragedy. Audits always find something. The question is if this 'something' will be given a continuation or not. Under normal circumstances in most of the cases, there should not be any continuation. However, outsiders must be discouraged and kept out and you are one of them.

A project commissioned by the Research Executive Agency (REA), an Agency of DG Research, was (according to the Commission) successfully implemented. Two years after implementation, however, was subject to an audit as the Agency (more than one thousand staff), had to justify its existence.

The auditors were asking for documentation, which at the time was not required for the contract they had signed but was to be provided for future contracts. REA was keeping some high-level academics in such agony and they were so confused they did not notice that the documents asked by the auditors were not foreseen in the contract.

In this chapter, I will provide some boring technical details, but this will be useful to any reader who might have had (or will face in the future) a problem with REA or DG Research. They constitute a solid argument in asking for "equal treatment". Because, I assume, our Europe has nothing to do with the Animal Farm in which "all animals are equal but some animals are more equal than others".

Contract: No. 980008 signed by Pablo Fernandez Ruiz on 26 August 2003. Mono-contractor was the European Science Foundation (ESF), a non-profit scientific foundation based in France.

Scope: Provision of scientific, technical and administrative management of a European Cooperation in Science and Technology (COST) project, within the framework of the specific research and technical development programme integrating and strengthening the European Railway Agency (ERA).

Duration: 18 months starting on 01/07/2003 Grant to the budget — Maximum community contribution: € 20,123, 400 — Rate of funding: 100%. Subsequently, eight amendments have been signed by Robert-Jan Smits and became a rolling contract.

Following these amendments, the duration of the project was set at 54 months, the maximum community contribution became €80,000,000 covering the following costs:

• Direct costs for installing and operating the COST Office in Brussels — all the costs (direct and indirect by nature are considered as direct costs for the contract).

• Direct costs for Science activities (organisation of conferences - grants for projects presented by researchers - dissemination).

• Direct costs for Support to COST technical Committees and Governance 20% flat rate indirect costs.

The COST Office was set up and monitored jointly by the Committee of Senior Officials (CSO) made up of representatives of the Commission and the Member States although it was exclusively funded by the Commission.

According to the Annex I —version 25/11/2004, ESF commits itself to calculating the actual indirect cost it incurs for the contract. In case the actual indirect costs are lower than the 20% Flat Rate, "ESF would use the possible available amount to cover all commitments it would have to face in the execution (or termination) of the COST contract. After ensuring the coverage of such commitments, possible remaining money would be invested in any European scientific networking activities that ESF may propose to develop in dialogue with appropriate collaborative bodies, the Committee of senior officials, to enhance the COST program's scope of activities" (This is also called "Return to Science Principle").

During the audit, it was noted that ESF never calculated the actual indirect costs in order to check if there was remaining money. Moreover, in its cost statements, ESF calculated also the 20% on the transfers of funds to the researchers for the grants (it should be noted that the same remark was made by the Court of Auditors following one of its audits). However, all the direct and indirect costs incurred by the COST Office for these transfers were already charged as direct costs.

In a first instance, the auditors rejected the 20% calculated on the transfers. In addition, they calculated the actual indirect costs and noted a substantial amount of unspent money.

The Legal Service was consulted and in its reply said: "The payments to the grant holders are "financial transfers from ESF, acting in its capacity as coordinator". It may be understood that transfers are not a cost and that the 20% may not be calculated on them. However, the Legal Service then stated that due to the wording of the contract, the Commission may not attempt to recover the indirect costs calculated on those transfers.

Concerning the insertion of the "Return to Science Principle" in the contract, the Legal Service states that DG RTD's question assumes, which is invalid under EC/EU law, namely that EC/EU grants may not generate profits for the beneficiary. Hence, the Legal Service advised not to rely on any clause the underlying assumption of which is contrary to EC/ EU laws. By doing so, the Legal Service did not really reply to the question whether the "Return to Science Principle" is enforceable.

The final audit report has been ready since August 2012. Based only on the non-compliance with the "Return to Science Principle", the non-eligible costs amount to €5,476,432.

In September 2014, a letter was sent to ESF to ask about its intention concerning the non-eligible amounts. The following three suggestions were outlined:

• implement the "Return to Science Principle" (out of the contractual life period of the contract, which is illegal)

• Transfer of these funds to the new COST Association (this suggestion does not comply with the Financial Regulation).

• Return them to the Commission.

In its reply, ESF rejected all three suggestions.

To make the issue understandable, there were two audits conducted on ESF. The first audit was June 16-20, 2008 and provided for a recovery of over €10,000,000. For this case, the Legal Service of the Commission with a NOTE to the Director General suggested that it would be better not to ask for such recovery as the initial contract, may be invalid under EU/EU law. Thus between the lines, it said that it would be better to keep one's mouth shut. Thus the whole issue was forgotten as if the audit had never happened.

The second audit, which was conducted March 31 to April 3, 2009, suggested the recovery of €5,476,432 and ESF refused. In 2015, DG RTD decided to cancel the audit and not to recover the €5,476,432 which is not eligible.

A minor detail is that the Director who signed the eight amendments of the contract, reportedly violating EC/EU law, and the Director General who closed the audit dossier without asking for a recovery a few years later, is the same person.

It should also be mentioned that OLAF was informed in 2008 about potential irregularities. As DG RTD launched an audit, OLAF requested to be informed about the outcome. The results of the audit have never been communicated to OLAF.

EUROPEAN COMMISSION
DIRECTORATE-GENERAL FOR RESEARCH & INNOVATION

The Director-General

Ref. ARES (2016) 580516 - 01/02/2016

Brussels,

By registered letter with acknowledgment of receipt

Basil A. Coronakis

CEO New Europe Group
Avenue de Tervuren 96
1040 Brussels
Belgium

****

Subject: **Your application for access to documents – GestDem Ref No 2016/162**

****

2.1 Protection of commercial interests

Pursuant to Article 4(2), first indent, of *Regulation (EC) No 1049/2001*, access to a document has to be refused if its *"disclosure would undermine the protection of commercial interests of a natural or legal person, including intellectual property"*.

****

In light of the arguments presented in this section, the exception laid down in Article 4(2), first indent, of *Regulation (EC) No 1049/2001* applies to the requested document. Consequently, we redacted all sensitive commercial information, the disclosure of which might undermine the protection of the commercial interests of the third party.

****

Yours faithfully,

Robert-Jan Smits
Director-General

1.5 SPECIFIC AUDIT CONSTRAINTS

During the fieldwork, ESF declared not to be able to calculate its actual indirect costs and therefore was not in a position to provide information on possible remaining monies to be reinvested. This is in contradiction with ESF's commitments laid down in the Annex I of the contract (see section 1.3.3).

After analysis of the accounting system used by ESF, the EU auditors were of the opinion that such a calculation was possible and intended to analyse ESF indirect costs during the initial on-the-spot mission in June 2008. However, ESF explained that it did not have to justify the use of the flat rate and asked the EU auditors in writing to refrain from auditing the indirect costs (see annex 2 of this report).

Based on an opinion issued by DG Research legal service, a second mission on the spot was performed in March 2009 in order to complete the audit work. During this second audit, ESF cooperated and provided the requested information. Thanks to information access finally accepted by ESF and thanks to juridical support provided by EU legal services, EU auditors could finalise the audit process.

1.6 AUDIT FINDINGS

The analysis of the ESF project accounting shows that a significant difference exists between actual direct and indirect costs of the COST contract incurred by ESF and the 100% contribution claimed to and paid by the EC.

All Direct costs recorded by ESF in the COST account (non eligible costs and transfers to final beneficiaries included)	EUR 69 995 908
Total BG costs allocated to COST 980008 (actual indirect costs)	EUR 4 527 658
Total Actual costs of COST 980008	**EUR 74 523 568**
EU contribution	EUR 80 000 000
ESF surplus on COST 980008	**EUR 5 476 432**

As a consequence, after having covered all its commitments related to the execution of the contract as foreseen in Annex I to the contract, remaining monies exist for an amount of EUR 5 476 432. This is corroborated by the fact that an amount of EUR 5 245 000 is recorded in ESF equity at the date of the financial audit (see annex 3 of this report) of which EUR 3 448 000 have been accumulated by ESF as *"Provisions for contingencies linked to COST contract"*. During the audit, ESF declared that these provisions could also be used for other purposes than the COST contract.

ESF committed itself to reinvest in research activities "possible remaining monies" after having ensured the coverage of its contractual commitments, but it did not yet honour such a commitment at the date of the audit. ESF omitted also to report to the EC the level of the actual indirect costs.

These significant remaining monies, not spent on COST research activities, are the result of two financial mechanisms used to calculate the indirect costs claimed:

Firstly, the application of the 20% flat rate on EU funds transferred to final beneficiaries and secondly, the application of the 20% flat rate on the direct costs of the COST Office in Brussels despite the fact that the totality of the costs incurred by the COST Office in Brussels are already included in the direct costs claimed.

202

8/4 THE AUDIT OF THE EUROPEAN SCIENCE FOUNDATION

1.5 SPECIFIC AUDIT CONSTRAINTS

1.6 AUDIT FINDINGS

The actual indirect costs incurred by ESF in its headquarters in Strasbourg (EUR 4 527 659) are significantly lower than the amount claimed (EUR 13 337 147).

Regarding personnel costs, auditors note that bonuses are paid to ESF staff. However, since the bonus system was not part of ESF usual accounting practices before the financing by the EU of the COST 980008 contract and because these bonuses do not respect the criteria of necessity for carrying out the project, these bonuses are not eligible. Due to the financial specificities of the contract, adjustments on personal costs would not affect financial conclusion of the audit.

1.7 RECOMMENDATIONS

In performing their audit work in June 2008 and March 2009, EU auditors noted mainly that:

1. Despite a specific provision included by ESF in Annex I to the contract foreseeing that potential remaining monies would be reinvested in European scientific networking activities (in order to contribute to COST programme's activities or to enhance the COST programme's scope of activities), a significant amount of remaining monies from the EU contribution to COST FP6, not spent on the COST contract, has been imputed to the ESF reserves (EUR 5 476 432);

2. Despite its own commitment to reinvest potential surplus generated by the difference between flat rate and actual indirect costs, ESF has never put in place adequate procedures in order to identify and calculate actual indirect costs related to the COST FP6 contract;

3. Bonuses paid to the staff were charged to the EC contracts.

Consequently, on 26/08/2011, by mean of a contradictory procedure based on a draft audit report, ESF was recommended:

1. To inform DG RTD external audit services on its reinvestment intention as soon as possible and communicate a detailed and dated investment program no later than the end of 2011. ESF was informed that in the absence of such a reinvestment, in conformity to its own commitment, remaining monies would have to be considered as a profit which is in contradiction with Article II.24, §2 of the contract: "The Community financial contribution can not give rise to any profit for the contractors";

2. To develop the accounting system further and adopt appropriate procedures in order to set a flat rate corresponding to actual indirect costs. This recommendation was done with the view to guarantee that the non profit principle is respected and to ease identification of actual indirect costs as foreseen by the "Return to science" principle and in order to set a flat rate corresponding to actual indirect costs;

3. Not to charge to the EC contracts with the bonuses paid to ESF staff.

8/4 THE AUDIT OF THE EUROPEAN SCIENCE FOUNDATION

This report is the property of the European Commission and should not be distributed to third parties without the written approval of the European Commission

1.7 RECOMMENDATIONS

In performing their audit work in June 2008 and March 2009, EU auditors noted mainly that:

8/5 Personnel and Infrastructures, the Waste

In the Commission, salaries vary from a minimum of €4,000 per month for clerks to approximately €18,000 per month for the very top civil servants, tax-free. In addition, for what the Commission does, it employs approximately 20% more people than it really needs.

Nominal salaries are between 12% and 42% higher. But this is a gracious trick to avoid national taxes. The difference between the real salary and the virtual salary, is supposed to be taxes withheld by the EU, which remain in the budget. In this way, once the salary is supposedly taxed by the European Union, and as it is already supposedly taxed, no taxes are paid in the Member State. However, as all employees (except Belgians) on the top of their salary are paid expatriation allowance (16%) which means that they are tax residents in their country of origin and work abroad (for this reason they are paid an extra 16%). Therefore, all amounts withhold from salaries as income tax, instead of remaining with the EU budget, should be returned from the Commission, to the Finance Ministries of the country of origin of the employees. To avoid any misunderstanding EU vis-à-vis Member States has neither the status of an international organization (i.e. UN, WTO, etc.) nor it is a diplomatic service, thus EU employees are not covered by the Vienna Convention on Diplomatic Relations (1961).

Therefore, withheld taxes by the EU Institutions should be transferred to the Member States. This is not done because, so far, no Member State has raised the issue. It remains to see if any judge or prosecutor, from any Member State, will ask for a preliminary ruling of Court of Justice of the EU, on the grounds of Article 267 of the Treaty for the Functioning of the EU.

All institutions of the European Union, major and minor (i.e. Commission, Council, Parliament, Court of Justice, Committees as well as countless Agencies and other bodies) are using one single contract for all employees. Procedures, documentation and archives are same for all. Whether an employee is a translator in the Commission serving in Luxemburg or a translator for the Parliament based in Strasburg, hiring and firing procedures are the same.

However, from there on there is no coordination, at all. Each of the various institutions is using their own system. Often, different sections in the same department use different software. This differentiation minimises transparency, as there is no central database and money is easily wasted for no real reason.

For everything that happens in life, there is of course a reason and in this case there are more than one. More jobs, more opportunities for direct or indirect benefits (where there are purchases there are always opportunities for benefits), less political supervision and less public scrutiny, are certainly some of them.

Additionally, employees of all grades at the Commission and other Institutions enjoy 30 working days annual leave, around 17 days per year for various religious and national holidays, plus a bonus of 12 days per year. That is more than three months. What is the bonus? Good question. Every Commission employee has the right to get one day of sick leave without a medical certificate every month, just by claiming headache or bad mood.

Finally, their superiors evaluate the performance of each of the 25,000 permanent employees of the European Commission, every year. This evaluation is considered a very serious test for all staff regardless of grade, gender and nationality.

If an employee is found "insufficient" he or she is demoted by one grade. If again evaluated "insufficient" for another two consecutive years (total three consecutive, not cumulative years), then he or she is fired. It must be added, that the bureaucratic procedures (report, committees etc.) required to justify insufficiency, are so many and so complicated that since 1957 (the year the European Union was founded), only seven employees have been dismissed!

On February 14, 2018, President Jean-Claude Juncker presented his thoughts "for a Europe which delivers." The question, however, is what it delivers and for whom.It was a series of practical actions that would make the European Commission more efficient and will improve the relation between leaders of the EU institutions and citizens.

To be honest, if the Commission wanted to do something for the citizens, it should start by reducing its operational costs, starting from the merger of certain services thus reducing the operational costs. There have been some attempts in this directions with the merger of certain personnel services in Brussels and Luxemburg. Impressive those they know nothing of Brussels and the System. Maximum 20 employees less who retired and were not replaced.

Of the necessary changes that would really mean cost reduction no body speaks. The first real change should be in the Directorate General Translation. Today there are about 4,000 translators who can be easily be reduced to 3,000 while reducing the cost to half. However, no body dares because there should be dismissed 4 Directors General, and at least 20 Directors and over 100 Heads of Unit. And while nobody is permanent employee but all of them have the backing of Prime Ministers, Ministers Cardinals and Bishops and nobody in Brussels wants to enter in to the logic of confronting these people. That EU institutions employees are not permanent, but nobody is fired, says a lot.

To change DG Translation, must change the organigramme changing verticalization from linguistic to thematic. Also most translators must be transferred in their countries. Today, over 70% of translators work from 10% to 50% of their working time, remotely, from home. Why not make it 100% and relocate them in their home town? Translators will be happy, the budget will save the 16% of their salaries (expatriation allowance) and new appointees will be paid local salaries.

Today, only in the Commission are translated 2,5 million pages every year, in 24 languages. Under s tacit unwritten agreement, every translator translates 5 to 6 standards pages per day, from one foreign language (only) to his language.

The cost of translation for each page to the Commission is € 180 per page. If same page were given for translation to outsources and Commission services were limited to make only the final control, the cost, all inclusive, would drop to € 90 per page.

Another way to reduce costs concerns the office buildings. Presently, the Commission services are spread throughout the European quarters of Brussels, in about 70 buildings. Rents beyond imagination!

What ordinary people do not understand is why the Commission does not buy a large area in the outskirt of Brussels (prices are very law) and build there the administrative center of Europe. However, there are other facets to consider yet I do not wish to present, as may lead to far-fetched scenarios.

8/6 It's Your Money

The European Commission and the European Parliament maintain offices in all Member States. Such offices are necessary for more than one reason. They are there to communicate the European Union and to be the "gate" for citizens in Member States to enter and get know the Union. What is it? How does it work? What does it mean to be a citizen of Europe and how can you benefit from membership?

Both institutions deploy their own offices in Member States, with their own buildings and personnel. Citizens do not understand why money for buildings and general staff is being spent twice. It would be logical for both institutions to share the same facilities and administrative personnel.

The excuse of these offices is well justified. To communicate Europe, noble endeavour! The real reason of their existence in Member States is to spy on the national politicians, government and opposition identify the Commission-friendly politicians and executives of the public sector and help them in their career through the most efficient Brussels circuits and manipulate both leaders and citizens (through friendly media).

In practical terms, they do exactly what the CIA and FSB are doing, though with no risk and better pay.

Offices of the European Parliament, manage to send at the expense of the Parliament, a few journalists to Strasbourg once a month. This could be well settled centrally, from one place which could be in Strasbourg avoiding the familiarisation between Parliament representatives in Member States and certain journalists at the expense of other journalists, whilst also cutting down on expenses.

The most important activity of the Parliament's office in Member States, however, is to secure the approval by national Parliaments on certain "hot" issues. This is pure lobbying activity and, for the Member States, unfair.

As for the offices of the Commission, the so-called Representations (in Member States), the whole thing is wrong.

First, they behave in a grand style, giving themselves in many cases diplomatic status, with the tolerance or the ignorance of the Member State and of course enjoy the relative privileges.

Embassies, what embassies? Indeed, it would be like Italy opens an embassy in… Napoli. Perhaps in this case it is needed, but what about Great Britain opening an embassy in Cardiff?

What do these "embassies" really do?

Their main duty is to manipulate local officials to align with the plans of the System and collect privileged information. In practice, they do what the CIA does in Latin America, but with a much better salary and zero risk. The whole concept is sickening. Member States are considered enemies of the Commission to be spied upon. On the contrary, the Commission is their Secretariat.

Another duty of the "embassies" is to monitor local media and report to Brussels confidentially what the media say, as mentioned earlier. The same job, yet objective and impartial, could be done much cheaper from any Member State, globally. This could well justify a press-monitoring Agency in one Member State, like in one of the Baltic States, which are well- advanced in technology matters with low operational costs.

What should they be doing?

Representations should be wide open to the public and should be staffed only with non-nationals who speak the local language. In this way many shortcomings such as manipulative interventions in national policies, will be avoided while visiting citizens will get a better sense of the European Union.

They should manage to put visiting officials from Brussels in touch with the public. In this context, they should arrange for visiting officials to speak about Europe at schools, universities and civic organisations. There is a voluntary programme called "Back to School" where EU officials are encouraged to speak about the Union at schools in their hometown. However, it does not work. Citizens in Member States are keen to learn about Europe, but nobody tells them anything.

Lastly, a rather critical question. The offices of the European Commission in Member States are marginally justifiable. All central governments in Member States maintain communication services in provincial cities. However, what is the reason of the European Parliament keeping offices in Member States? Do you know of any National Parliament, in any Member State maintaining office in any city of the country?

INSIDE THE SMALL RING

9/1 The Big Players and the Poor Relatives

To understand the "Sin City", that is the European quarters of Brussels where in 84 buildings are hosted the Commission services, first you must understand how a complex system works and who the big players are, where they acquire power from, and how checks and balances are maintained. In the chapter "The Dark Side of the Moon," the basics of complexity under "Complexity and the European Union" are presented. Now, we will speak about the big players.

Playmaker is the System. You already have an idea about what it is, about its composition and how it operates. The System is the basic component within the Brussels complex and is composed of top-level functionaries: The President of the Commission and his Head of Cabinet, the Secretary General and a selected number of Directors General; plus, the three big Member States, France Germany and, whether we like it or not, still and only God knows until when, the United Kingdom. They are the overlords of the Union.

Second to the overlords come the many other smaller players, such as the big influence groups, which include religious groups and others. The Permanent Representatives of certain important Member States, Italy, Spain and Poland also have a considerable role to play in matters concerning their countries, analogous to the political leverage of their Commissioners.

As for the various national delegations of less important countries visiting Brussels to resolve their problems with the System, the so-called "poor relatives," they have no chance. Indeed, they usually return home with empty hands, big words and no outcome.

This results from the misevaluation of the correlation of powers, the pragmatic standing of the affairs of the System and the misperception of going to Brussels well prepared and with valid arguments.

The System is extremely well prepared. We are talking about the top and among the best-paid administrators in the world. Each of them has mastered his field of specialisation and knows how to navigate the 110,000 pieces of legislation that make up European law. The battle of the "poor relatives," is lost before it has even started.

The "poor relatives" arrive to Brussels thinking they are sharp, intelligent and well prepared. They approach the System with various "provincial" tactics. But nothing works.

The only chance to get something is to politicise the matter, but this is not easy because the System masters the art of driving negotiations where it wants. Needless to say, that politicization of an issue, especially for countries of secondary influence, is not easy. This is possible only if the Commissioner of the country takes the matter seriously and provided that he fully controls his Cabinet. Indeed, whatever will be possible to be achieved, it will happen only if the Cabinet of the Commissioner decides to do it.

If politics enters the negotiations of the Commission's techno-structure, the System gets into difficulties because they know very little of politicking and they will try to stop the matter in the Cabinet. Politicization of a matter means that the case will be handled by the Commission This is the last thing they want, as they do not know what deals other Commissioners and the Commissioner of the country concerned may have reached. Therefore, if the issue is well politicised, the "poor relatives" may return home with some results.

In this case, they should approach matters with a very low profile, without fanfare and without sensationalised TV shows because the System has eyes and ears all over the empire and does not like to appear to have lost.

Finally, the "poor relatives" should realise that to elevate an issue one level up and raise it from technocratic to political is not easy and cannot be laid out by the administration in the Member State concerned. It must be perceived and methodised by the political personnel of the country.

9/2 Lobbying is King

In Brussels, you can do anything and everything, except the impossible. This takes some time and... some money. However, it is a game for the big kids.

In most Member States, if you mention the word "lobbying," even at a social occasion, people will look at you with suspicion and, if by coincidence or not, a Member of the National Parliament is present at the gathering, he or she will find an excuse to leave. In most Member States, the word "lobbying", is blasphemy. In Brussels, it's a cult.

Lobbying in Brussels is an institution and even more, it is a religion. It is a monotheistic religion where money is god.

Lobbying in the capital of Europe is a cardinal element of everyday life and contributes to the economy of an undefined number the Eurocrats and their satellites. Besides money, beneficiaries also enjoy all kind of fringe benefits. These include dinners, luxury holidays, and gifts of any kind and size. Fringe benefits include even private expensive cruises and luxury male, female or bisexual... escort services.

Not many years ago, a top politician of the EU Institutions, accepted a gift a 10-day cruise for him and his friends. The value of this otherwise "symbolic" gift, according to the advertising of cruise boat for a 10-cruise was one million Euro. The advertisement, disappeared from the web sites of the luxury yachts rental brokers when a question was tabled in the European Parliament

"Lobbyists" in the transparency record of the European Commission include NGOs, representatives of organisations from Member States (municipalities, regions and industry groups), lobbying firms, Agencies etc. They usually have more than one "executive" exercising the sport and are all supplied with the special EU badge that allows entrance to the Parliament facilities in Strasburg and Brussels.

You can find details of all these people in the transparency records of the European Commission, in a list that is available to all.

Besides the official "lobbyists" who count approximately 9,550, there is also an unknown additional number of unofficial lobbyists, estimated at over 10,000, who under many different identities secure entrance to the temples of the System. They are former Members of Parliament, former Members of the Commission and former officials of the System, Members of Permanent Representations and embassies, journalists and foreign correspondents, lawyers and consultants of all kinds. There are also the "parachute" lobbyists from Member States coming to Brussels for specific issues.

The unofficial lobbyists are not listed anywhere, and they have various ways of getting in and out of the corridors of the System. But do not worry, if you come to Brussels to resolve your problem, you won't have to look for them because they will find you.

The most disadvantaged among them, and this must be said, are the big Agencies with heavy corporate structures and rules. Agencies, even though they avail the best know-how for "orthodox" lobbying, always follow the ethical and professional rules. But this is not because they are good Christians or Jews. They must do so because they belong to big PR and lobbying conglomerates where they do everything by the book. Furthermore, bank transfer conducts all their financial transactions. In Brussels, however, in terms of "efficient" lobbying, bank transfer is not considered the best practice.

9/3 Lobbying with the Formers

Several "former," although retired, are very active and very effective in Brussels lobbying. All kinds of formers: Former Members of Parliament; former Commissioners; former Directors General of the Commission; former Parliamentary assistants; and former System executives. Not to mention formers from other important European organisations. Even former Ministers and Members of National Parliaments come to Brussels for a "good cause", usually related to their former portfolio.

In this game, former Ministers and former Members of National Parliaments from Member States, bring their own clients to Brussels. They usually come with one case at a time, mostly concerning complaints on competition, internal market (public procurements), the environment, energy, or infringements on the misuse of community funds.

Formers in Member States have access to companies and organisations with Brussels concerns, and they have sufficient inside information to approach usually worried businessmen. The wheelers-and-dealers with plenty of cash, who are self-described as big in the small and marginal Member States with no connections in Brussels, are terrorised if they realise that the Brussels services are interested in them. An invitation by OLAF to testify as "witness" or "person concerned" is enough to bring in this category of operators, a heart attack.

So, when a former Minister is approaching them on something that makes them lose sleep, they cooperate and pay immediately, usually cash in advance.

These kinds of "parachute" lobbyists are not few. Usually they know one or two executives of the Commission, people who they worked with when they were visiting Brussels in their ministerial capacity. They also know several Eurocrats coming from their own country and a few Members of the European Parliament. Of course, all these contacts are mostly useless, but still good for "name dropping" back home to secure the client. In most cases, they work together with an established Brussels lobbyist for the job to be done. And, of course, the income is shared accordingly. The "lion's" cut, however, in all such cases usually goes to the client detector.

Often, lobbying with the formers is a kind of one time "hit and miss" business. It has no formalities like a code of conduct, invoices, bank transfers and other trivialities. Even though it costs more, in many cases it is efficient because it has few, if any "red lines." Yet lobbying informally with formers, does not always bring about the desired results. Only a few power brokers of this kind (i.e. until recently Directors General of the Commission and a few others) can deliver. They work with utmost confidence for a few large and important clients and cannot be approached by peasants coming from the province with a "basket full of eggs and fresh fruit." Even to speak with them requires something more than that.

9/4 The Lawyers

There is a New York joke about lawyers. It goes something like this: ten lawyers at the bottom of the Hudson River is pollution, but 10,000 lawyers at the bottom of the Hudson is a solution. If you change the name of the river to Zenne (Senne in French, the river crossing Brussels), the joke is just as funny. That's wishful thinking, however, as Zenne is not deep enough.

I leave aside Belgian lawyers who work with the Belgian justice system. They are good professionals and they perform ordinary legal activities with moderate charges reflecting value for money. This chapter is not about them. This chapter is about the lawyers who deal with the System. Some of them are quite a different species of jurists.

First there are the big international law firms with large numbers of agents specialising in all facets of Community Law. They have expensive premises, highly sophisticated staff and once you enter their offices you must be ready to put your hand deep in your pocket. They maintain good PR relations with Commission officials and, depending on the case, they produce results.

Big law firms do not opt for any "unorthodox" approaches when handling a case, unless you are a rather small client who potentially can disturb the System. In this case, do not be surprised if they will "sell" you to their Commission "friends." In Brussels, there are no friends or enemies, only clients and competitors. However, big law firms know well the Community Law and how (if they want to) their clients can benefit from it.

Indeed, there might be few Brussels lawyers, who exceptionally and for some cases of importance to the Commission services, might not exert all their abilities if they are asked to do so. The point is that these few would never antagonise the System for a small client, if asked. The issue is that a small client coming from a remote place of the empire will never know in advance who those few are. Consequently, one must be very careful.

A few years ago, a Commission officer (Head of Unit level), extremely intelligent and with deep knowledge of the rules, became furious at the way the Commission was handling a case. This gentleman, acting as an ordinary citizen, based on Regulation (EC) 1049/2001 asked the Commission to release certain documents. The Commission ignored the Regulation and refused to release the documents. The gentleman took the Commission to the Court of Justice of the EU for failure to comply with Community Law. At that time, the matter was a hot topic in the corridors of the "sublime port." Imagine, a medium-rank Commission officer taking the Commission to Court!

In this context, he received an offer from a lawyer he knew, a big gun in Brussels, who offered to represent him for free. The gentleman accepted and despite the case seemingly being a piece of cake and the lawyer one of the best in Brussels, he lost at the First Instance.

The lawyer proposed to continue with the appeal, but the gentleman thanked him and asked for the dossier. Initially, the lawyer refused to give the dossier back and told the plaintiff that he would appeal the ruling for free. However, as the good lawyer insisted to keep the dossier, the gentleman warned him that he would complain to the Brussels bar. Only then he did get the dossier back. Then, he wrote the appeal himself (despite the fact he was not a lawyer) and hired a local lawyer from his village to support the case in the Court of Justice of the EU, in Luxemburg. This new lawyer spoke no working EU language and did not even know what the Berlaymont building looked like. Yet, he won the case on appeal.

There are a great number of law firms and individual lawyers working specifically on EU matters. However, any lawyer, if he or she is a member of the bar of any Member State, can work with the Commission and can bring any case to the Court of Justice of the EU. For this reason, and as the law market in Brussels is very competitive, most Brussels lawyers try to keep national lawyers out of their playground.

Dealing with EU law requires attention. Operators in Member States often violate Community law as they lack even basic knowledge. As they do not know how the System works in Brussels, they can easily panic and become the victims.

To perceive the magnitude of the problems in this field, I will tell you another story. It may sound far-fetched and fantasy, but it may well be real.

A "clever" Brussels lawyer learns that in the Member State of his origin, where he has contacts and good knowledge of the local players, a big company committed violations in executing a Community co-financed project. Nothing unusual so far. The "clever" lawyer travels immediately to the Member State and meets urgently with the "big boss" of the company.

The "clever" lawyer informs the "big boss" that his company is under scrutiny in Brussels. The first visit serves just to pass the message and establish a line of communication with the company.

The "big boss," who understands his company violates Community law by default, asks his lawyers to find out. Usually, the lawyers of the company can find nothing, probably because there is nothing to find.

Also, because investigations of the Commission on violations of Community Law are kept confidential. The Services want to avoid interference from the Member State in the initial phase of the investigation, so nothing is disclosed.

The "big boss," rather disappointed and worried, calls the "clever" lawyer and asks him to investigate the matter.

The "clever" lawyer prepares a Complaint under the name of a third person and mails it to the Commission. In some cases (as for instance could be in our case), the "clever" lawyer has a good personal contact in the Directorate General where the Complaint is addressed. Complaints of this kind usually end with the Department of Internal Market (DG MRKT). Then, as it may happen, all by "coincidence," someone who our good "clever" lawyer knows is assigned to examine the Complaint as case-handler. What a joy!

The case-handler finds the Complaint substantiated and worth investigating. Thus, a preliminary investigation is opened. The "clever" lawyer calls the big boss and says: "Dear friend, I was right, somebody launched a Complaint against your company and the Commission is working on it. Therefore, you should not be surprised when you will receive the letter to testify as witness or even as person concern." In few weeks invitation letter arrives.

From there on, the sky is the limit. Use your imagination to guess what may happen especially if the company is listed in the stock market. The "big boss" is losing sleep. The company goes on red alert. The "clever" lawyer is hired to work on the case. In this context the "clever" lawyer gets a substantial amount to find a copy of the Complaint.

By strictly enforcing rules, the Commission never releases Complaints to the parties concerned and the name of the complainant is considered top secret. However, in some cases, a copy of the Complaint (with the details of the complainant covered) can be obtained for a few hundred thousand Euros. Most probably not from the Commission but from the "unknown" complainant.

Back to our story. The case may take months or years. There is a lengthy, slow process of investigations, letters are exchanged, interrogations, on the spot Commission audits and visits are made to the Commission. The well-paid "clever" lawyer is omnipresent.

The case will come to an end when the Commission is about to conclude its investigation. At that point, the "clever" lawyer informs the "big boss" that the Commission is seriously considering proceeding with funds recovery, financial penalty, inclusion of the company in the "black list" and referral to OLAF for further follow-up with the national Prosecutor. This will exclude the company from future co-financed or other EU-funded programmes.

The "clever" lawyer also claims that he has some contacts in the System, which for a large amount of money could close the file with minimum damage. From there on, things are simple. The "big boss" pays the formal invoices, as well as the cash agreed. The initial complainant, without much publicity, withdraws the Complaint. This information is never communicated to the company concerned. The Commission sends to the parties concerned the letter of closing the case. After the final act of the tragedy, the "big boss" gets back his sleep and "everybody goes happily to the beach," as Melina Merkouri said in the Jules Dassin film "Never on Sunday."

The good news is that this story is imaginary. The bad news is that some business operators in marginal Member States may probably recognise this story and see themselves...

Brussels is not full of "clever" lawyers, but you may find some of this kind coming mostly from the new Member States and the South. This "Sin City" is full of all kind of lawyers: lawyers who know the law, lawyers who know the "judge" (in this case the proper "systemic" officials), intelligent lawyers and "clever" lawyers. They are all hunting for clients, as Member States are full of businessmen violating EU law who land in Brussels with no knowledge and no contacts.

Of course, there are lawyers in Brussels who working mostly independently but also in big legal firms, who know very well EU law. They also know very well and realistically how the System works and can fight within the mainstream and against it, if necessary.

One such case is the lawyer who came to Brussels a few years ago, from a small, marginal Member State. This young lady lawyer, although in good formal relations with the System dared to take on former President of the European Commission Jose Manuel Barroso to the Court of Justice of the EU for the John Dalli case (read more about this in the Dalli scandal in the last chapter).

The young lawyer substantiated the case against the sitting President of the European Commission extremely well. It was accepted by the Court (there is no such precedent). Because of the Court accepting the application, Barroso lost his third term as President of the European Commission in 2014. All this because of one ordinary and intelligent lawyer who was not corrupted by the System.

WE CITIZENS OF EUROPE

10/1 Get the Hell Out of Here

Over the years, the European Commission has successfully managed to keep citizens far from the European making.

The Commission is the government of the governments of Europe and rules, to the smallest details, everyday life of half a billion people. Most of these rules are issued without European citizens or their elected representatives having the minimum knowledge or even an idea of what others with no political legitimisation have decided for them. When they learn about it, it is too late to react.

Even most Member States governments do not have full knowledge of what is coming or what is about to come. This often happens because they are deliberately kept out of the substantial process of European policymaking.

In several cases, when "improper" questions are asked and reservations are raised by some "ignorant" from a minor Member State, the Commission deals with the issue usually at two or three levels up. That is, a Head of Unit pays a visit to the Minister in the Member State and in a nice, yet cool, manner explains that the "higher echelons" in Brussels are in a hurry to pass a certain Decision. The visitor explains in a rather vague and generic way that the Commission thinks that this Decision is very important for the democratic and efficient functioning of the European Institutions with ultimate beneficiaries the Member States.

Then, in smooth manner, the Minister is told that there is a gentleman, down below in the hierarchy of his services who does not display the right spirit to understand the importance of this great endeavour and with his approach is delaying the process.

The identity of the "higher echelons" is for the Minister's imagination to define. According to the fantasies of the Minister, the "higher person" (who sent to him a personal emissary!), could be anybody. Anyone between the Director and the Director General without excluding the Commissioner or even the President of the Commission himself!

Nothing else is needed, as the "curious" employee will be transferred to logistics, from where he will not see Brussels anymore unless as a tourist.

Of course, the Commission, before proceeding with new legislation, undertakes a procedure involving consultations with all Member States at the level of Permanent Representations and stakeholder representatives. Permanent Representatives are under continuous instruction by their governments. However, in many cases of small countries, in ambiguous cases, the Permanent Representative prefers not to open new collision fronts with the System and opts to appease it. Such cases, in most instances, will never be reported to the Member State, and with this eternal "give and take" process, the Permanent Representative will gain in his personal contacts in the Brussels System.

As for the stakeholder representatives, these are the same people working for years with the services on a permanent basis. In the context of this working relation, they have learned very well how to behave to survive in Brussels.

The institution of the Ombudsman is an excellent invention, which is supposed to be at the service of the citizen but serves as an airbag for the System. In dealing with the EU administration, once an issue comes to a point where the administration wants to block the process to neutralise you, they will advise you to file a complaint "with the Ombudsman."

Do not do it. The result of your Complaint to the Ombudsman, after many months or even years of delay, will be a simple recommendation. This recommendation is not binding. In addition, once you file a complaint with the Ombudsman, all other actions (investigation etc.) are frozen until the (non- binding) Ombudsman report is published.

10/2 EU Citizens' Rights

The rights of EU Citizens are many. Some are well hidden, other are widely publicized. There are many sites, mostly sponsored by various EU programmes, which will inform you about them. But they tell you what they want you to know, not what you should know. This is downplayed and hidden among a plethora of useless information.

So you will learn many facets of general-purpose rights, such as those referring to freedom, data protection, dignity and the like, valid in all Member States and all over the western world. Furthermore, there are citizens' rights stemming from the Treaties, which concern free movement of people and capital within the Union, etc.

EU citizens, however, have many more rights than what the sponsored sites tell you in detail. EU citizens have rights enabling them to penetrate the System from the back door, which though open, is well-hidden and well-protected.

The most important of such rights are: the right to access documents of the European Commission, the European Parliament, the European Council and the European External Action Service; the right to file complaints with the various institutions and the Ombudsman; and the cases where the citizen, can take the European Commission to the Court of Justice of the EU, without prior application to national Courts.

Equally important is Regulation 45/2001 on processing of personal data by the Community institutions and bodies and on the free movement of such data. Citizens have the right to get their data.

These are important for all citizens to know and this is what this chapter will tell you about. The rest, you can easily find on the europa.eu website.

10/3 Access to Documents and Personal Data

Access to documents and to personal data are two Regulations, which allows you to communicate directly with the System. It is one of the rare instances when you can play with, enjoy and even challenge the System.

It costs nothing and, if you do not get what the law entitles you to get, then you can take the System to the Court of Justice of the European Union. Think about it: any EU citizen can take the European Commission directly to the Court of Justice of the EU, without bringing the case before any national Courts at all.

You need no lawyer to request an EU document. It can be done with an email or a letter addressed to the Secretariat General of the European Commission (Sg-Acc-Doc@ec.europa.eu address Rue de la Loi 200, Brussels 1000). And don't forget to copy your correspondence to New Europe, the largest independent media group in Brussels.

If you are not satisfied with what the System gives you, then you can take the European Commission to Court. This will cost you only the lawyer fee (if the lawyer is a friend most probably, nothing) and a trip to Luxembourg. This means that if you are a lawyer or if you have a close friend who is a lawyer, the entire venture will cost you only the trip. Filing of the case does not require the physical presence of the lawyer in Luxembourg. This can be done by mail. As for the language, you can choose any of the 24 official languages of the EU, both for the Access to Documents request and the Court case.

A few years ago, I personally engaged in extensive correspondence with the Commission asking continuously for documents concerning the case of a great scandal. The case involved real theft of public funds and the Commission. More specifically, it concerned the Cohesion Fund (DG REGIO) that had promoted the deal. The Commission tried desperately to refuse me access to the documents. My technique was simple. I asked first for the final documents approving the project and closing the file. Once received, I went through the references in the document in my hands and immediately asked for all documents referred to in the document granted. The story continued like this for a few months and in this way, I had in my hands all the details involving payments and the responsibilities of the Commission. This cat and mouse game was continuing for a while. Until in one of my requests, I received the documents requested with a cover letter signed personally by the Director General who said, "please find the documents you requested, but so far as you have requested too much, therefore do not ask for anymore documents because we will not give you anything else."

I replied to the good Director General, with whom I became friends after he retired, "thanks for sending me the documents requested. I appreciate your comment; however, I wish to inform you that I will keep asking you for documents for as long as you serve in the Commission and you will keep sending them to me. By the way, based on Regulation (EC) 1049/2001, please provide me the following contracts concerning... etc." After a few days, I received the documents requested with a handwritten note on a yellow sticker, "always at your service, best..."

Regulation (EC) 1049/2001 gives EU citizens the right to request and receive from any of the major EU institutions, Parliament, Commission, Council and EEAS, any document with few exceptions explicitly stated in the Regulation. Indeed, Article 4 of the Regulation restricts the release of documents related to foreign, defence and economic policy, as well as to documents revealing personal data or involving commercial secrets of enterprises (business proprietary information).

Furthermore, no documents are released on ongoing (not completed) investigations and audits, the same rule used in the US for requests under the Freedom of Information Act (FOIA). Such documents can be released after the case is closed.

Upon applying, the applicant will receive confirmation of receipt and will also receive an answer with the documents requested within 15 working days. But if the demand is complicated (or embarrassing), the Commission can take an additional 15 days. Then it has either to deliver the documents (all or part) or refuse to do so, stating the reason that applies to each document withheld. In case of total or partial refusal, the citizen has the right to reply to the withholding service/ institution, insisting on the release request (confirmatory application). The institution is obliged to reply within 15 days. Eventually, the institution will reply providing the documentation requested, or it may refuse.

Any refusal of the confirmatory (second) application (request), entitles citizens to take the Commission to Court within two months. This is something quite embarrassing for the System, but not the end of the world.

Before Regulation (EC) 1049/2001, access to documents was extremely complicated. The procedure involved many decisions, different for the various institutions and, given the manipulative state-of-the-art skills of the System, it was quasi-impossible to get anything. The soup turned sour during the negations for accession of Sweden and Finland, two countries very sensitive to transparency matters, which set as a prerequisite for their accession the adoption of a Regulation allowing citizens to get documents from the institutions with no difficulties, something similar (but not the same) to the American "Freedom of Information Act."

Regulation (EC) 1049/2001 is very explicit, leaving no room for arbitrary interpretation and does not allow the System to exert its "discretionary powers."

We recommend downloading this Regulation, which is available in all EU languages, and study it carefully. Then start asking informed questions! Start with your questions on co-financed projects in your country. You are entitled to receive everything if you use the right wording.

Often when the Commission releases documents that it cannot refuse, yet does not want to release, it is covering with black marker many important facets of the content of the document (redaction). It claims it does this for personal data protection purposes and/or protection of business proprietary information. Unfortunately, most of the time such redaction is an excuse that you cannot challenge because you do not know what was removed. Under these circumstances, you can appeal to the Court of Justice of the EU and at the same time to the European Data Protection Supervisor who has the power to review the redacted documents and check.

In requesting documents, you must be very specific about what you ask because the strongest ability of the System is to avoid giving out anything. Indeed, if the request is not carefully phrased the System will escape like an eel. This is very important because if you fail to put forward the right request, the System will not accept a second request from the same person asking the same or similar things as before. In this case, if your request is refused because it is vague (sometimes referred to as "fishing") do not insist. Ask a friend/ associate to file a properly worded request for the same document and follow the procedure from the beginning through your friend.

The Access to Documents Regulation, is the biggest setback the Commission System has, but it's also a great advantage.

By using Regulation 1049, citizens acquire knowledge and become extremely dangerous for the System. This is the reason the Secretariat General of the Commission is working to invent excuses to pass a new Regulation on Access to Documents watering-down the existing one. If it succeeds, it will be the last nail in the coffin of the European Union and Jean Claude Juncker will be remembered in history as its gravedigger. Yet, under the present configuration of the European Parliament it may prove impossible. As for the next Parliament, it will certainly be more citizen-friendly than the present.

On the other hand, abolishing on rendering ineffective the Regulation on Access to Documents will unveil that many officials of the Commission are useless as they exclusively work in inventing obstacles to hide the truth. Pathetic as in bottom line they are paid by the citizens to cheat them!

However, as the excuses that the Secretariat General will invent to water-down the existing Regulation, the reply of the political leadership of the Commission should be very simple: Publish everything releasable on the internet.

The issue of personal data is. a very sensitive matter and Regulation (EC) 45/2001 explicitly provides that EU citizens can have access to all personal data processed by any services in any EU Member State as well as to European Institutions as well as to the names of the controllers and processors of such data. The Regulation does not leave room for refusals and all data must be released within three months.

Furthermore, there is Directive 95/46/EC (effective since May 25, 2018) on the protection of individuals with regard to the processing of personal data and on the free movement of such data. Such Directive is an important element of EU privacy and human right law.

10/4 The Complaint

The Complaint is the citizen's most powerful weapon. However, the inventiveness of the System to disorient citizens when they get close to "hot" matters is impressive. This becomes particularly true when citizens realise violations of Community Law and the Commission decides it must whitewash.

However, if a citizen believes, understands or even thinks that EU law has been violated by a Member State, or by the European Commission services or by a private or public enterprise, he or she has the right to file a Complaint with the European Commission. The latter, must examine the case and decide if it must open an investigation process called an "infringement procedure" or not.

The Commission tries its utmost to discourage citizens from filing Complaints. There is an unwritten law in the System, that the wrongdoing of its services should not be unveiled, especially if such wrongdoing occurred in the "interest of the service." This is the modern version of the "raison d'état" introduced by Cardinal de Richelieu five centuries ago, which ultimately led to the French Revolution. Point is that all wrongdoings of the Commission, are supposedly committed in the "interest of the service."

We must admit that the System works late hours. The higher you rise in hierarchy, the more hours you put in, without claiming overtime. Indeed, if you pass by any of the 80 or more buildings the Commission occupies in Brussels in the evening, in certain rooms there are lights, visible from the outside. People are working hard you will think. If you look at the plans of the building, you will see that evening lights are mostly in the offices of Directors, Directors General and Heads of Unit. What are they doing? In the late hours, when the plebeians are out, the praetorians with the help of the patricians are manipulating Decisions, which must be approved by the College.

If you search online about what a citizen can do if Community Law is violated, you will get an extremely large amount of information, hundreds of pages where you will be informed clearly of all the innocent manners you have recourse to. They will tell you to call Europe Direct, or appeal to the Ombudsman, an institution with no real executive power and many other disorienting, harmless things. They will also send you to the "Petitions Committee" of the European Parliament. Yet you should consult with a crystal ball if you want to do something real and effective. So, here we are.

If you think that EU law has been violated, by anyone, file a Complaint with the European Commission. You need no forms and you pay nothing. Furthermore, you can write it in any of the EU official languages, including yours.

Write your claim in an email substantiating your case with documentation, and address it to the Commission. In the subject line, you should type the word "Complaint." You should send it to a few recipients, to be sure that it will be given attention. Therefore, you should address your complaint to the Secretariat General (SG-PLAINTES@ec.europa.eu) and cc it to the relevant DG and, if you suspect fraud, to the Antifraud Office OLAF, as well. And of course, copy your correspondence to New Europe.

In filing a Complaint with the European Commission, you should be aware of the following details.

Your name and the text of the Complaint are treated by the Commission as "secret" information in the sense that they cannot reveal your name to anyone. If they do, they are in breach of the Code of Conduct and consequences are grave. Even if theoretically someone can lose his job, often names are revealed because your Complaints will pass through several functionaries. Consequently, you can ask a lawyer friend to file the Complaint "on behalf of his Client." Your name should be notified, only when you take the Commission to the Court of Justice of the EU. Of course, a client of the lawyer could be anybody, so any name can be submitted to the Court. This is important to know because certain Member States are very vindictive when ordinary citizens bring cases to the Court in Luxemburg.

The name that will appear in the Court file does not really matter. What does matter is for the Commission services to know who is behind the Complaint. Indeed, they need to know because, depending on who the complainant is, they will take seriously the Complaint. To this effect, if the Complaint is on an important issue, the Commission will use all tricks to find the name of the Complainant to manipulate the case further, if necessary.

Your Complaint must be accompanied, if possible, by supporting documents. These documents you can get by the Commission through the Access to Documents procedure

One additional element to keep in mind is that if you are not satisfied with the response of the Commission, or if the Commission does not open infringement procedure, there is no recourse because of the "margin of discretion" of the Commission. You can have recourse to the Court of Justice of the EU, only if the Complaint concerns a breach of Competition Law by an undertaking and you have an interest to act. For this reason, DG Competition will try to forward the Complaint to another DG. For instance, if you file a Complaint to DG Competition against a state-controlled energy company on the grounds of de facto monopoly, they will forward it to DG Energy which may well close the case without you having the opportunity to appeal. In this case, you must insist with the Competition Department. You can also take the Commission to Court for the "Competition Complaint" you submitted as the Court will judge if it is a Competition case or not.

Finally, in writing your Complaint on any matter, try, if there is the case, to substantiate violation of the penal law as well. In this way, if you do not get a satisfactory response you will have the possibility to take the issue with the national or the Belgian Prosecutor. Of course, the System, will not be very happy about this.

10/5 Take Them to the Court, it is Cheap and Easy

Citizens can take the Commission directly to the Court of Justice of the European Union (CJEU) in Luxemburg.

Reasons for appealing to the CJEU are limited and well- defined. However, for such cases, it is easy as no fees and not complicated procedures for appealing are involved. The brief can be written in any of the 24 EU official languages. Any lawyer registered in a bar of any Member State can file legal charges.

The reasons a citizen can take the Commission to the CJEU without previously appealing to the Courts of the Member State, are the following.

In the case of refusal to release, partially or totally, documents asked according to Regulation (EC) 1049/2001 (see Access to Documents). The deadline is two months, after the final total or partial refusal of the release.

In the case of violation of Community law in matters of competition. The deadline is also two months, after you receive a final non-satisfactory reply from the Commission on your Complaint.

In the case of actions implicating the contractual liability and non-contractual liability of the Union due to damage caused by Union bodies or its employees in the performance of their duties, as well as from legislative activities of the European Institutions (Article 340 of TFEU). The deadline for acting is five years from the date the damage occurred. The Court of Justice of the EU recognises the liability of the European Institutions acting illegally under European law. Also, when there is a direct causal link between the damage suffered by the claimant and the illegal act of the European institutions or their agents.

The System has a strategy of encouraging individuals to render Member States liable in the case of damage caused by European law being poorly applied. This means that citizens have to appeal to the national courts. This is a procedure, which will cost money and take time, while the results may be dubious.

The approach in such cases should be different. Take the European Commission to the CJEU for damages for neglecting to launch infringement procedure to the Member State for not complying with EU law. The legal base in this case will be the non-contractual liability of the European Commission and the damages, because of which, the citizen has suffered.

THE COMMISSIONERS

11/1 Designated Commissioners

This chapter is dedicated to the Commissioners-designate, who have not been trapped by the System, yet. It is even more important, however, for sitting Commissioners, as they will pay attention to certain details that they were probably not aware of.

It is human nature to magnify the irrelevant and ignore the important.

Once the government of any Member State decides to appoint its Commissioner, the first to be informed is the Commission. Immediately after, the Head of the EU Representation in the country is visiting the designated Commissioner and informs him or her, in a very reverential manner addressing him or her as "Mr or Ms Commissioner," that he was sent by the Commission to brief and assist.

The designated Commissioner will learn the first "real" things about the Commission form the Head of the EU Representation. Or so will believe. In this section, we will learn that the Commission in its internal operational mode is functioning based on certain customary attitudes and unwritten rules. We will learn also that the unwritten rules are of prime importance and must be respected. This will not be said bluntly, but in an innocent way. It will be stated between the lines.

If the designated Commissioner has enough guts, he/she should reply, "unwritten laws are dictated only by God and I am an atheist." It is the best way to cut a long story short, but it never happens this way.

There is no modern democratic state with unwritten laws. Exceptionally, the European Commission and the "honourable societies" in Italy work with "unwritten laws," but they are not related what so ever to democracy.

Unwritten laws are valid mostly for incoming Commissioners from weak countries, and not for all. Contrary to the unwritten laws of the Commission, there have always been and applied before it was changed recently, the French unwritten law. It says that Palais de l'Élysée (official residence of the French President) appoints the French Commissioner as well as his Head of Cabinet. Even though this unwritten law was valid until recently, nobody from the System dared to challenge France. Thus, gradually some Commissioners tacitly followed the French precedent. Under these circumstances, the unwritten law concerning the Head of Cabinet has been "de facto" abolished. Now, a presidential (written) circular provides that the Head and Deputy Head of Cabinet cannot be both same nationality. However, there are still Commissioners who for the appointment of their head of Cabinet obey the abolished unwritten law in order to make the System happy.

The perception of small state Commissioners is a state of mind. You are a minor Commissioner if the System drove you to believe that you are a Commissioner of less importance because you are coming from a marginal country. It is not correct. All Commissioners are equal, full stop, as all have one vote in the College.

Once the designated Commissioner is nominated, the System will "take care" of him or her from the first moment, to the extent that he/she will not be able even breathe independently and gradually he/she will be isolated from the external world.

This is the first step to make the Commissioner a prisoner of the System and make him or her feel dependent and gradually, one of them. If the Commissioner comes from a new or small country, with some rare exceptions, he/she will never manage to penetrate the inner circle. He/she will be led to believe so but should always be reminded that he/she will never become part of the System because he/she will never be trusted.

Finally, the first thing a Commissioner must do, is to control all incoming correspondence and all calls. Indeed, in most cases, not even 5% of what arrives to the office of the Commissioner comes to his/her attention. As to the replies to the 95%...

11/2 The Hearing in the Parliament

Between the nomination of the Commissioners by the Member States and their official enthronement, there will be a hearing at the European Parliament for each one of them, individually. The hearing will confirm (or not) the appointment of the Commissioner. Only after a successful hearing does the nominee officially becomes Commissioner for five years.

After that, the Member State has no authority over its Commissioner, whatsoever. Upon approval by the European Parliament, Commissioners can only be dismissed only under certain well-defined circumstances. Member State have nothing to do with this.

Only the President of the Commission has the right to ask for a Commissioner's resignation without stating any reason or explanation. This prerogative of the President is purely political and is explicitly provided by Article 17 of the Treaty.

If the Commissioner violates EU law, the President may bring the issue to the College, which will decide whether to refer the case to the Court of Justice of the European Union.

If the European Parliament revokes its confidence in any Commissioner, he or she may be dismissed at any time.

The hearing at the European Parliament is not such a big mountain to climb. However, the System will present it to the Commissioner as a very difficult test, which can only be passed with the preparation and assistance of the System. It will be only the beginning of pushing the Commissioner into a trap for the next five years, where he/she will become a "prisoner" of the System. The trap will consist of a set of musts, obligations, rules and procedures and the Commissioner will be convinced that only the System can help him/her to rise to the occasion.

For a mature politician, the hearing at the European Parliament is a piece of cake. All questions are simple, political and not technical. With common sense, basic knowledge of European affairs and political understanding, questions at the hearing can be replied. Knowledge of the policy intentions of the President and of the policies of the Commissioner's portfolio is necessary. Some high-ranking officials of his/her DG coming from his own country can easily inform the Commissioner on the specifics.

It is very important for the Commissioner to select his mother tongue as the language of the hearing. This will give him more time to reflect, as there will be simultaneous interpretation. Furthermore, as there might be questions concerning his/her own career in his/her country of origin, they should be prepared for this and identify possible nasty questions. They should be ready with a simple, 10-word denial on every case and bring along various documents to deposit as evidence. Pertinent or relatively relevant, it does not matter, as long as they have a kind of affinity with the subject. The documents should be in the national language and should be filed with the chairperson of the hearing. Of course, no matter how relevant the documents will be to the case or not, this will be helpful for the battle of perceptions. The hearing lasts three hours and it takes at least a couple of months for the documents to be translated. Therefore, all documents presented during the hearing are mainly tabled to create impressions.

In recent years, it has become practice of the Parliament to reject at least one Commissioner-designate in each term. This way, the

Members of Parliament think they have real powers. Who will be rejected, however, is agreed beforehand between the two biggest political families in the European Parliament (EPP and S&D). Usually, the Commissioner-designate to be "scarified," if intelligent enough, will sense the looming danger and will behave accordingly.

In the last three parliaments, three Commissioners-designate were rejected, one in each parliament.

The first was the Italian Rocco Buttiglione, who was supposed to take the portfolio of Justice and Media. When he was asked his opinion about gays he said something like: "I do not know about gays, all what I know is that in Bergamo, we call them ricchioni!" The Parliament, where a silent community of gays is quite active, rejected the appointment. That was in 2004.

In 2009, we had the case of Rumiana Jeleva. Coming from Bulgaria, a country with rough political antitheses and sometimes grotesque political reactions, Jeleva presented herself in the Parliament, briefed not by trusted people but by the Services of her DG. She was given a German Head of Cabinet. She came to Brussels, impressed by what was happening around her, and found her Cabinet practically ready. She had fallen into the trap of the System. Then Jeleva, a typically stubborn Bulgarian, wanted to have the hearing in English while she made the mistake to refer in her speech, by name, one of her adversaries, a Member of Parliament from the Liberal Party (ALDE). Jeleva was with the EPP Popular Party.

Mentioning the name of the political adversary during the hearing gave the right to her adversary, Antonia Parvanova, to speak up and defend herself. Parvanova, a sharp, intelligent medical doctor with good political culture and understanding of the Brussels machine, practically "executed" Jeleva in no time. The then Prime Minister of Bulgaria asked immediately after the hearing for Jeleva to resign, and she did.

In 2014, we had the case of the interim Slovenian Prime minister Alenka Bratusek who nominated herself as Commissioner. The System discussed the matter with the Slovenian nomenklatura dealing with Brussels and the self- designated Slovenian Commissioner was rejected.

To cut a long story short, the hearing in the European Parliament, for an experienced politician, is, as stated before, a piece of cake. The System, however, will try to "sell" it to newcomers in such a way as to trap them into its net from the very beginning. The Commissioner-designate will be kept busy reading and learning useless technicalities in preparation for the hearing and, in the meantime, the System will manipulate the making of his/her Cabinet.

As for the language of the hearing, do not speak English unless you are a native English speaker. In all official events, starting from the hearing, you can speak your own language and reply to all questions in your own language, as well. This is the reason the EU has a huge interpretation department which works on translation of documents and simultaneous translation, in 24 EU languages.

The hearing is neither a trial nor an interrogation for Commissioners-designate, but it is their first public appearance.

11/3 The Making of a Cabinet

Each Commissioner has his own team, known as the Cabinet, which consists of up to 17 persons, including six AD grade functionaries (Administrators), the rest being of AST grade (Assistants) and AST/SC grade (Assistants/Secretaries).

In theory, Commissioners can structure their Cabinet the way they want. In practice, they do not. Many things depend on the personality of the Commissioners, their targets, their vision for Europe and their country and finally how strong their willpower is.

Cabinets are the battering ram of the System. Nothing and nobody can resist the Cabinets. On the other hand, Cabinets can bring the change we need. For this to happen they must first be appointed by the Commissioner and not by the System. Also, the cardinal members of the Cabinet must not see the Cabinet as a launching platform for their own career in the Commission, but as a solid step to make a political career in their Member State of origin.

The way in which the Cabinets are structured render them the "long arm" of the servants of the System. Their aim is to obstruct any initiative of the Commissioner that is not approved by the inner circle of the System and promote policies decided by the System. If the Commissioner is against such policies, the Cabinet will find the way to stop him/her from raising reservations in the College.

However, the manipulation of the Commissioner is not the role of the Cabinet. Cabinets must assist Commissioners to pursue European policies and assist them to formulate new policies they think are right for Europe and its citizens. They must also assist the Commissioner to look after the interests of his own country within the limits of EU law and make the Commission citizen-friendly, which it currently is not.

Often Commissioners, swept by the inspirational winds of Brussels, forget where they came from and become "Commissioners of Europe." This is correct because they are Commissioners of Europe. However, they are also citizens of their own country where they will return after five years. And, ultimately, they will not be buried in *Cimetière d'Ixelles*, but somewhere in their birthplace, probably next to their Head of Cabinet, if they manage to win the System and have their own trusted associate to lead their office.

Therefore, it is crucial for the new Commissioners to avoid being manipulated. Upon announcement of their nomination, the System is put on red alert and uses any means available to position the Commissioner under its control.

First, the System creates the proper climate of "terror" around the hearing, magnifying the non-case, especially if the Commissioner is not too familiar with Brussels. The formation of the Cabinet is the next matter to settle and usually, the services "manage" to put it together with the hearing. While the Commissioner-designate is busy studying for the exam (which is not really an exam), it is easy to manipulate the formation of the Cabinet by bringing to the Commissioner a ready, and apparently fine-looking, solution.

If the Commissioner gets seriously involved in the selection of his Cabinet staff, the System will put forward several obstacles, ethics, customary procedures, unwritten rules, the relations of the Commissioner with the Cabinet of the President and others. Therefore, the Commissioner, anxious about the coming hearing, is likely to let it go. More so, he will feel secure that two of the six executive positions, one of which is the Head or rather the Deputy Head of the Cabinet (in most cases it happens that the selection of the Deputy Head is left for the Commissioner), will be left for him to select from people in his own country.

It should be noted that the Communication of the President C20149002, on page 5, states "The Head of Cabinet or the Deputy Head of Cabinet shall be of a different nationality from that of the Commissioner."

The position of the Head of Cabinet, depending on the personalities involved, may prove more powerful than the Commissioner (even though no Commissioner will ever accept this fact).

Therefore, Commissioners must appoint a "non-systemic" figure that they can trust to fill this position. More so because the distance that separates the Head of Cabinet and his Deputy is larger than the Pacific Ocean.

11/4 Why Cabinets are Important

The decision-making process of the Commission is standard. The various DGs present to the corresponding Cabinet the dossiers with the issues requiring a College Decision. The Cabinets examine the dossiers of the draft (proposed) Decisions to be introduced to the College and brief the Commissioner.

According to the instructions of the Director General or his assistant, they emphasise the importance of the aspects the services wish to highlight and downplay the others.

The Cabinets, after "consulting" with their Commissioners, decide which dossiers will be brought to the College for a Decision to be taken. Early in the afternoon each Monday, all Heads of Cabinets meet to discuss the various dossiers and decide on the classification of the dossiers into A and B. Dossiers under B will be discussed during the College meeting on Wednesday and a final decision will be taken by the College after a debate.

However, only a few are selected for discussion in the College. The Commissioner in charge of a selected dossier that needs to get a specific decision from the College has to negotiate the matter with his or her colleagues in the days before the meeting in order to secure the necessary majority. Usually, Commissioners negotiate on a qui-pro-quo basis except on certain major political issues and at the end of the day, everybody is happy.

Dossiers classified under A are practically already approved by the Heads of Cabinets. As such, these do not need further discussion in the College. In this case, the College formally approves the decisions "en bloc," as presented by the Cabinets, without any discussion.

Under these circumstances, it becomes crystal clear why the services want, at all costs, to control the Cabinets with their own people and especially the position of the Head of Cabinet.

Once somebody gets one of the six AD positions in a Cabinet, and if proves to be intelligently cooperative with the System, will subsequently secure a meteoric career. That is, from Plebeian will become Patrician, and by the time will leave the Cabinet will have secured a good post in the hierarchy. Indeed, after serving in the Cabinet, depending on how helpful and cooperative one was with the "house," also known as *"la maison"*, they will get a post as Head of Unit or Director. Heads of Cabinets aim directly at a position of Director and exceptionally Director General.

Another "capacity" of the Cabinet is to kill the ideas and initiatives of the Commissioner that are not in line with the philosophy and interests served by the System.

This is the key and therefore the Commissioner must secure his own people in his Cabinet. Once someone gets a post in the Cabinet, they will do whatever is possible to satisfy the System. This often means going against the choices or the interests of the Commissioner. However, the manipulation will be so extremely sophisticated and smooth that the Commissioner will probably never notice what is going on. Therefore, the Commissioners must select their own team for their Cabinet and keep the "services" at bay.

AND YET, IT MOVES

12/1 The European Union Must Adapt

Systems that do not adapt, disappear. The dinosaurs disappeared 65 million years ago because they did not adapt to new Earth geo-climatic conditions.

The most recent and pertinent case in the contemporary geo-political world is that of the collapse of the Soviet Communism on 29 December 1991. It disappeared overnight, after a reign of terror that lasted 74 years, because the gap between ordinary citizens and the communist nomenklatura became unbridgeable. The Kremlin, too big and too strong to adapt, was living in its own world and had abolished the two-way communication exchange with the people.

A rather similar situation, or close to it, is the European Union of today. Of course, the EU cannot be compared to the Soviet Union as the EU is an association of democratic nations ruled by a non-political, very strong administration, which throughout the years, in the absence of leadership, became autocratic.

The Soviet Union was a cruel dictatorship with the only advantage being that its people never sensed freedom and were led by a merciless super-dictator yet in a highly-politicised context.

The fundamental European Institution, the Commission, which theoretically corresponds to the government of Europe, has developed into an organism that is too big to adapt in the emerging new socio-political conditions. By acquiring more authority over its citizens, the European administration has exceeded its capacity limits and cannot control the embodiment of its rule -over-regulation, which is its own creature.

For the first time in post-war European history, social evolution is not linear. The new parameters, which formulate our social landscape, are thus not predictable by civil servants who can handle perfectly linear phenomena but not dynamic changes. Such situations can be handled only by politicians. For the administrations, two plus two makes four, not any and more not less. But in politics two plus two might make four. It might.

European society is trapped by a closed system of striving over-regulation that results in galloping unemployment and deepening austerity. In parallel, Europeans are subject to a mass influx of immigrants and refugees of different religious and social cultures.

Both problems are very recent and involve millions of people. A strong administration can handle isolated interest groups, as well as individual citizens, under normal conditions. But millions with acute, survival problems cannot be effectively handled without the cooperation and support of society.

European governments and the EU, because of the growing terrorist threats, have opted for more security and less freedoms.

The current leaders of the traditional 15 EU Member States are of a small political calibre. They cannot handle serious crisis such as the socio-political crisis, which they think is economic, and the predicament over immigrants. They left the problems with the administration to address. All problems of the European Union today are, however, political and cannot be addressed by civil servants.

The situation is worsening as all matters are of a deep political nature and the administrators in charge of them are only addressing what they know, with more restrictions and increased regulations that is so overstated that they cannot handle the situation.

At the top of the agenda is immigration – the main social issue of the day. To address it within the framework of our political system, values, and interests requires determination and the cooperation and support of citizens.

Unemployment is also a major problem in that it requires the cooperation of the people in order for it to be resolved. The System believes that unemployment will be reduced with big investments, which means even more austerity to finance these big investments.

Wrong.

To conclude, nothing can be done when citizens do not trust their administrations anymore. It seems the European Union, as an oasis of freedom, democracy, and prosperity, is being driven to its eventual end.

A partial or total failure of the European Union will bring to power in most of the Member States newcomers to politics armed with ideas that will be difficult for society to absorb and adapt to.

The only way to avoid this is for the citizens of Europe and the governments of the Member States to understand and assume their historical responsibilities and make the peaceful changes we need to survive.

They only need knowledge of the truth and determination, both of which they have. Knowledge is power, and the truth is the most powerful weapon.

12/2 A New Start without Euro

The European Union must reform in order to survive and return to what we dreamed of, while meeting the hopes and expectations of its citizens. Reforms are, however, quasi- impossible as will it be extremely difficult to peacefully deprive people, especially the intelligent "merciless killers-types", the sort of privileges that they do not reserve, but have accumulated over the years.

"Quasi" implies that it can be done.

For the European Union to survive and prosper, we must restore the political powers back into the hands of elected politicians and deprive the Brussels nomenklatura from the extraordinary powers that they have accumulated over the years. Downsizing the privileges and the powers of the Commission employees, will facilitate the process of saving Europe.

This, will make somehow easier the abolition of Euro common currency as it favoured only one country while the rest drown in austerity, recession, and unemployment. To be liberated from the Brussels stranglehold, the United Kingdom, withdrew from the EU because of the heavy-handedness of Brussels.

Abolish the Euro with a fast track procedure with a summit that will approve a new Treaty, without groupings of currencies or interim situations will be the challenge of the century. Once completed, this will be followed by a period of chaotic disorder on the international currency markets, the banks and big conglomerates, but it will only be temporary, and it can be short. The markets and enterprises know how to survive and to profit in times of crisis. The return of the

European nations back to their national currencies will bring major inflation and, therefore, jobs and hope.

It should be understood that the Euro is not a national currency, but a union of currencies and cannot last forever as a result. No union of currencies has had a lengthy shelf life, and all were abolished when the socio-economic differences among the participating nations became unmanageable.

The abolishment of the Euro will create chaos, that is true, but as always, the chaos is followed by period of order and stability. This is the beauty of it. Chaos always creates order.

A new treaty for the abolishment of Euro should also provide that all foreign and domestic loans must be converted into the newly re-introduced national currencies the moment that the Euro is abolished. The exchange rates at the moment of the Euro abolishment, must be same as when the various countries first adopted the Euro.

Germany for example. When it entered into the Euro, the Deutsche Mark (DM) exchange rate was 2 DM for 1 Euro. The exchange rate in the current case will be the same and all German loans - whether domestic or foreign - will be converted into DM at the rate 1 Euro equals 2 DMs. If the DM will later devalue, this will be the problem of the creditors. No business is risk free and here we must only look for society to keep the calm.

More importantly, the Euro is rapidly losing ground in the conscience of European citizens. Ordinary people are now more concerned about their country joining the Eurozone in the first place. With the exception of very few people, the Euro has only brought problems to Main Street, in the form of austerity, unemployment, recession, and salary reductions.

Italians recently turned the political landscape of the country upside down when 53% voted for anti-establishment, and in practical terms, anti-Euro candidates. Italians are clever people and will channel these changes in an intelligent manner. Italy is a country where the omnipotent Commission, which is fighting the mother of all battles to keep the Euro alive, can do nothing. Italians are politically smart and experienced and they know vert well how to handle timing.

The first anti-Euro eruption exploded in Greece in 2015 when 61% of Greeks voted in a national referendum to withdraw from the Euro. The director of the Commission's office in Athens claimed publicly that he had visited the President of the Hellenic Republic on the evening of the Referendum and told him that if the Greeks did not ignore the result of the poll and thus, remain in the Eurozone, an emergency meeting would be convened in Brussels the following Monday morning to move to kick Greece out of the Euro and the EU.

A couple of days after this statement, which in simple terms was a successful attempt by the Commission to blackmail the Greek government to force them to stay in the Eurozone, I asked the Commission's Spokesperson Service to explain who sent the message conveyed to the Greek President and to explicitly reveal what the content of the message was.

The reply was astonishing:

"Dear Basil,

Please publish the following statement and attribute it to a spokesperson of the Commission:

«There were no instructions given by the Commission to the Head of our Representation to undertake specific demarches at the time and on the issues mentioned. Any relevant activity was based on his own initiative in the framework of his duties. The role of the Commission and of President Juncker in keeping Greece into the Eurozone whilst actively supporting with positive measures its return to growth, is universally known".

Sincerely, "

That the Commission did not immediately fire the employee who, "with their own initiative" lied to a sitting president of an EU Member State, means that the employee acted on instructions. In this matter there is no more to say as everything is clear.

Europeans, in their conscience, have repudiated the Euro and the sooner it is abolished, the better we will be, but it must be abolished orderly and minimise the collateral damages.

12/3 The Role of the European Parliament

The salvation of Europe is now gradually passing into the hands of the politicians and the citizens. Both national parliaments and the European Parliament are full of parliamentarians who are ready to "do something" about it.

The issue is very current it is a just cause and communication wise, it is a convincing argument. Adding to the panic of the System, which is not capable of addressing crises, and the political change in Italy, it is now the great opportunity to channel fundamental changes, as the reactions will be minimal.

The authority of the European Parliament must be expanded, which can be done by amending the internal regulation of the Parliament. This can be achieved without the approval of the Council.

Parliamentary questions must be replied in a satisfactory manner. The Members of Parliament ask serious questions that require serious replies, but instead receive a lot of nonsense with references to 'Decisions and Regulations', but no firm response to the question that was asked.

The Parliament is the supreme European institution and must be respected by all.

In amending its internal regulations, the Parliament must establish a Special Transparency Committee where all of the Members of Parliament who do no receive satisfactory replies will submit their claims and force the Commission to reply. At the same time, the functionaries responsible for inadequate replies must be dismissed.

A similar approach must be applied when the Commission refuses to release documents and personal data to citizens under Commission Regulations EC) 1049 and 45 of 2001. In this case, the Commission will claim that any citizen can take the Commission to court, which is a useless argument as very few citizens will take the time to file a court case and wait for a decision on a release. By the time the court hands down a ruling in favour of the citizen, the document will most likely be useless. As an example, when a citizen asks for information on the awarding of a tender, the reply that will have to come through the court, meaning the data received will be useless by the time the awarded project is finished.

In cases where a citizen has taken the Commission to court over the former's refusal to release certain documents, once a decision has been made, the Commission functionaries responsible for the refusal must be immediately dismissed.

Statements and replies to questions by the Spokesperson Service must be also scrutinised as certain "hot" matters are only addressed indirectly, which causes disinformation, or 'fake-news', to be generated. The Spokesperson Service must reply honestly and clearly to all questions as fake news has no place in a democracy. Again, the Parliament must provide guarantees for that.

The Parliament must abolish the Commission's "discretionary power". No civil servant, regardless of the positions, has any discretionary power in a democracy. The Commission shouldn't either.

12/4 Your Commissioner Will Get You Europe Back

Your Commissioner is the Key.

The Member States who wish to benefit from EU membership and who are willing to regain their dignity and their role in European policymaking must make their peaceful revolution by choosing their Commissioner with new criteria – this is a revolution.

Europe must change to survive, and this can only happen if the Member States, regardless of size and political leverage, all benefit from their membership. The Commissioners must go beyond being the "Ministers of Europe" and look after the interests of their countries.

This is a very sensitive political matter as the Union cannot survive in the medium to long-term if the Member States are not fairly and honestly treated. Therefore, the "Ministers of Europe" must become watch-dogs for the interests of their countries while securing the interests of Europe as a whole. This is a question that comes down to who can possibly better secure the national interests of the individual Member States in Brussels than the national Commissioners?

In many Member States the Commissioners are chosen based on intra-party domestic equilibria and complicated political expediencies. An individual who is very strong, often the ruling party or the head-of-state, themselves, want to get rid of a difficult opponent, and may park him or her in Brussels as a Commissioner for five years.

This approach is completely wrong. Indeed, it is the basic reason that most countries are marginalised in Europe and thus lose both money and opportunities. The EU is not only about obligations, commitments, and contributions, it also offers great opportunities for development and growth through programmes and co-financed projects that are especially designed for the economically weaker Member States.

Of course, all of this depends on the know-how that the national administrations display when approaching Brussels. To this effect, the Commissioner, his team in Brussels, and support from home are the key players.

The Commissioners have three essential roles starting with the theoretical concept that they are supposed to be the "Ministers of Europe". For all practical purposes, the Commissioners are representatives of their countries and look after the interests of their home nations. This is not because they do not believe in Europe, but because Europe is not what it should be. To diffuse the national dimension of the role of the Commissioners, President Jean- Claude Juncker, in reference to his own country Luxemburg, defined it as "the country that I know better."

But it does not work this way.

Each Commissioner must also act as a political leader for Europe according to his or her assigned portfolio. This role gives the Commissioner special powers in policymaking based on the extent of their portfolio for the entire European Union. Some of these powers are extremely efficient negotiating tools in the hands of the Commissioner and the country that he or she comes from. That some Commissioners are not fully aware of this capacity, and most do not use it, is another issue that reflects the personality and the political aims of the Commissioner and the degree that is trapped by the Cabinet.

Third, the Commissioner is a Member of the College, the collective body that in practice is the closest equivalent of a ministerial cabinet of Europe. The role of the Commissioner in this collective body is of an unambiguous importance to each Member State if the Commissioner is aware of his or her real powers.

It is true that each Commissioner, despite portfolio, may have an opinion on any matter and can express it in voting when comes to collective decisions at the supreme level of the European Commission, the College of the Commissioners. The College vote is always the result of checks, balances and compromises. This is how the Commissioners achieve collateral benefits for their countries in the perpetual give-and-take process that defines Brussels.

Under these circumstances, the choice of the Commissioner is an opportunity for the Member States to be duly and efficiently represented every five years by someone who has the ability, experience and determination to help his or her country and get it benefit from every opportunity. To be able to exert its powers, it is "sine qua non" prerequisite for the Commissioner to fully control his Cabinet.

The Member States must understand that large and small decisions that affect all issues have an impact on the everyday life of citizens who depend entirely on the European Institutions. This is where the real political power and executive decision-making has been transposed from the national governments to the European Commission, a administrative body with no political legitimization to take political decision and not in the Council or the European Parliament.

The European heads-of-state and the opposition leaders need to understand that the post of the Commissioner is not a parking spot to exile their intraparty political rivals. It is the battering ram of the country in the fight with fortress Europe.

When the time comes to appoint a new Commissioner, the governments and political parties in the Member States must stay together and select the best, the most prominent, sharp, and capable politician that they have for the position of Commissioner. Together with the Commissioner-designate, they must choose a team that will support him or her in Brussels.

The Member State and Commissioner must then negotiate a portfolio reflecting the size, importance, and particular expediencies of the country. The Commissioners will continue to bring to Brussels two or three trusted assistants and faithful secretaries, which the System methodically and systematically pays to marginalise.

To bring the change we need, the Commissioner must bring along a team of approximately 25 people, 20 executives, and 5 assistants. Some will staff the Cabinet of the Commissioner, while the others will be based in the Permanent Representation of the country supporting the Commissioner and their office.

Each one will be assigned general and specific competences that correspond to the Commissioner's portfolio. During the Commissioner's five-year term, a rotation should be applied so that most of the team spends at least a couple of years in the political quarters of the Commission. This experience will be extremely useful when they return to national politics or become top executives in the public administrations of their countries.

Serving under such conditions in Brussels and being involved in the daily routine will give the team members from the various Member States the opportunity to work and socialise with colleagues from other countries, and develop networking skills. This will prove very useful in strengthening relations among European countries when these people will assume political or administrative roles in their respective countries.

In this way, through the process of developing honest relations among administration executives from all over Europe, the European idea will be consolidated.

The qualifications for the Commissioner's team are very important. The selection should not take place with the usual "who you know" approach, but for once with the "what you know" method. Educational background, languages, smart thinking versus empty talk, and a determination to use success in Europe to launch a national political career or in the national administration should become the criteria.

Two important elements to consider:

(a) Under no circumstance should any member of the team have even hidden ambitions to make a career in Brussels in any capacity that goes beyond representing their country diplomatically or in the Parliament. If the Commissioner sees any change in the attitude of a member of their team, that person should be immediately replaced.

(b) Though all will be supporters or members of political parties in their countries, once in Brussels they must leave their party IDs behind.

As the Commission will not like this innovation at all, the Commissioner's team stationed in the Representation should be given an attractive name and purpose so that the "system" can digest it, *volendo o nolendo* as my Italian friend would have said.

The new section in the Permanent Representations could be given the catchy name "Team Europe." The scope of this new unit could have the noble task to better understand Europe and bring it closer to its citizens. It could be specified that the unit's goal will be achieved in cooperation with the Commissioner and his Cabinet, as well as with the Commission Services and the European Parliament.

This 'Team Europe' will be the political watchdog of the Member States in Brussels. Its task will be to help the Cabinet of the Commissioner, as well as Members of Parliament, with superior intelligence monitoring and advice. Team Europe could help the Cabinet in the preparation of draft legislation, considering the Member State's interests, as well.

As to internal rules are just simple internal rules, non-comparable to Regulations, Directives or even Court Decisions, which the System violates at will through its undefined "discretionary powers." The Commissioners can therefore violate internal rules at will and can even change them.

12/5 More National Politicians in the Commission

The root of the crisis in the European Union, which could lead to the Union's dismemberment, is a lack of political leadership in the executive ruling body of the 27 Member States – the European Commission.

Each of the Member States are entitled to propose one Commissioner for a five-year term to act as the political leadership of the Commission, the *de facto* government of Europe.

This creates a political body of 27 politicians who originate from 27 different European countries, speaking 24 different languages, of different political orientations that include the Christian Democrats, Socialists and Liberals. Furthermore, they do not know each other, they know very little about the rules of the game in Brussels and often find themselves in the position of being subjected to a forced education about the in-and-outs of the System.

Most Member States do not appoint their best politician as Commissioner, but instead often select an individual that the head of state wants to marginalise.

These 27 politically and culturally heterogeneous politicians are supposed to rule the "monster" that is the European Commission. As the most sophisticated administrative body in the world, the Commission is staffed by an army of some 30,000 loyal foot "mujahideen" tasked with mastering 110,000 pieces of European legislation. They are all immovable and accountable to no one, except their boss. The present ruling scheme of the European Commission does not leave any room for political control.

The first thing that should be done for Europe to survive as it should be and not how it currently is, is to enhance the political presence of the Member States at the Commission and curtail the supernatural powers of the administration by making the Commission political.

The present structure of the Commission, with one Commissioner per Member State, goes back seven decades when the EU was comprised of only six nations, with two Commissioners each, and dealing mostly with agricultural matters. With 27 current members, the European Commission rules over the every-day life of a half a billion people, right down to the smallest detail and is headed only by 27 politicians.

Every Member State should be sending not only a single Commissioner, but at least five politicians, that would include two alternate Commissioners and two deputy Commissioners to lead directorate generals, agencies, and independent services.

The System became ever stronger over the years, it evolved into a self-reproducing, non-transparent, and independent leviathan accountable to no one. Under the circumstances, it is practically impossible for an ordinary Commissioner to make any sort of political decision even when it is within their portfolio.

In a Directorate General that employees roughly 2,000 people, the Commissioner theoretically has direct control of their 17-person Cabinet. In reality, however, the Commissioner in question does not control even half of the staff.

All the staff of the Directorate and related agencies are under the direct control of the Director General and the few systemic praetorians of the Cabinet. Therefore, the first thing to do is to increase the number of appointed politicians from the Member States to serve in the Commission.

Political appointees from the Member States should ideally originate from the major political parties of the country and be selected based on merit. To increase the number of appointed politicians, a new Treaty needs to be adopted. Since the stakes are very high and a catastrophe is something that can no longer be excluded as an outcome, any such a decision can be provisionally made by a majority vote in the Council in order to be implemented as quickly as possible.

Led by Germany, a few of the big Member States continue to use the present administrative scheme to politically and financially dominate the Union. They not only want to maintain the status quo but are preparing the ground to decrease the member of Commissioners and thus further reduce the possibility of any sort of political control of the Commission and instead turn it into their own secretariat that would dominate Europe.

This is the current and unvarnished reality. Unfortunately, the will of those who want to see the System, as it is presently constituted, continue to prevail. Thus, as a potential catastrophe of the Union may originate only by uncontrolled "bottom-up" developments, there is only one way out for the Union. Escape forward in the context of an unconditional generous compromise.

12/6 Eradicate the power of the Cabinets

Each Commissioner is allowed to have an office of up to 17 people, of which six are functionaries (AD), who work in close cooperation with the inner circle of the Commission and do everything the System asks with or without the knowledge of the Commissioner. The others are secretaries, assistants, and drivers. Career-wise, the future of the functionaries in the office of the Commissioner depends entirely on how much cooperative they will be with the System.

From their first day on the job, in most cases, Ads behave in a way that is aimed at satisfying the System without the Commissioner having real knowledge of what they do in his name.

As a result, the first thing to be done is for the Cabinet of the Commissioner to stop handling dossiers. Consequently, the staff in the office of the Commissioner must be limited to three or four individuals who will exclusively service the Commissioner, including the two executives of their choice, one of which the head will be from the home country of the Commissioner. The Commissioner and the Alternate and Deputy Commissioners will then handle the various dossiers directly with competent units, and the Director General will be notified, but will only be involved when asked by the Commissioner.

Today, all dossiers require a College Decision. However, before presented in the College, are discussed among the Heads of the Cabinets. They decide which dossiers will be discussed in the College (procedure B) and which will be approved *"en bloc"*, without any discussion (Procedure A). What is of paramount importance in this particular manner is that the content of most of the dossiers is ignored by the Commissioner as the System thinks that they should not be bothered with "irrelevant matters" even if they concern issues that are involve millions of euros.

The Cabinets, the way they are structured, are designed to exclusively serve the inner circle of the Commission and to keep the Commissioner under control, while at the same time giving him the impression that he has a role.

By abolishing the super-powers of the Cabinets, the political leadership of the Commission will return to the Commissioners.

12/7 End the Despotism of the Directors General

A major setback for the long-term survival of the European Commission is the status of the Directors General under the present appointment schemes, which the College must view as a priority in that it directly concerns the Commissioners and the political functioning of the Commission.

There are 46 sitting Directors General, nearly double the number of 27 Commissioners. The reason for this is simple as the System exerts easy control over the College and leaves the Commissioners without any room to exert even the slightest for of political control.

Every five years, the new Commission will assume its duties on November 1, nearly six months after the May Parliamentary elections. Shortly before the end of the term of the outgoing Commission – roughly, in the latter part of October – the System will prepare for the rotation of the Directors General and decide on their re-positioning for the next half decade. That term will begin on January 1, only two months after the new Commission begins its mandate.

In one of the last College weekly meetings, when all of the outgoing Commissioners think only of their political future and nobody cares of the Commission anymore, it is passed a College Decision, under "Procedure A" (approved by the College without even looking at the content of what they approve), a Decision providing for the appointments of the Directors General for the next five years.

As a result, the new Commissioners who will assume their duties on November 1, two months after, on January 1, will be visited by an individual who will then present himself as their new Director General for the next five years.

All of the Directors General meet as regularly as once per week. In one such recent meeting. a Director General unveiled certain personnel changes he had decided for his DG and when asked what his Commissioner thinks about the changes, he replied smiling, *"when I will need my Commissioner's opinion, I will ask him".*

What must change is simple and it will produce transformative results. In one of its weekly meetings, the College must rule that the Commissioners have the undisputed authority to hire and fire Director Generals at will. They must also rule that once a Commission functionary becomes Director General, regardless of their age, they will be dismissed after five years and will no longer have the possibility to ever return to work for the European Commission unless they return as a political appointee.

The System will most likely unanimously oppose and obstruct such a cardinal change. However, a College Decision passed with simple majority will be enough to break down the existing situation and contribute significantly to making Europe better and even democratic.

12/8 Lifting Immunity

All Commission employees, regardless of their status or position, enjoy diplomatic immunity. In this context, they are not susceptible to lawsuits or prosecution in regard to their duties as EU employees. European Commission employees can, therefore, violate EU laws at will while claiming that they are exercising their duties,

---

This is a standard practice, especially in the case of contract awards.

If for any reason an employee of the Commission violates an EU law and a Prosecutor requests the European Commission to lift their diplomatic immunity, the College, as is the standard practice, will refuse and the criminal investigation will be closed, before opened.

The immunity of EU civil servants must be abolished, and all employees must perform their duties responsibly and lawfully as it happens with all civil servants, all over the democratic world.

Lifting the immunity of EU employees - other than the Commissioners, who are political appointees - is a must and will restore accountability of EU staff. The abolishment of immunity must not be retroactive otherwise certain Commission services might be decimated.

The abolishment of embassies among the Member States is another hot button issue. Is it logical for Denmark to have an Embassy to Italy when the various ministers of the two countries meet regularly and speak at any time there are issues to address?

The European Commission and the European Parliament should have luxury premises with large numbers of employees in the Member States when they can have dedicated employees in each important ministry that follow EU matters?

The real reason, of course, is that the Commission with this type of offices, spies on the Member States.

12/9 Transparency

To help restore accountability, the irrational immunity that EU civil servants currently enjoy must be abolished and a mechanism put in place to ensure that all actions for payments from the EU budget are uploaded to the internet and made available to the public. This would include all of the documents involved in a transaction, from calls for tenders to the evaluation of offers, award protocols, intra-service memos, and even notes for files and emails.

To further guarantee that the EU bureaucrats are held accountable, European citizens should be given the right to appeal to either Belgian or national Prosecutors, as well as to the European Prosecutor, once the newly formed body becomes functional.

The internet and the threat of the Prosecutor, regardless of whether they are European or national, will secure transparency and force EU civil servants to obey the law.

12/10 Reform the Reforms

In 2000, during the Romano Prodi Commission, the European executive unilaterally introduced a series of self-styled administrative reforms that proved catastrophic for the future of the European Union. The reforms, known as the "Kinnock Reforms", were secretly and carefully designed by British authorities and were introduced to Brussels as a *fait accompli* by the then-British Commissioner responsible for Administration, Neil Kinnock.

The reforms provided for extensive outsourcing of consulting services in many areas, including policy issues. They also abolished the Commission's fund for its employees and passed its assets on to the EU budget.

Given the nature of the outsourcing, the main beneficiaries have been overwhelmingly Anglo-American companies. Under the circumstances, outsourcing should minimize to secondary jobs and the relevant Commission services must be restored. It is outrageous for the government of Europe to outsource policy matters.

As to the civil servants' fund. In the event that the European Union somehow dissolves, would see pension and retirement benefits paid out by the individual Member States, and not by Brussels, which would see civil servants' pensions reduced drastically.

Therefore, one of the first things to do will be to restore the fund of the EU civil servants in order to secure their pensions, in the case something goes wrong. Such funds exist in other international organizations even after the organizations have been abolished. For example, the last pension of the predecessor of the United Nations, the Society of the Nations, was paid to last in life official of that organization, two years ago.

The Kinnock Reforms did, however, provided positive changes into how the European Commission functions, especially in matters of transparency and financial control. The changes that were ushered in, no matter how positive they were at the time, must now be all reviewed from zero base, examining how they help the European Union better guarantee its own future.

12/11 The Sensitive Posts

A major shortcoming when it comes to how the European Services function is the fact that key sensitive posts are occupied by the same executives for more than the five-year limit provided by the staff regulation.

When the System wants to keep an executive in their same post for many years, it usually employs a scheme whereby it regularly changes the name of the position or ads and removes secondary duties from the position's job description.

Hypocrisy is one of the basic characteristics of the System, where everybody is happy. This is a detail that must be taken into consideration.

One of the most flagrant examples of this practice is case of a Commission official responsible for personnel matters. Using various dubious mechanisms, the executive in question has kept the same position for almost 15 years. In much the same manner, the head of a unit that awards contracts in SG Energy has been in the same post for over 10 years and has reportedly even refused a promotion.

Under the circumstances, a brief revision of the staff regulation will be enough to restore order when it comes to the very delicate matter of sensitive posts.

Serving in sensitive posts must be reduced to three years. Functionaries that serve in sensitive posts must stay there up to three years, not one day more, and after the three-year term, must be subject to a mandatory transfer to another Directorate General, not related to the previous. Furthermore, same sensitive positions must not be occupied by the same nationality twice over a period of 30 years.

The claim that employees need time to be used to the post, is only an excuse. The job is simple, functionaries have higher education and more time is needed only to know better all players (beneficiaries, middle-men, etc.).

12/12 Yes, We Can Make It

As previously mentioned, major organisations that fail to or refuse to adapt ultimately disappear. If the European Union does not adapt, it too will vanish overnight and this it will not occur in an orderly way.

The big Member States that exploit the smaller nations will never let their "colonies" to be free. But socio-political grassroots changes, however, cannot be manipulated and certainly cannot be avoided by Regulations or Treaties.

Most of the personalities involved in perpetuation of the European myth, believe that the interested parties who want Europe to survive are much stronger than the those that want it dissolve. They believe that the European Union will certainly survive. However, only two things are certain in life - death and taxes. The second is sometimes not nearly as certain and nothing else is guaranteed, including the future of the European Union.

So uncertain is the future of the EU that if it, indeed, does not change in order to meet the hopes, needs, and expectations of the diverse peoples of Europe, it will crumble under its own weight from the pressures that are already rapidly spreading and impossible to reverse under the same conventional way of thinking.

Germany and the Brussels nomenklatura will not permit even the slightest change in the normalisation of intra-European relations, which would secure the salvation of the Union, because they stand to lose both financial benefits and power. They continue to and will block any initiative that could turn the Union from a merciless administrative machine into a human political entity.

As grassroots changes have already begun in Italy, Slovenia, Hungary, Spain, and Poland among others, there is no time to lose. Germany and the Brussels establishment must adapt, otherwise they will not avoid perpetuating the own downfall.

A logical person knows that when they are affected by gangrene, they either to have amputate the stricken limb or die. Too much wealth and too much power means they have to give some in order to keep some to avoid losing everything.

The European Union was created seven decades ago when the United States invited French Charles De Gaulle and the Chancellor of West Germany, Konrad Adenauer, to discuss ways to unite Europe in an effort to avoid a third pan-European war in the 20th-century, as well as ways to fundamentally sort out any outstanding Franco-German disputes.

It is and was in the best interest of the United States, the main determining power of the Western world with over 4,018 nuclear warheads and a combined fleet of over 100 aircraft carriers and ballistic missile submarines to keep the European Union united. But a united Europe that serves only Germany's interests is certainly not in the best interests of either the Americans or the Europeans.

With this in mind, the citizens and politicians of Europe can and must convince both the Germans and the establishment in Brussels that is better to amputate its infected leg today rather than die tomorrow.

To conclude, will recall two historical facts. The French Revolution of May 5, 1789, result of a bottom-up eruption, and the humiliating unconditional surrender of Japan of August 15, 1945 signed on September 2, 1945 on USS Missouri. After the chaos, in both cases, order was restored and ordinary people lived better, much better.

Printed in Great Britain
by Amazon